ADVANCE PRAISE

"While in the astronaut training 'pipeline' for an Apollo mission, I served as CAPCOM and Lunar Module Checkout astronaut on Support Crews for Apollos 9, 10, and 13. In fact, I was the CAPCOM who answered that fateful call from Apollo 13, 'Houston, we've had a problem!' Follow the riveting stories from those exciting and historic days of the Apollo program in this book by Dr David Chudwin, my fellow graduate from the University of Michigan."

JACK LOUSMA, Astronaut, Apollo 13 CAPCOM, Skylab 2 Pilot and STS-3 Commander

"Seeing Apollo 11's launch through the memories of a wide-eyed teenage outsider is remarkable: a homegrown reminiscence from someone fortunate to be a witness to humankind's greatest engineering triumph."

FRANCIS FRENCH, Space historian and Director of Education, San Diego Air and Space Museum

"During the 50th anniversary celebration in 2019 of the historic Apollo 11 Moon landing, millions of people all around the world will remember where they were and what they were doing when the Eagle landed on the Sea of Tranquility with astronauts Neil Armstrong and Buzz Aldrin on board. But this book's author, David Chudwin, was actually there, as a teenager, with his camera and a notepad, as a bonafide member of the press when the mission blasted off from Cape Kennedy on 16 July 1969. The photos Chudwin took as a teenage space reporter are compelling, but it is the story of how his experience with Apollo 11 changed his life that is so profound and marvelous."

JAMES R. HANSEN, Neil Armstrong's biographer, author of *First Man: The Life of Neil A. Armstrong*, and co-producer of the film of the same name

"History is a subject best understood after viewing it through multiple lenses. How wonderful to have this new perspective from David Chudwin, who has crafted a vivid memoir about covering the Apollo 11 Moon flight as a young journalist. His sharp recall of details frames the events in a rich tapestry of historical context. David's ambition and 'don't give up' work ethic are an inspiring call to action for all types of young explorers to pursue their interests and follow their dreams."

JAY GALLENTINE, Award-winning space historian and author of *Ambassadors from Earth: Pioneering Explorations with Unmanned Spacecraft*

IN MEMORY OF

CLAUDIA ZIFF CHUDWIN

[1953 - 2018]

"Doubt thou the stars are fire;
Doubt that the sun doth move;
Doubt truth to be a liar;
But never doubt I love."

WILLIAM SHAKESPEARE
(*Hamlet*, Act 2, Scene 2)

Published by
LID Publishing Limited
The Record Hall, Studio 204,
16-16a Baldwins Gardens,
London EC1N 7RJ, UK

524 Broadway, 11th Floor, Suite 08-120,
New York, NY 10012, US

info@lidpublishing.com
www.lidpublishing.com

A member of:

www.businesspublishersroundtable.com

Printed in the Czech Republic by Finidr
ISBN: 978-0-9991871-2-8

Cover and Page design: Matthew Renaudin

I WAS A TEENAGE SPACE REPORTER

FROM APOLLO 11 TO OUR FUTURE IN SPACE

DAVID CHUDWIN

LONDON MADRID MEXICO CITY
NEW YORK BARCELONA MONTERREY
SHANGHAI BOGOTA BUENOS AIRES

TABLE OF CONTENTS

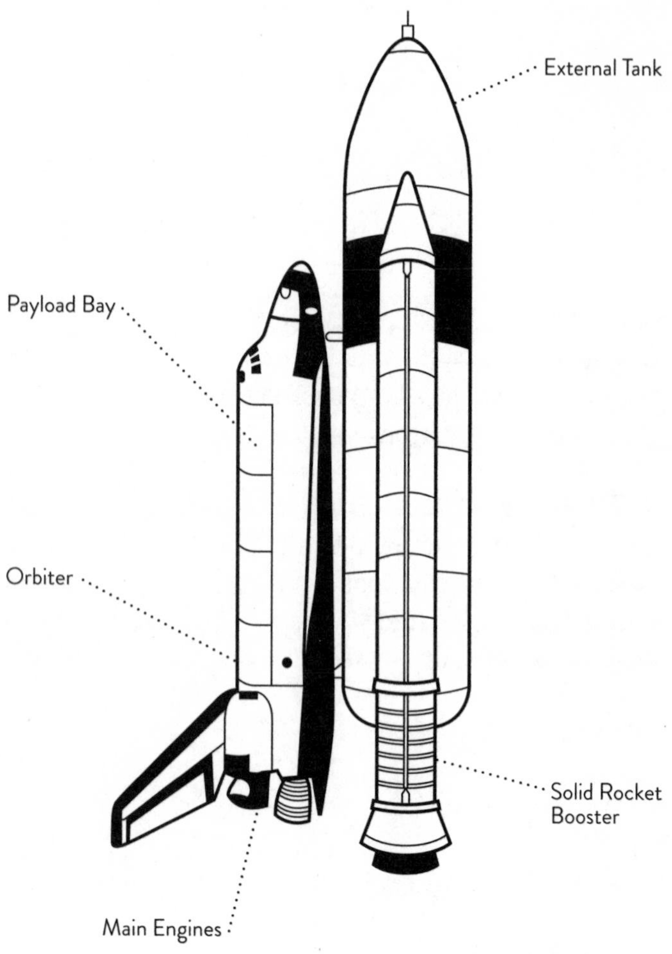

Figure 1: Space shuttle.

INTRODUCTION

I am a very lucky individual. As a 19-year-old college journalist I covered the launch of the first Moon landing mission, Apollo 11, from Florida. I was one of the only teenagers to have official NASA press credentials for that historic event in July 1969, and the only journalist representing college newspapers. As a result, I had extraordinary access to the astronauts, rocket scientists, launch pads, rockets and control centres there.

On 16 July 1969, at 9:32 a.m., I watched in person as Neil Armstrong, Mike Collins and Buzz Aldrin lifted off from NASA's Kennedy Space Center on a Saturn V rocket on their way to the Moon. Four days later I reported from the NASA News Center there on humankind's first steps on the Moon.

Now that the 50th Anniversary of Apollo 11 approaches, it is an appropriate time to look both backwards at that mission, and forward to our future in space.

For you and others not born yet, Neil Armstrong and Buzz Aldrin's landing on the Moon on 20 July 1969 is almost ancient history; indeed, a 50th anniversary confirms that fact.

In many ways the world was quite different then, with no mobile phones, personal computers, the internet, Facebook or other social media.

By recounting Apollo 11 through the eyes of a teenager who was there, I hope that you experience the excitement, fears, planning and hard work that led to the first landing on another celestial body. It was not at all clear that the complicated plan requiring rendezvous of two spacecraft in lunar orbit would work. The astronauts themselves estimated they had only a 50-50 chance of success on the first try.

I was captivated by space exploration from early childhood. The first part of this book talks about how I grew up with the space program. It was not my choice to be born in 1950 in the United States, but it was fortunate timing with respect to the Space Age. I was seven years old when Sputnik launched, nine when the Mercury astronauts were chosen, and 11 when Yuri Gagarin and Alan Shepard became the first Russian and first American, respectively, in space. I then watched with pride how the United States caught up with and surpassed the Russians in space milestones.

As I entered high school, I had opportunities as a teenager to meet astronauts in person as they visited the Chicago area. In high school, I became a writer and an editor of my school paper. This interest in journalism continued as I entered the University of Michigan in August 1968 as a freshman. I joined the staff of *The Michigan Daily*, the independent, student-run newspaper on the Ann Arbor campus, where I became a reporter and eventually Managing Editor.

The next part of this book relates my experiences as a teenager at the Kennedy Space Center. I flew to Florida on 13 July 1969 representing *The Daily* and the College Press Service, a consortium of college newspapers. There I was an eyewitness to history, covering the last steps of the Apollo 11 crew on Earth, their launch on 16 July, the landing on the Moon on 20 July, and the subsequent visit of the crew to Chicago the next month after their safe return.

This experience changed my life. I became obsessed with space exploration, voraciously reading about it in newspaper articles, magazines and later websites and social media. I began to realize that space exploration is part of human progress – the expansion of human habitation from the prehistoric plains of Africa to all the continents, then navigation of the oceans, and more recently flying to the edge of space with airplanes. The further expansion of the human species to the solar system and beyond, starting with the Moon and Mars, is the next step forward.

While it is important to recount the past, it is perhaps even more vital to understand that our future is going to be in space. The final section of the book looks forward to the rockets, spacecraft, and orbiting space stations that will take you and other young people further into the solar system.

The Saturn V rockets and Apollo spacecraft are monuments to the past. However, the development of the Space Launch System rocket, the Orion spacecraft and orbiting stations such as the Lunar Orbital Platform-Gateway are paving the way for trips back to the Moon and to Mars. The children and young adults of today will crew these missions, so there are great opportunities for you to participate in these exciting voyages in the decades ahead.

I hope you and other younger generations will have the same enthusiasm for space exploration that my contemporaries and I had in the 1960s. The future of the human species lies in exploring and colonizing the Solar System, starting with the Moon and Mars, as discussed in the Epilogue.

You and the young people of today will be the explorers of the future, travelling to space stations in Earth orbit and around the Moon. The first men and women to return to the lunar surface, orbit Mars and eventually land on Mars have already been born.

While the excitement of the first landing on the Moon was unique, there are many firsts in space to come. Come along and enjoy the ride!

TIMELINE

December 1903
Wilbur and Orville Wright made the first powered flight in their newly invented airplane.

March 1926
Robert Goddard launched the first liquid-fuelled rocket.

June 1944
Germany's V-2 rocket became the first vehicle to enter outer space, reaching 176 km in altitude.

July 1950
The Author is born in Chicago, Illinois, USA.

October 1957
Russia launched Sputnik, the first artificial satellite to orbit the Earth.

November 1957
A Russian dog named Laika was the first animal launched into in Earth orbit, but did not survive.

January 1958
Explorer 1 became the first US satellite in orbit around the Earth.

April 1959
The United States chose its first astronauts, the 'Original Seven'.

April 1961
Russian cosmonaut Yuri Gagarin became the first human to orbit the Earth.

May 1961
Alan Shepard was the first American in space during a brief suborbital flight.

February 1962
John Glenn orbited the Earth, the first American to do so.

October 1968
The US space program resumed crewed flights with three astronauts in Earth orbit aboard the Apollo 7 spacecraft. The Author wrote his first editorial about space exploration for *The Michigan Daily*.

August 1968
The Author enrolled at the University of Michigan and joined the *The Michigan Daily*, the student newspaper on the Ann Arbor campus.

December 1968
Frank Borman, James Lovell and William Anders orbited the Moon aboard Apollo 8, becoming the first crewed flight to leave Earth orbit.

January 1967
Astronauts Gus Grissom, Ed White and Roger Chaffee died in an Apollo spacecraft, during a test on the ground, from a fire in the cockpit.

March 1966
Gemini 8 astronauts Neil Armstrong and David Scott made the first emergency landing from space in the Pacific Ocean after the first space docking.

December 1965
Astronauts aboard the Gemini 6 and Gemini 7 spacecraft performed the first rendezvous in space, flying in formation and coming within one foot of each other.

March 1965
Russian cosmonaut Alexei Leonov was the first human to walk in space.

June 1963
Russian cosmonaut Valentina Tereshkova became the first woman in space.

June 1965
Edward White made the first spacewalk by an American astronaut.

March 1969
The Apollo 9 crew tested the lunar landing module in Earth orbit.

May 1969
Apollo 10 astronauts Thomas Stafford and Eugene Cernan flew to within 50,000 feet of the lunar surface in a dress rehearsal for landing. The Author and a friend decided to go to Florida for the next mission.

June 1969
The Author received an official NASA press pass to cover Apollo 11 for the College Press Service.

July 1969
The Author flew to Florida on 13 July, two days after his 19th birthday.

Apollo 11 astronauts Neil Armstrong, Michael Collins and "Buzz" Aldrin blasted off from the Kennedy Space Center on 16 July. The Author viewed their 'walk out' and launch.

The Apollo 11 lunar module landed on the Moon on 20 July and Neil Armstrong became the first man to walk on the Moon.

August 1969
The Apollo 11 crew visited New York, Chicago and Los Angeles on 13 August. The Author covered the Chicago parade.

May 1973
The United States launched its first space station, named Skylab, which was visited by three astronaut crews.

July 1975
The Apollo-Soyuz Test Project marked a new era of cooperation in space between the United States and Russia with the docking of their crewed spacecraft in Earth orbit.

June-July 2003
Spirit and Opportunity were launched to Mars; they were the first Mars rovers capable of sophisticated robotic exploration.

October 2004
SpaceShipOne, designed by aerospace engineer Burt Rutan, became the first crewed private craft to enter space, flying twice within two weeks to win a $10 million prize.

February 2003
The Space Shuttle Columbia broke up during reentry, killing seven astronauts.

November 1998
The first element of the International Space Station was launched into Earth orbit, starting a construction project that continued until 2016.

January 1986
The space shuttle Challenger disintegrated after launch, killing all seven astronauts onboard.

February 1986
Construction of the Russian Mir modular space station in Earth orbit began. Mir was occupied by Russian and foreign cosmonauts until 2001.

June 1983
Sally Ride became the first American woman to orbit the Earth.

April 1981
The United States launched the first Space Shuttle, Columbia. With crews of up to seven astronauts, shuttles carried astronauts and cosmonauts into Earth orbit. There were 135 shuttle flights over 30 years.

July 1976
The Viking 1 and 2 robots successfully landed on Mars and sent back pictures and scientific data.

September 2008
Falcon 1, launched by SpaceX, became the first privately developed liquid-fueled rocket to reach Earth orbit.

June 2009
The first flight of SpaceX's Falcon 9 rocket, which has been a mainstay of the commercial satellite launch business.

May 2012
An unmanned Dragon spacecraft carried supplies to the International Space Station in the first commercial cargo flight.

December 2017
US President Donald Trump signs a directive ordering NASA to return humans to the Moon as a precursor to a trip to Mars.

August 2012
First man on the Moon Neil Armstrong died at age 82 following cardiac surgery.

PART ONE

MOON LAUNCH

Figure 2: Launch of the Apollo 11 crew on a Saturn V rocket towards the Moon on 16 July 1969 from the Kennedy Space Center, Florida.

PROLOGUE

Figure 3: Apollo 11 astronauts Mike Collins and Buzz Aldrin walk out of the Manned Spacecraft Operations Building on 16 July 1969 on their way to the Moon. Spacesuit technicians Joe Schmitt and Ron Woods accompany them.

© David Chudwin

It is 4:30 a.m. Eastern Daylight Time, 16 July 1969, and a loud, metallic ring from an old-fashioned, wind-up travel alarm clock wakes me up.

Outside the motel room it is dark. The chirps of the crickets and croaks of the frogs are the only noises. It is still warm and humid, as one would expect for a July night in Florida. With a sense of excitement and purpose, I roll out of bed and jump into the shower. I hope to be an eyewitness to history later today.

Through a series of coincidences and just plain good luck, I am at the Sea Missile Motel in Cocoa Beach, Florida, to report on the Apollo 11 mission to the Moon for college newspapers. In a few hours, astronauts Neil Armstrong, Edwin (Buzz) Aldrin, and Michael Collins are scheduled to be launched to attempt humankind's first landing on the Moon. The notion that men can reach the Moon, safely land, walk on the lunar surface and safely return to Earth is indeed a radical one. It will take almost a miraculous synthesis of men, machines, computers and celestial mechanics to pull this off.

Almost as miraculous as this planned journey to the Moon is the fact that I am at the Sea Missile Motel getting dressed to see the start of this adventure. I just turned 19 years old on 11 July and, accompanied by a friend, I am the only college journalist as such to have NASA press passes. I am accredited to cover the launch for the College Press Service, a group of college newspapers.

I dress and carefully lay out my plastic-encased NASA press badge, my old Kodak Retina camera loaned to me by my Dad, two rolls of 36-exposure Kodachrome colour slide film, a small spiral notebook, a blue felt-tip pen for note taking and the keys to my rental car. This is 1969, so I do not have a notebook computer or a mobile phone like those that all reporters will be using in the future.

At the same time, my best friend and compatriot in all matters relating to space is also preparing for the day ahead. I have known Marvin Rubenstein since the fourth grade at McDowell School on the South Side of Chicago. We share a similar passion for space and have gone to several space events together beginning with the visit of astronauts Jim McDivitt and Ed White to Chicago in June 1965 after Gemini 4, the second manned Gemini flight. Planning this trip has been a joint effort as well. It is Marv who suggested a trip together to the Kennedy Space Center for an Apollo launch while I made most of the arrangements and got the NASA press credentials. Marv is not a reporter but comes along as a friend and to help.

We check our motel room again to be sure we are not leaving anything important behind and walk out into the warm, humid Florida air. We make our way through the darkness and I start up our rental car. Both of us are half asleep, and we speculate whether the astronauts will actually take off today. There is so much that can go wrong, including a myriad of mechanical problems and poor weather.

I drive a relatively short distance on Highway A1A to the NASA Apollo 11 News Center, a two-story industrial building that is being used by NASA as a temporary press center. NASA press facilities at the Kennedy Space Center itself would be overwhelmed by the over 3,500 journalists from around the world here to cover this historic launch.

Adjacent to the News Center are several buses to transport the journalists to the Kennedy Space Center facilities. We wait, sitting in the buses for a while as the first hint of dawn appears in the eastern sky. The buses then travel together north to the Kennedy Space Center gates, where we are waved through by the security guards.

The buses head on to Kennedy Space Center grounds towards a building known as the MSOB, a NASA acronym for Manned Spacecraft Operations Building. (In 2014 the same building will be renamed the Neil Armstrong Operations and Checkout Building, or O&C.) The Apollo 11 crew has spent the last few nights in the MSOB, which contains the astronaut quarters. Besides bedrooms, there are a separate kitchen and dining room, as well as rooms where technicians are helping them into their spacesuits.

The buses stop a couple of hundred yards from a lighted, roped-off area near an entrance to the MSOB. Parked near the entrance is a large shiny white NASA van to transport the astronauts to Launch Pad 39A, where their Saturn V rocket is waiting for them. The press is ordered to stay behind the ropes to witness the astronauts leaving the MSOB and walking the short distance to the NASA van. This event is appropriately called 'the walk-out'.

As soon as the buses stop and the doors open, there is a mad rush as grown men sprint from the buses to grab the best positions behind the ropes to see the astronauts. These are reporters, not only from the United States, but from around the world. It is a close approximation of a rugby scrum. Marv and I are able to get a fairly good position in the third row.

As the 200 or so reporters jostle for position, the crowd inches forward to the point that I feel hemmed in by the mass of people. It is the first hint I have of mild claustrophobia.

We stand there at around 5:30 a.m. as the astronauts inside the MSOB eat breakfast with select fellow astronauts and NASA officials. Then they are suited up in their white spacesuits. The scene inside is witnessed by artist Paul Calle, the only 'civilian' present, who makes pencil sketches of the men and their activities for the NASA Art program. Years later, Paul and I compare our experiences that morning inside and outside the MSOB.

As we wait, I check that I had loaded photographic film into my camera. There is nothing automatic about this camera from the 1930s, but it does have a high-quality German lens. I set the f-stop and speed and hope the pictures will turn out.

After we wait impatiently for about 40 minutes, astronaut Deke Slayton, the Director of Flight Crew Operations, walks out of the building, down the steps, and is interviewed at 6:10 a.m. by a television reporter. Deke is wearing a reddish, short-sleeved sport shirt. Those of us assembled cannot hear his live comments (**Figure 4**).

Fifteen minutes later, at 6:25 a.m., there is a stir in the crowd of reporters. We can see, through the open door of the MSOB, individuals start to scurry around in the corridor. A white dot is visible in the distance down the corridor, and within a few seconds the dot moves towards us and becomes a man in a white spacesuit. Neil Armstrong leads the procession.

Astronauts Armstrong, Collins and Aldrin walk briskly down the hall in their spacesuits, carrying portable air conditioning units, to the applause of NASA and contractor employees, and then outside, down the ramp from the MSOB towards the transfer van.

Collins also carries a paper bag. Many years later, I hear from Collins himself what is in that bag. It contains a frozen fish nailed to a trophy plaque – a gag gift for Guenter

Figure 4: Astronaut Deke Slayton, director of flight crew operations, is interviewed before the 'walk-out' of the Apollo 11 crew on 15 July 1969.

© David Chudwin

Wendt, the 'Pad Leader' in charge of the white room area near the top of the Saturn V. It is a tradition for astronauts to exchange gag gifts with Wendt before they are sealed in their spacecraft.

As the three astronauts walk out towards the van they are accompanied by two white-garbed suit technicians and two silver-uniformed, red-helmeted firemen. Slayton follows the assemblage at the rear.

There are loud cheers from both inside and outside the MSOB as the men walk through the door. Hundreds of flashbulbs go off. Photographers jostle for position, elbows flying, as we try to get off as many shots as possible. I manage to take five photographs and pray they will turn out when I get the Kodachrome film developed.

All three astronauts are smiling. Armstrong cocks his head a little, Collins looks serene and Aldrin has a big grin. Armstrong and Aldrin each give a 'thumbs up' as they approach the van. Armstrong waves to the crowd.

The whole scene is surreal – three spacemen in white spacesuits and their entourage of spacesuit techs, firemen and NASA officials, being cheered by onlookers as frenzied photographers and movie and television cameramen attempt to record their 'walk-out'.

Once the astronauts and their attendants are aboard, the astro van drives off slowly towards Pad 39A.

The whole event lasts only a couple of minutes, but it is one of the emotional high points of my own voyage. It is a surreal scene that leaves my heart pounding. Those of us in that small crowd at the MSOB are privileged to see the last few steps on Earth of the first human beings who would land on the Moon. Marv and I are perhaps the only teenagers present.

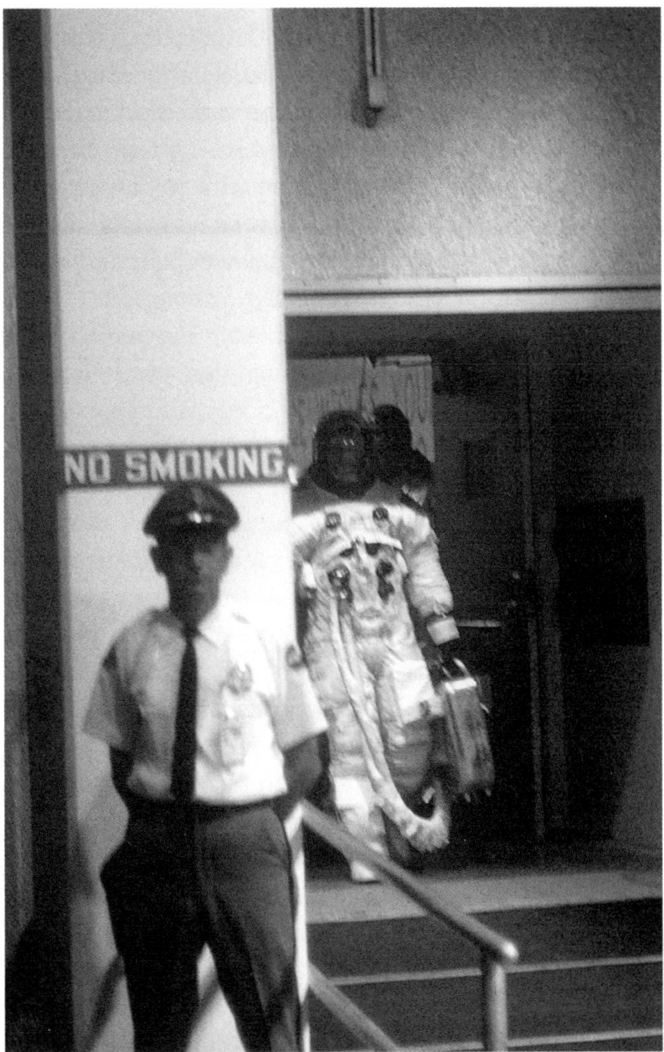

Figure 5: Astronaut Neil Armstrong walks out from the entrance of the Manned Spacecraft Operations Building on 16 July 1969 on the way to the Moon.

Marv and I then leave the area in a NASA bus, headed for the launch viewing area. We are exhilarated to have been eyewitnesses to history that morning, but more is yet to come.

Considering the circumstances and my primitive colour film camera, I am very happy with my own photographic results when the film is developed later at home.

Three of the five pictures turn out well. The first image shows Armstrong walking through the door of the MSOB, carrying a portable breathing unit. A NASA security guard stands at ease under a 'No Smoking' sign, carefully scanning the crowd of reporters and other observers. By today's standards, however, security at the event is not that tight (Figure 5).

The second picture is the 'money shot'. It shows all three crewmen walking down the ramp in their spacesuits, Armstrong with a sweet smile (see Figure 33 page 113).

In the third image, I miss Armstrong's 'thumbs up' outside the MSOB because another photographer's head gets in the way, but I do catch Mike Collins and Buzz Aldrin. They are followed by the two white-helmeted spacesuit technicians – the late Joe Schmitt, to Aldrin's right, and Ron Woods in the back. (Years later I would become friends with Woods, who became a space artist, and a collector of his art.) Behind them are two red-helmeted firemen and Slayton in civilian clothes (see Figure 3 page 12).

The last two images showing Aldrin and Collins entering the van are blurred and show only partial views of the astronauts because my camera view is obscured by other journalists' heads.

How we got to the Kennedy Space Center to cover the Apollo 11 walk-out is a long and lucky story, and more adventures await us later that day.

CHAPTER 1

ORIGINS: 1950-59

Figure 6: Walt Disney (left) and Wernher von Braun collaborated on segments about space exploration for *Walt Disney's Disneyland* on television in 1955-57.

I was born in Chicago on 11 July 1950, a day which numerologists say is lucky (11/07/50), although I have never been partial to superstition. My father was a physician, specifically a newly minted radiologist, having been discharged from military duty the year before. In 1946, he had married my mother after meeting her at the University of Wisconsin, where she was an undergrad and he was a medical student in military uniform. They spent most of the ensuing three years in the US Army Medical Corps, stationed in post-war Germany.

In 1952, when I was two years old, we moved from our Chicago apartment to a new house at 9104 South Merrill Avenue, in a newly constructed middle class neighbourhood on the South Side of Chicago. Later, in 1958, my parents and my two younger brothers and I moved a couple of miles away to a nicer tri-level house with air-conditioning at 8759 South Blackstone Avenue. These were my two main haunts during my formative years.

I was definitely a child of the 1950s. My mother stayed home as a housewife while my father went to work each day wearing his bow tie. We had a home-cooked dinner every night together as a family – fast food was a thing of the future. (McDonald's didn't open its first franchised restaurant until 1955.) After dinner, we then watched the latest television shows, first on a set with a small round picture tube and then on a newer model with a rectangular black-and-white screen.

My favourite comedies were *I Love Lucy* and *Leave It to Beaver*. My favourite adventure show was *Davy Crockett*, with the frontiersman played by Fess Parker in a coonskin hat. In fact, my sixth birthday present was a faux coonskin hat.

However, the program that sparked my imagination the most was *Walt Disney's Disneyland*, which debuted in October 1954. The variety series, produced by Walt Disney, had several segments on the possibility of space travel. These segments were produced in collaboration with *Collier's* magazine and former German rocket scientist (and ex-SS officer) Wernher von Braun (see Figure 6 page 21). The exciting television shows depicted men being launched into space and rendezvousing with a round, spinning space station, as well as travelling to the Moon and Mars.

At this time space travel was just a dream, the stuff of science fiction, which even some scientists called impossible. This Disney television series and a number of earlier *Collier's* magazine articles (1952-54) ignited public interest in space flight by projecting realistic and practical plans for human space travel.

Besides magazine articles and television shows, both fictional and factual books describing humans in space were published in the 1950s. I loved science fiction, especially Robert A. Heinlein's imaginative novels for young readers, which were introduced to me at eight years of age by a friendly librarian at the small Chicago Public Library branch near our house. My favourite was *Have Space Suit – Will Travel*, the improbable but engaging story of Kip Russell, a teenager who wins a space suit in a contest and ends up defending humanity with the help of a girl nicknamed Pee Wee and an alien creature called 'The Mother Thing'.

One of the first books I ever actually owned was *Space Pilots* by Willy Ley, published in 1957. This illustrated book was my eighth birthday present, and I still have my original copy. Written by German-born rocket scientist Ley, *Space Pilots* factually discussed the future selection, training and missions of the first astronauts. It was aimed at impressionable young people like myself, providing a blueprint for their aspirations to fly in space.

I caught the bug, and had visions of being a space pilot like the ones depicted in the book. My goal was to become an astronaut when I grew up.

On 4 October 1957 speculation about space travel turned into reality as the Soviet Union launched Sputnik, the first artificial satellite to orbit the Earth. I was seven years old at the time. The US had plans on the drawing board for such an unmanned satellite, but a combination of inter-service military rivalries and bureaucratic foot-dragging delayed a US launch.

Sputnik emitted a 'beep, beep, beep' radio signal that was heard around the world. But, in 1957 the Cold War was a serious concern – we actually did 'duck and cover' drills at school, as if that would save us from a nuclear bomb. There was intense competition between the United States and the Soviets in all types of endeavours, including scientific and engineering achievements. Sputnik was a slap in the face to the US and its beliefs in American superiority.

Sputnik ignited a sharp political debate in the US about whether America was losing its technical edge. In American politics, the opposition Democrats at the time, led by Senator Lyndon B. Johnson of Texas, went on the offensive. They pushed through legislation establishing as of 1 October 1958 a new National Aeronautics & Space Administration (NASA), which combined several existing non-military US space efforts, and appropriated more money for space exploration. The 'space race' was on.

The Sputnik debate also ignited in me, a somewhat precocious seven-year-old who was a voracious reader, a deeper interest in space. Science fiction and an interest in astronomy had given me a keen sense of wonder about the universe. The unmanned satellites orbited first by the Soviets and then by the US (Explorer 1, on 31 January 1958) raised the possibility of men riding aboard larger satellites. At that time, society was still quite sexist so the idea of women riding rockets was barely considered until later decades.

Today space travel is taken for granted, but in the 1950s there were serious medical concerns as to whether humans could actually survive the vacuum and microgravity of space. I read all I could about the subject, clipping newspaper articles about space from the now-extinct afternoon newspaper, the *Chicago Daily News*.

Besides the unmanned Sputnik in 1957 and Explorer 1 in 1958, the other key event of the 1950s concerning manned spaceflight occurred when NASA named its first seven astronauts at a press conference on 9 April 1959 in Washington D.C. I was eight years old at the time. All were military test pilots but they dressed in civilian clothes for the occasion.

Alan Shepard, Virgil 'Gus' Grissom, John Glenn, M. Scott Carpenter, Walter Schirra, Donald 'Deke' Slayton, and L. Gordon Cooper put actual faces on the hitherto abstract notion of 'astronaut' (see **Figure 7** page 26).

With the exception of Glenn, who had set flying records as a US Marine aviator and appeared on television before, these men were plucked from relative obscurity to become heroes and role models for my generation. That they were all too human was lost in the hoopla promoted by NASA and by *Life* magazine, which won an exclusive contract for their personal stories.

CHAPTER 2

THE EARLY SIXTIES: 1960-64

Figure 7: The "Original Seven" Project Mercury astronauts (upper row) Alan Shepard, Virgil "Gus" Grissom, Gordon Cooper (bottom row) Walter Schirra, Donald Slayton, John Glenn and Scott Carpenter.

© NASA

As the 1960s dawned, the winds of change were starting to blow across America.

A young Massachusetts Senator, John F. Kennedy, was running for president and asked that America 'do better' than the complacency of the 1950s. Rock and roll continued its rise in the music world. US college students began to become involved in anti-segregation marches and later in the Peace Corps, first proposed by Kennedy in a campaign speech on 14 October 1960, on the steps of the Michigan Union in Ann Arbor (a place I would frequently pass eight years later).

In 1960, I was turning 10 years old. I was a good student, but I wore glasses, was overweight (my 'fat period') and was not athletic (right field was my permanent baseball assignment). By all criteria, I was what is now known as a 'nerd' and certainly not one of the 'cool kids'. At first I resented this. It took me decades to accept the fact that I was not one of the 'cool kids'. But over time, not only did I accept that fact, but I reveled in it. In later years, as I became a physician and writer, I understood that it was the 'nerds' of the world who accomplish so much in science, engineering, medicine and technology. This realization gave me a sense of satisfaction and peace.

In the 1960s my circle of friends at our elementary school in Chicago weren't the 'cool kids'. One of my best friends was a dark-haired boy named Marvin Rubenstein. We had common interests and would hang out at each other's houses. His kitchen was full of loud conversations and laughter (his mother was from New York and his father from the West Side of Chicago) and the wonderful aromas of all kinds of food and bakery goods.

Our friendship was based on shared interests in science and space. But there was also an element of competition in our friendship, which became more prominent as years passed.

Marv and I compared the latest news about the newest Russian satellites, including their animal passengers. The first dog in space – Laika aboard Sputnik 2 – was stranded in orbit in November 1957, sacrificed on the altar of space exploration.

Compared to the Soviets, the United States had a late start. Ambitious plans for unmanned scientific satellites were delayed by repeated rocket explosions in full view of the world. Russian programs were cloaked in secrecy so that failures were generally neither announced nor seen on television.

NASA, the new US civilian space agency, began in the early 1960s to develop a space infrastructure. NASA absorbed old government research sites such as those at Langley Field (Virginia), Ames Field (California), Lewis Field (Ohio) and Cape Canaveral (Florida). NASA also planned new facilities such as the Manned Spacecraft Center south of Houston and the Marshall Space Flight Center (MSFC) near the Redstone Arsenal in Alabama.

Each of these research centers specialized in specific tasks. For example, the Manned Spacecraft Center was responsible for the astronauts and the spacecraft they piloted. MSFC was delegated the task of developing and building the rocket boosters they were to ride. Cape Canaveral oversaw space launches (except for polar orbits, which originated from Vandenberg Air Force Base in California).

President Eisenhower in 1958 nominated T. Keith Glennan as NASA's first Administrator. An engineer by training, Glennan had been serving as the President of the Case Institute of Technology in Ohio. As NASA Administrator, Glennan began the task of bringing together the disparate and sometimes fractious units that comprised the new space agency.

These centers at the time were semi-independent fiefdoms, zealously guarding their budgets, personnel and responsibilities in colossal bureaucratic turf wars. NASA Headquarters in Washington was a relatively small operation with program managers, budget officers and a public relations staff.

Glennan resigned at the end of the Eisenhower administration in January 1961. He was replaced by James Webb, not an engineer but a Texas oilman and an experienced political wheeler-dealer who was a protégé of Vice President Lyndon B. Johnson.

In the Kennedy administration, Johnson was also head of the National Space Council. Previously, he had been one of the figures instrumental in the creation of NASA. As chairman of the powerful Senate Space Committee before he became Vice President, Johnson had an influential voice in NASA appointments and budgets. Therefore, the decision in 1961 to locate the Manned Spacecraft Center in his home state of Texas was not an accident.

Amid this bureaucratic and political wrangling, the seven Mercury astronauts began their training at sites across the United States. The astronauts were initially based at NASA's Langley Research Center in Hampton, VA; it was only after September 1963 that the newly constructed Manned Spacecraft Center in Texas opened for business.

The astronauts were constantly on the move, flying jets from one training facility to another.

After competitive bidding, in January 1959 McDonnell Aircraft in St. Louis won contracts to build one-man Project Mercury capsules. The astronauts made frequent trips to St. Louis to consult with engineers there and monitor production of their spacecraft. The Mercury capsules were small, and detractors such as Gen. Chuck Yeager, the first man to break the 'sound barrier', described Project Mercury pilots as 'Spam in a can'.

For the first two suborbital missions, the plan was to use a modified Redstone rocket, an intercontinental ballistic missile (ICBM) built by Chrysler Corporation at the Redstone Arsenal in Alabama. For subsequent orbital flights, the rocket of choice was a modified Atlas ICBM manufactured by Convair in San Diego. The astronauts inspected their future rocket boosters during regular trips to Alabama and California.

They also flew to Johnsville, Pennsylvania, to train on the large centrifuges of the Naval Air Development Center; to Chapel Hill, North Carolina, to study the stars at the Morehead Planetarium; to Nevada for desert training at the USAF Survival School; and to Panama for jungle survival training, among many other training sites.

The main pacing factor in the US space program in 1960 was the reliability of the booster rockets, which had a disturbing propensity to explode on ignition or shortly afterwards. Marv and I watched on television the spectacular explosions of these unmanned rockets at Cape Canaveral. Not only were the rockets destroyed, but also their valuable satellite payloads.

Meanwhile Russian satellite payloads, including animals, became increasingly larger and more sophisticated. For example, on 19 August 1960 the dogs Strelka and

Belka were sent into space aboard the Sputnik 5 satellite and recovered alive. However, Russian space research was considered a state secret and the future plans of the Russians were not known.

On 12 April 1961, I came home late in the afternoon from school. My Dad was lying on the couch, reading the *Chicago Daily News.*

"Did you hear about this?" he asked, holding up the newspaper with a large headline 'MAN IN SPACE'. The lack of cellphones and computers meant that news spread dramatically slower than the instant news cycles of today.

The Soviets had announced that a Russian pilot, a major named Yuri Alekseyevich Gagarin, had become the first human being to travel to space, successfully completing a one-orbit, 108-minute trip around the Earth aboard Vostok. Very few details about the Vostok rocket, Vostok capsule, launch or landing were made public at the time.

We know now that a multi-engine Vostok rocket lifted off at 6:07 a.m. Greenwich Mean Time (GMT) from the secret Tyuratam launch complex about 160 miles from its ostensible location near Baikonur, Kazakhstan. Gagarin was cramped in a 2.3-metre-diameter, ball-like Vostok descent capsule, which was attached to a cone-shaped equipment module. The spacecraft was placed into an orbit with a high point of 177 nautical miles. The ground track took Gagarin over the Soviet Union, then south over the Pacific Ocean to Patagonia, then north over Africa and back to the Soviet Union.

Retro-rockets fired over Angola slowed the capsule down enough so it descended over Soviet territory. Parachutes further slowed the speed, but a soft-landing mechanism had not yet been perfected. As planned,

Gagarin ejected out of the capsule at 7 km altitude and parachuted to a soft landing near the city of Engels, 280 km west of the planned landing site.

Major Gagarin was flown to Moscow, where he received a hero's welcome. The Russians were justifiably proud of their achievement in safely orbiting the first human being in space. They mounted a massive propaganda campaign with Gagarin as its centerpiece to tout the superiority of Communism.

When I saw the headline, my heart sank. I had truly hoped that an American would be first in space. In 1961 the Cold War was very real, and the Soviets had reached an important milestone of space exploration before the United States. I was very disappointed, but at least the flight proved the naysayers wrong about the ability of humans to withstand the microgravity and vacuum of outer space.

Meanwhile, NASA had long before announced that the first American manned space flight would merely be a suborbital mission in which a Mercury capsule would be shot up into space and then come down in a parabolic arc. In February 1961 NASA publicly named astronauts Alan Shepard, Gus Grissom and John Glenn as the possible crew for this first US manned space flight. Internally, Shepard was the leading candidate.

The first launch attempt on 2 May 1961 was scrubbed due to bad weather, as was another on 4 May 1961. At that point, when he was identified as the pilot during these attempts, Americans learned that Shepard was to be the first American to fly in space.

The third time proved to be the charm as Shepard blasted off on 5 May 1961 at 9:34 a.m. Eastern Standard Time aboard a Mercury-Redstone rocket. His Freedom 7 capsule flew to an altitude of 116 miles before arcing back down to Earth. The entire flight lasted only 15 minutes. Shepard was picked up from the Atlantic Ocean by personnel from a US Navy aircraft carrier the USS Lake Champlain.

Ocean landings were the only way to safely return astronauts from orbit in the 1960s and 1970s because it was much more difficult technologically to safely soft land on the ground. It wasn't until the space shuttle program, beginning in 1981, that astronauts were able to come back from space on land without splashing into the ocean.

While Shepard's flight was not as impressive as the Soviets' orbital mission, it was greeted with great enthusiasm in the United States with headlines, parades and a White House appearance for Shepard. I watched the coverage on our black-and-white TV and saved the next-day newspapers. I was excited because the US now at least had a toehold in space.

In the second and final U.S. suborbital flight on 21 July 1961, Gus Grissom was launched aboard a Mercury-Redstone rocket to an altitude of 103 miles in a 15-minute, 30-second flight. What was remarkable about the mission was that Grissom's Liberty Bell 7 capsule sank after the ocean landing, almost carrying him with it. A drenched Grissom was plucked from the water by hovering helicopters. The hatch of the capsule had blown open prematurely after the ocean landing, the cause of which is a controversy to this day. Some blamed Grissom, but most of the evidence pointed to a faulty hatch design.

Meanwhile, unmanned test flights of the more powerful Atlas rocket, designed for an orbital flight, continued after the first Mercury-Atlas rocket (MA-1) exploded.

Finally, in November 1961, a chimpanzee named Enos was sent on a two-orbit flight in a Mercury capsule that was successfully recovered from the ocean by a US Navy ship, the USS Stormes. This MA-5 chimp mission validated the Mercury-Atlas system and preparations began to launch John Glenn into orbit.

Excitement was building for the first US manned orbital mission. The plan was for Glenn to ride his Friendship 7 capsule for three orbits around the Earth, but first he needed to get launched. A series of 'holds' (delays) and 'scrubs' (postponements) delayed the launch as an anxious nation listened on radio or watched on television.

The flight was originally scheduled for 16 January 1962 but was postponed on that date due to fuel tank problems. The flight was rescheduled several times but then repeatedly scrubbed – 20-27 January due to bad weather each day, then 1 February due to a fuel leak, and again on 14 February due to poor weather conditions.

Finally, on 20 February 1962, Glenn successfully rode his Atlas rocket into orbit around the Earth. The mission lasted 4 hours 55 minutes. The Friendship 7 capsule with Glenn aboard landed in the Atlantic Ocean to be safely recovered by a US Navy ship, the USS Noa. An American had finally orbited the Earth.

There was jubilation around the world at Colonel Glenn's success, carried out in the full glare of publicity and openness, in stark contrast to Russian secrecy. President Kennedy flew to meet Glenn. Accompanied by his wife Annie and Vice President Johnson, Glenn attended ticker tape parades in his honour across the US.

I was 11 years old at the time of John Glenn's flight and I followed it as best I could, considering that I had to go to school to attend sixth grade. I watched the television newscasts after school and that night. I also saved newspaper front pages and clippings about Glenn's flight and other space news, for which I purchased an oversized scrapbook. Today, I still have the scrapbook and its successors with their yellowed newsprint contents. *Life* magazine was a valuable source of colour pictures and 'inside' – but carefully manufactured – stories of the astronaut families.

After Glenn's flight, there were three additional Project Mercury orbital missions: Scott Carpenter in May 1962 (three orbits); Wally Schirra in October 1962 (six orbits); and Gordon Cooper in May 1963 (22 orbits). There was a push for an extra Mercury flight (MA-10), to be piloted by Alan Shepard, but NASA management wanted to focus on the two-man Project Gemini – the next milestone in manned space exploration.

I was in the eighth grade when Project Mercury concluded in 1963. Following this, a series of national events ensued that would have long-lasting effects both on the US as a nation and on me personally.

On 22 November 1963 I was walking back to school during the lunch break when my friend Eric Forsman came up and excitedly asked, "Did you hear? The President has been shot." I gasped and we went inside our classroom, one of the only ones in the school that had a television. Broadcast journalist Walter Cronkite was on the air and we knew immediately that something was wrong – instead of his usual suit coat, Cronkite just had on a white shirt and tie.

There was a lot of confusion immediately afterwards about the condition of President Kennedy in Dallas, but then Cronkite read a bulletin that the president was dead. Some of the girls in the classroom started sobbing. I was saddened and shocked by the unexpected assassination of the popular young president.

The days that followed were marked by the sounds of muffled drums and horseshoes on pavement as John F. Kennedy was returned to Washington and buried at Arlington National Cemetery. The grief was profound across the nation because the assassination had been such a surprise; it had been two generations since a president had been assassinated.

Kennedy had been a strong supporter of the space program. He thought that space was a technological playing field on which the United States could succeed in competing with the Russians. He also enjoyed associating himself with the Mercury 7 astronauts, whose young, brave, dashing personas fit the hopeful and heroic tone he sought for his presidency.

Kennedy laid US prestige on the line when he stated in a speech to a Joint Session of Congress on 25 May 1961: "This nation should commit itself to achieving the goal, before this decade is out, of landing a man on the moon and returning him safely to the Earth" (**Figure 8**). He reiterated this goal even more forcefully in another speech at Rice University on 12 September 1962.

His untimely death made the country and its new president, Lyndon B. Johnson, feel almost obliged to carry out this pledge made by the fallen president. Of course, Johnson already was a big supporter of the space program, especially since the Manned Spacecraft Center had opened that year in his beloved Texas.

Figure 8: President John F. Kennedy before a Joint Session of Congress on 25 May 1961 setting a goal of landing a man on the Moon before the end of the decade. Vice President Lyndon B. Johnson is at upper left.

© NASA

As the grief-stricken nation entered 1964, NASA was intensively testing a new, two-man spacecraft called Gemini. Two unmanned test flights of the spacecraft with its Titan II booster rocket – on 8 April 1964 and then on 19 January 1965 – were both successful. Gus Grissom and John Young were named as the prime crew for the first crewed Gemini flight. Grissom called his capsule the 'Molly Brown', a sardonic reference to the Titanic-themed Broadway show *The Unsinkable Molly Brown* and to his sunken Mercury capsule, Liberty Bell 7. However, NASA did not approve and there was no radio call sign for the crew other than 'Gemini 3'.

Just as 1964 was a time of transition for NASA from Project Mercury to preparing for Gemini, it was also a time of change for me.

In June 1964, along with my friends Marv, Eric and others, I graduated from the eighth grade. There was a formal graduation ceremony with hats and robes. I had started to thin out and was taller than some of my classmates – puberty was starting to work. I was ready and eager to go to high school, which in this case was Bowen High School on the South Side of Chicago. The place was a melting pot of nationalities, colours and religions; there were even 1950s-like bikers who had cigarette packs twisted into the arms of their white T-shirts. I looked forward to starting there in September.

CHAPTER 3

THE MID-SIXTIES: 1965-66

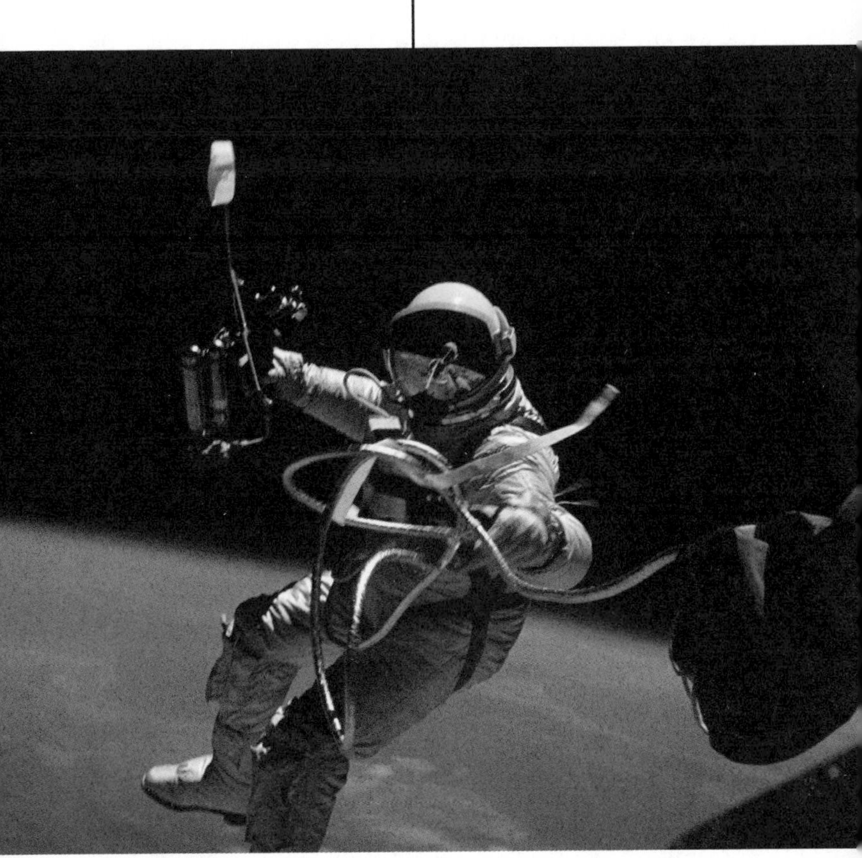

Figure 9: Astronaut Edward White takes America's first spacewalk on 3 June 1965 in this photo by his Gemini 4 commander James McDivitt.

The year 1965 was a time of new beginnings, both for the space program and for me personally.

On 18 March 1965, the Russians again surprised the world by carrying out the first spacewalk, more formally called 'extra-vehicular activity'. Cosmonaut Alexei Leonov floated outside his Voskhod spacecraft, attached by a tether, for about 12 minutes. He had difficulty returning inside due to a swollen spacesuit, but Leonov bled off some of the pressure to allow him to safely re-enter the spacecraft. (Later Leonov commanded the Russian crew of the Apollo-Soyuz joint flight and made several visits to the US, during which I met him twice.)

Five days later, on 23 March 1965, the US launched its first two-person space flight. A modified Titan II rocket sent Gus Grissom and John Young into space for three Earth orbits aboard a Gemini capsule. The pair tested the manoeuvring rockets that would allow Gemini to change its orbital plane and eventually rendezvous with other spacecraft – skills essential for any lunar landing.

The mission, designated Gemini 3, is also remembered for a contraband corned beef sandwich, procured from a deli by backup commander Wally Schirra, which Young carried and ate aboard. The corned beef incident provoked a Congressional hearing and public criticism of Young, who took it all in his stride with his 'aww, shucks' attitude.

While the success of Gemini 3 buoyed US space hopes, NASA officials were frustrated that the Russians had again upstaged them with Leonov's spacewalk. The first US spacewalk was moved up to the next Gemini flight (Gemini 4) with astronaut Ed White named as the first American spacewalker.

Throughout this time, I was still collecting newspaper clippings about space activities. I also started to audio-tape TV coverage of the launches using a reel-to-reel tape recorder I received as a birthday present in July 1963. I still have these tapes today and have converted some of them to digital files.

In early 1965 I saw an article about sending philatelic envelopes, also called 'covers', to the Navy for postmarking aboard the USS Wasp, the planned Gemini 4 prime recovery ship. I sent two stamped envelopes, which I received back after the flight with a design (cachet), which had been printed on the ship, and the ship's postmark. This was the start of a large 'space cover' collection, which has continued to grow over the last 50 years.

I followed the Gemini 4 flight, the second manned Gemini mission, with great interest. I was excited about the planned first American spacewalk by Ed White. Moreover, astronaut Jim McDivitt, the commander of Gemini 4, was of interest to me for three reasons. First, McDivitt was the first astronaut to command a multi-person space mission without having had previous space experience. Second, McDivitt was the first of the 'New Nine' astronaut group selected in 1962 to be named a commander. Finally, and most importantly to me, Jim was a Chicago boy, the first astronaut to fly from my neck of the woods. Later, we would share ties to the University of Michigan, where both he and I went to school, but that was still in my future in 1965.

Gemini 4 was launched on 3 June 1965 for a four-day mission. On the third orbit, McDivitt and White opened the hatch and White floated in space for 20 minutes. He used a 'zip gun' powered by pressurized oxygen to manoeuvre himself. White enjoyed the experience so much that he had to be ordered back into the spacecraft by Flight Director Chris Kraft. The call from the ground, in no uncertain terms, was, "The Flight Director says get back in!"

McDivitt took spectacular pictures that were released after the flight. Later, McDivitt was nominated for a Pulitzer Prize for his photography of the spacewalk (see Figure 9 page 39).

The rest of the flight after the extra-vehicular activity was also highly successful. The pair landed to a hero's welcome aboard the USS Wasp, the audio coverage of which was my first live space recording on my reel-to-reel tape recorder. I put the microphone next to our TV to record the live television coverage.

After the flight, President Johnson ordered the crew to go on a cross-country tour. My friend Marv and I learned about a planned visit to Chicago. A special program for high school students was scheduled to be one of McDivitt and White's stops in Chicago. Marv immediately went and got us the two tickets given to our high school so we could meet our first live astronauts.

The two astronauts flew to Chicago on 10 June 1965. Their entourage included Vice President Hubert Humphrey, Gemini Program Manager Charles Matthews, and NASA manned space chief Dr George Mueller (whom we would later meet again in 1969).

Marv and I were among the 6,500 students who saw McDivitt and White at the Arie Crown Theater in McCormick Place, a white stone-coloured convention center on the shore of Lake Michigan. I took a few pictures with an Instamatic camera.

We had seats towards the front of the large theater and when it was time for a question & answer session, Jim McDivitt was just a few feet away with a portable microphone. This was the first time I had encountered an astronaut in person. Even though he had just turned 36, McDivitt looked old. Perhaps it was the greying, crew-cut hair or the pale skin from being inside spacecraft trainers all day (**Figure 10**).

The two astronauts expertly answered the mainly softball questions from the high school children, and then they were off to other events that day. Mayor Richard J. ('The Boss') Daley pulled out all the stops to give them a hero's welcome.

The Gemini 4 visit was my last event under the auspices of Bowen High School in Chicago. For a variety of reasons, my parents decided to move away from the city of Chicago to the South Suburbs. They found a beautiful, unconventional ranch house in a small village, Olympia Fields, about 20 miles south of the city and I had just turned 15 when we moved there in August 1965.

I was excited about going to a different high school (Rich Township Central) but unhappy about losing close contact with my friends, including Marv. Before my family moved from the city, my friends threw me a memorable surprise party that summer (**Figure 11**).

Unfortunately, I remained only in sporadic contact with them, Marv included. The lack of email, social media or cellphones at the time made communication more difficult.

At the same time, in August 1965, Gordon Cooper and Charles 'Pete' Conrad flew for 8 days in Earth orbit aboard Gemini 5 – this was considered at the time a long-duration mission. The crew designed a patch showing a pioneer

Figure 10: Gemini 4 Commander Jim McDivitt answers questions from high school students including the Author in Chicago on 10 June 1965. McDivitt and Ed White were the first astronauts encountered in person by the Author.

Figure 11: High school friends hold a surprise party for the Author before he moves from Chicago to the suburbs in August 1965. The Author is in the upper row at center. His friend Marvin Rubenstein is at lower right.

© David Chudwin

Conestoga wagon. The original patch had an inscription 'Eight Days or Bust', but timid NASA managers insisted that the inscription be covered up lest that goal not be accomplished. (It was, despite problems with pesky fuel cells.)

I started my sophomore year of high school at Rich Central just after the Gemini 5 flight was successfully completed. The suburban high school was a different environment, with a new building, middle-class student body, broader course offerings and an honour system that extended to unlocked lockers.

However, there were still the proverbial high school cliques. By natural association, I ended up with 'the brains'. I joined several clubs and started writing for *The Torch*, the student newspaper. The satisfaction I received from writing sparked an interest in journalism that has continued to this day (**Figure 12**).

Sports reigned at Rich Central, and athletes were at the top of the social order. To avoid complete disdain, I joined the sophomore track team. I decided that throwing the shot-put required the least athleticism on my part, but I still had to do long practice runs with the rest of the track team. At least I had a team to mention when asked the ever-present question, "Are you on a team?" I did end up getting a sophomore letter for track, which is still in my study. All the running also helped me slim down; my 'fat period' was a thing of the past.

The next Gemini mission in 1965, Gemini-Titan (GT)-6, was supposed to be the first rendezvous and docking mission in space. A rendezvous involves two spacecraft flying together in close proximity, while docking means two spacecraft becoming physically attached. The plan was to use an Atlas booster to launch an Agena rocket stage

Figure 12: The Author (right) as one of the Editors of his high school newspaper, *The Torch*. Students were required to dress up for these yearbook photos.

into Earth orbit, which would serve as a target. Astronauts Wally Schirra and Tom Stafford would then blast off in their Gemini spacecraft to chase after the Agena target. The nose of the Gemini spacecraft would dock with the Agena target receptor. All was ready in October 1965 when there was a major problem – the Atlas-Agena target rocket exploded after launch.

NASA managers, faced with up to a six-month delay in bringing the Atlas-Agena back in service, came up with the ingenious plan of combining Gemini 6 with the follow-on flight. That mission, Gemini 7, with Frank Borman and Jim Lovell aboard, was designed to be a two-week, long-duration flight. With the unavailability of the Agena, NASA planners decided to make Gemini 7 the target in orbit for Gemini 6. Gemini 7 would be launched first, followed by Gemini 6 a few days later. The two spacecraft, Gemini 6 and Gemini 7, could not dock together, nose to nose, but they could rendezvous in close proximity.

On 15 December 1965, this goal was accomplished with great success. The two spacecraft flew together as close as one foot apart. The astronauts could see each other through the windows. There were also some of the expected inter-service US military rivalry signs, such as the football reference, 'Beat Army'. There was a lot of competition between US astronauts who were naval officers and those who were Army officers. The astronauts brought back some spectacular pictures (Figure 13).

The Gemini 7/6 mission was also a milestone in the 'space race' – for the first time, the United States pulled ahead of the Russians in space milestones by performing the first active and close-up rendezvous in space.

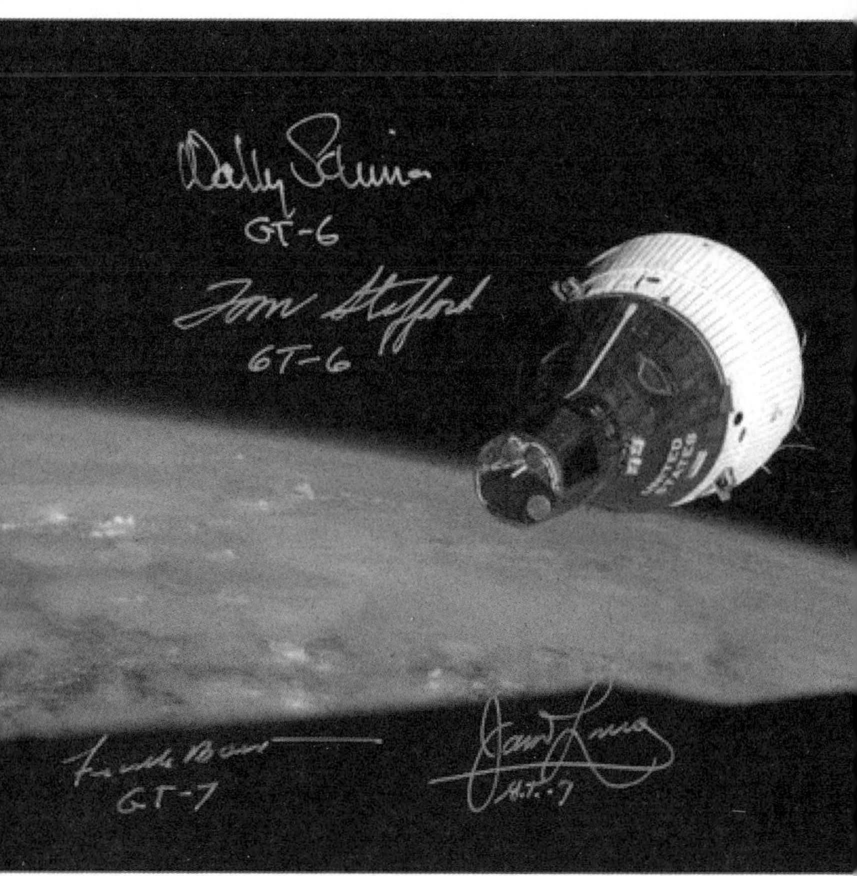

Figure 13: The Gemini 7/6 mission in December 1965 marked the first active rendezvous of two crewed spacecraft.

© David Chudwin/NASA

(The Russians twice had two capsules in orbit at the same time but they had not rendezvoused.)

As 1966 dawned, I was enjoying my new high school in the suburbs. My sophomore class had about 360 students, less than half of my Chicago school. The quality of education was, for the most part, also better. I excelled in chemistry and physics, although math was a challenge. I was also excellent in English and French.

I chose French as my foreign language for all the 'wrong' reasons. The class was mainly made up of girls, which I liked. Also, the teacher was a sweet lady who was Swiss.

I learned to write better due to the efforts of a tough but inspiring English teacher, Mr J.C. Dredla, who painstakingly commented on our essay submissions. Also, I learned to write succinctly as a staff member of *The Torch*. The 'who, what, why, when and where' required for newspaper stories would later help me communicate in my career as a physician.

The next Gemini flight, GT-8, was planned for March 1966. While almost all the astronauts were active duty military officers, the commander of Gemini 8 was to be a civilian – Mr Neil Armstrong, a former X-15 pilot who had flown that hypersonic vehicle to the edge of space. I had an affinity with Armstrong's fellow crew member because of the pilot's name – David Scott, coincidentally the same as my own first and middle names.

Armstrong and Scott successfully performed the first docking in space, easing the nose cone of Gemini 8 into the Agena docking receptor while both space vehicles were in Earth orbit. Shortly thereafter, the astronauts noted that the joined Gemini-Agena started to rotate. Armstrong, following emergency procedures, separated the two space vehicles and the spin became increasingly worse, up to one rotation per second.

Armstrong and Scott started to develop blurred vision and were on the verge of passing out. Armstrong was able to calmly troubleshoot the problem and used a separate reentry rocket system to control the position of their Gemini spacecraft. Later it was found that a small rocket thruster in the capsule's attitude control system had been stuck open.

Once the reentry rockets were fired, however, mission rules required the men to return to Earth, which they did on the next orbit. Originally scheduled to land in the Atlantic, Gemini 8 came down in the Pacific Ocean, many miles from any recovery ship. A secondary US Navy recovery ship, the USS Leonard Mason, raced to pick up the men and their capsule.

The Gemini 8 flight was significant as it successfully achieved the first docking in space and the first emergency return to Earth by an American crew. Furthermore, Armstrong's skilled piloting in the emergency burnished his reputation for coolness under pressure.

Later in 1966, I sent a colour photograph I had obtained from NASA by a mail request showing the Gemini 8 Agena launch to Neil Armstrong at the Manned Spacecraft Center. A few weeks later I received it back through the mail inscribed to me. While Armstrong stopped giving almost all autographs in 1994, in these early years he was generous with his signature. Years later I had Dave Scott also sign it to complete the Gemini 8 crew (**Figure 14**).

The crew for the next Gemini mission, GT-9, was veteran Tom Stafford and a rookie astronaut, Eugene Cernan.

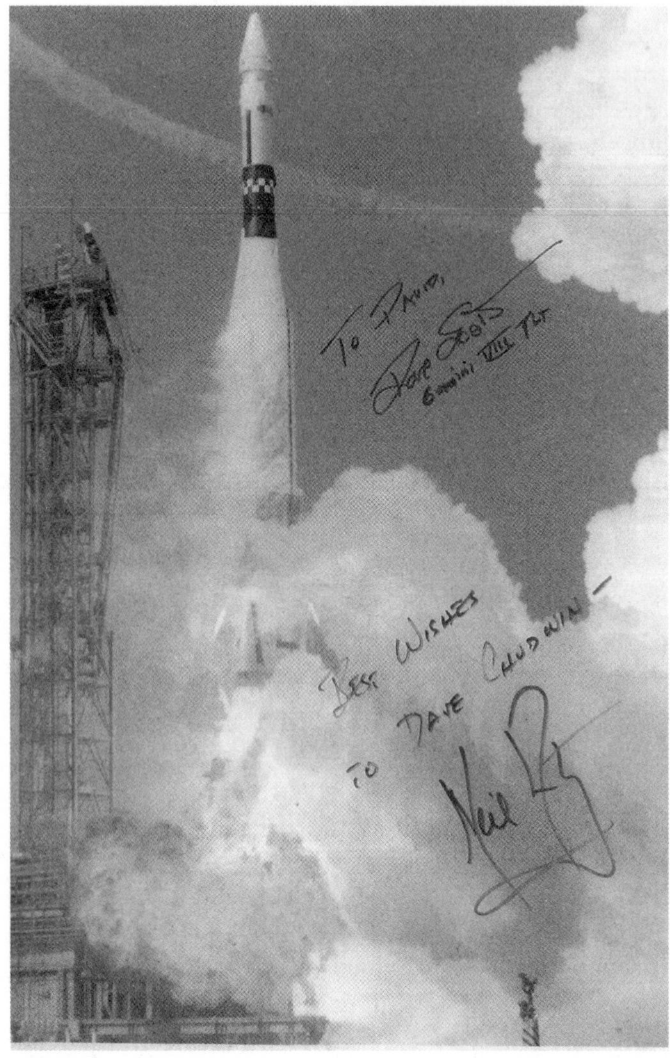

Figure 14: A NASA photograph of the Gemini 8's Atlas Agena target vehicle shortly after launch. The photo is inscribed to the Author by Gemini 8 crew members Neil Armstrong and Dave Scott.

Cernan was a native of the Chicago area, growing up in Bellwood, a gritty suburb with a large immigrant population just west of the city.

The two main tasks for the Gemini 9 crew were to dock with an Agena target stage and to perfect spacewalking techniques.

However, in May 1966, due to a booster malfunction, the Agena target vehicle for Gemini 9 blew up after launch and ended up in the ocean instead of in orbit. A smaller target device, called the Augmented Target Docking Adapter (ATDA), was quickly developed to be sent into orbit as the Gemini 9 target. The ATDA was launched by an Atlas rocket on 3 June 1966, and a few hours later Stafford and Cernan followed aboard their Gemini 9 spacecraft on top of a Titan II rocket.

When Gemini 9 rendezvoused with the ATDA, the astronauts saw that the two payload covers protecting the ATDA for launch had incompletely separated, looking like two long jaws. Stafford memorably described the ATDA's appearance as an 'angry alligator'.

The Gemini 9 spacecraft approached the target adapter but could not dock because the two payload covers, the 'jaws' of the alligator, blocked the docking receptor. Mission Control decided to settle for a rendezvous rather than a dangerous attempt to open the 'jaws'.

The success of Ed White's limited 20-minute spacewalk on Gemini 4 had given NASA officials a false sense of security about extra-vehicular activities, which involve astronauts in space suits floating in space. Cernan was scheduled for a more ambitious extra-vehicular activity on Gemini 9, but had to end it prematurely. During his spacewalk, Cernan became sweaty, overheated and exhausted as he struggled to do tasks without the hand holds and foot holds that went on to become mandatory. His visor fogged up, his heart rate increased and he became dehydrated from sweating. Cernan ended early what he later called the 'spacewalk from hell', after 1 hour and 46 minutes of frustration.

It was clear that more work was needed to allow successful spacewalks. The problems with the Gemini 9 extra-vehicular activity led NASA to redouble its efforts to find better techniques to move around in microgravity. For example, astronaut Buzz Aldrin and others proposed using neutral buoyancy underwater training to simulate working in space.

Despite the difficulties, the mission was deemed a success. Stafford and Cernan received a hero's welcome on their return. My friend Marv and I heard of plans for Cernan's hometown of Bellwood, Illinois, to hold a parade for the Gemini 9 crew and a public question & answer session. I wrote to Bellwood's mayor to try to get a couple of tickets and received a letter back that none were necessary; he sent me a schedule of events.

Marv had remained in Chicago, attending Bowen High School, while I was out in the suburbs, and we decided that the Gemini 9 welcome event would be a good opportunity for us to get together again. We went to Bellwood for the parade and public meeting.

Despite being only 35 years old at the time, Stafford was almost bald with a fringe of greying hair; he was also tall (six feet) for an astronaut. Also with greying hair, Cernan looked older than his 32 years as well.

At the parade assembly site, we were able to say hello in person to the astronauts and we talked briefly to them

CHICAGO SUN-TIMES, Mon., June 27, 1966

3

les For Astronauts

Figure 15: *Chicago Sun-Times* report of 27 June 1966 about the visit of Gemini 9 astronauts Tom Stafford and Gene Cernan to Bellwood, Illinois. The Author is circled in this photo showing Cernan answering questions at lower left.

as the parade got under way. I asked for Stafford's autograph on a copy of the parade route and he obliged.

We followed the motorcade on foot for a while and then headed for the meeting place. Along with Stafford and Cernan, members of the Cernan family were present, including his mother Rose and his sister Dee, whom we would meet again three years later. The astronauts made brief remarks and answered questions. The day's activities were reported in the *Chicago Sun-Times* (Figure 15).

For Marv and me, it was exciting to meet these men who had just travelled in space three weeks before. As impressionable teenagers (I was 15), the astronauts remained our heroes.

Later, there were three additional Gemini flights in 1966, practicing docking, and firing up the Agena engine to go to increasingly higher orbits, but most of all, training in extra-vehicular activity techniques. During the final Gemini mission, GT-12, in November 1966, Buzz Aldrin performed a successful 2-hour, 20-minute spacewalk, retrieving a micrometeorite detector and performing other tasks. The new techniques that had been developed paid off on the final Gemini mission, and what was to be the last American manned spaceflight for close to two years.

CHAPTER 4

DAWN OF APOLLO: 1967

Figure 16: Apollo 1 astronauts Edward White, Virgil "Gus" Grissom and Roger Chaffee perished in a fire in their capsule during a ground test on 27 January 1967.

© NASA

With Project Gemini coming to an end, focus shifted to Project Apollo, whose mission was to send men to land on the Moon by the end of the decade. The Apollo Command and Service Modules (CSM) and lunar landing module development had increasing delays due to technical problems. NASA announced in March 1966 that astronauts Gus Grissom, Edward White and Roger Chaffee would be the crew for the first manned Apollo flight, which was originally scheduled for the last quarter of 1966. I wrote to NASA in the summer of 1966 requesting a colour lithograph of the crew, which I received (**Figure 16**).

The possibility of a Gemini/Apollo rendezvous was considered until further schedule slippage in CSM development made this a moot point. Finally, the planned two-week flight, designated Apollo/Saturn 204 (AS-204), was scheduled for 21 February 1967. (The two-stage rocket to launch the Apollo CSM was named Saturn 1B, hence the name Apollo/Saturn. There had been three previous unmanned test flights of the Apollo/Saturn 1B combination so the crewed mission was designated AS-204). However, fate intervened.

In late afternoon on 27 January 1967, Grissom, White and Chaffee were dressed in their spacesuits and strapped in their spacecraft for a powered-up test on the ground. A spark from some damaged or faulty wiring set off an intense fire that raged almost instantly in the 100% oxygen atmosphere in the spacecraft.

Shocked NASA and contractor employees battled smoke to open the hatch. They found the largely intact bodies of the astronauts lifeless in their spacesuits. All three astronauts died of asphyxiation within a couple of minutes, long before the bulky hatch could be removed. Ironically, the first U.S. astronauts to die in a spacecraft perished on the ground and not in space.

I remember that the first television and radio announcements from the Cape about the tragedy were vague as to which astronauts were involved, what they were doing and what was their fate. NASA delayed the details so that the families could be notified in person by fellow astronauts. With full military honours, Grissom and Chaffee were buried at Arlington National Cemetery and Ed White at West Point.

Investigation boards were set up by NASA and Congress to determine how and why the men died. Major changes in the Command Module were recommended, including an oxygen-nitrogen atmosphere for the spacecraft, sole use of flame-resistant materials inside the craft, and re-engineered doors that would allow a swifter exit. NASA would not fly Apollo until this revised Command Module would be available.

I was a junior in high school at the time of the Apollo fire, which brought the risks of spaceflight into very clear focus. Three of the best and the brightest astronauts had perished, including Gus Grissom, whom many observers at the time thought might be the first person on the Moon.

Realistically, I finally began to understand and accept that my own chances of actually becoming an astronaut were close to zero. I had bad eyesight and was afraid of unprotected heights (being in an airplane was fine, but not being on a high ledge) – not the best recipe for an astronaut in those days. I understood that fate had declared that I would be an 'armchair astronaut' instead of the real thing. Although it was disheartening to realize that my childhood dream of becoming an astronaut was unrealistic, I knew that even those with the best health faced immense odds.

So, in high school, I immersed myself in a variety of non-space related activities, including plays, Student Council, *The Torch* student newspaper, the French Club, etc.

At the same time, there were a lot of changes going on in the US and in the world in 1967. The Vietnam War was raging and there was already strong opposition to American involvement in that Asian civil war

I had come to despise that war for many reasons. First, the US should never have gotten involved in what was a civil war between two Vietnamese factions. Second, the rationale for US involvement (containing Communism to protect the US) was faulty because there was no Communist monolith – the Russians, Chinese and Vietnamese all hated each other for historical reasons. Third, the US military was prosecuting the war with crazy rules of engagement, tying the hands of commanders on the ground, and a misguided emphasis on 'body counts' that led to increased civilian casualties. Finally, there was an inherent unfairness in a draft system where the wealthy got college and other deferments, while the poor were drafted and sent to 'Nam'.

Planning had started for a massive protest rally against the war at the Lincoln Memorial in Washington, to be followed by a march on the Pentagon scheduled for 21 October 1967. Over 100,000 people attended the rally and an estimated 30,000 went on to the Pentagon, where they were met with tear gas, beatings and arrests.

The civil rights revolution had been evolving since a march in Washington in August 1963. Spearheaded by a younger generation of leaders, the 'Black Power' movement started to gain strength in 1967. More traditional leaders, such as the Rev. Martin Luther King, Jr, also spoke out that year against the Vietnam War, noting that its $25 billion annual cost was taking money away from helping the poor, and that the military draft unfairly affected poor young African-American men.

The rise of feminism posed a challenge to entrenched sexism. The 1950s paradigm of men as the jobholders and women as homemakers was eclipsed by a movement for women's rights. The 1963 book *The Feminine Mystique* sparked a re-appraisal of the role of women in most spheres – an exception being NASA, where women, with only a few exceptions, were relegated to traditional roles such as nurses or secretaries. While the Russians had launched Valentina Tereshkova as the first woman in orbit aboard Vostok 6 in 1963, females aspiring to become astronauts in the US were rebuffed. For instance, Sally Ride, the first American woman in space, did not fly until 1983.

Finally, there was a cultural revolution going on in the Western World. The 'hippie' movement began with drug use, psychedelic music, anti-capitalism, anti-consumerism, 'free love' and 'dropping out' from society. Tens of thousands of hippies, mainly young people, made their way to San Francisco in 1967 for an ongoing happening of music, drugs and free sex that was later described as the 'Summer of Love'. While that movement affected musical tastes nationwide, it did not take hold as much in the Midwest as on the West and East Coasts.

The hippie movement was anti-technology and anti-big business. The movement was not, in general, supportive of the space program, other than the message of one world without political boundaries derived from pictures and views from space. The space program was seen as part of the 'military industrial complex' that ate up billions of tax dollars and propped up the hated Vietnam War.

In the middle of all this, I submitted university applications in the fall of 1967. Unlike many of my classmates, I did not want to attend the University of Illinois because I frankly did not like the campus. There were boxy red brick buildings set right next to flat farm fields, with the smell of fertilizer in the air when I visited. The Urbana-Champaign campus was no match for beautiful ones at the University of Wisconsin-Madison, Michigan State University in East Lansing and the University of Michigan-Ann Arbor. As a long shot, I also applied to Harvard and Yale, but did not even bother to visit, doing local interviews instead.

I had very good standardized test scores, an excellent grade point average, and participated in many activities in high school. I had done well in my classes and enjoyed most of them.

One class I did not like was gym, where my instructor was a big, muscular, former professional football player from Texas and now the head high school football coach. He vowed to get us physically fit so that if we were sent to Vietnam we would, he said, have a better chance of making it back. His workouts were brutal, although they did get me in shape.

So, as 1967 concluded, both the space program and my own status were in flux.

NASA was trying hard to recover from the Apollo disaster. The Apollo Command Module was extensively redesigned because of the fire. Wally Schirra, Donn Eisele

CARL
CAPT.
DAVE
"Take!" Scholars stay cool under hot lights.

Figure 17: The Author (centre) was captain of the high school's *It's Academic* team and appeared twice on Chicago television.

© David Chudwin

and Walt Cunningham were named the crew for the next flight. It was named Apollo 7 – Grissom's crew was posthumously designated Apollo 1 and unmanned Apollo tests were counted as Apollo 2 through 6, making the next mission Apollo 7.

I was enjoying my senior year of high school, happily engaged in a variety of activities, the most enjoyable of which was writing for and helping to edit *The Torch*. I also was honoured to be the captain of our school team competing on the *It's Academic* television quiz show, and appeared twice on television (**Figure 17**).

Our team won the first match but went down to defeat in the next one. I took a girlfriend to our high school senior prom, which included a chaperoned overnight bus trip.

I continued to follow the space program closely, intently watching television coverage, saving newspaper and magazine articles, and collecting space philatelic envelopes.

I looked forward to what developments the new year 1968 would bring.

CHAPTER 5

COLLEGE BOUND: 1968

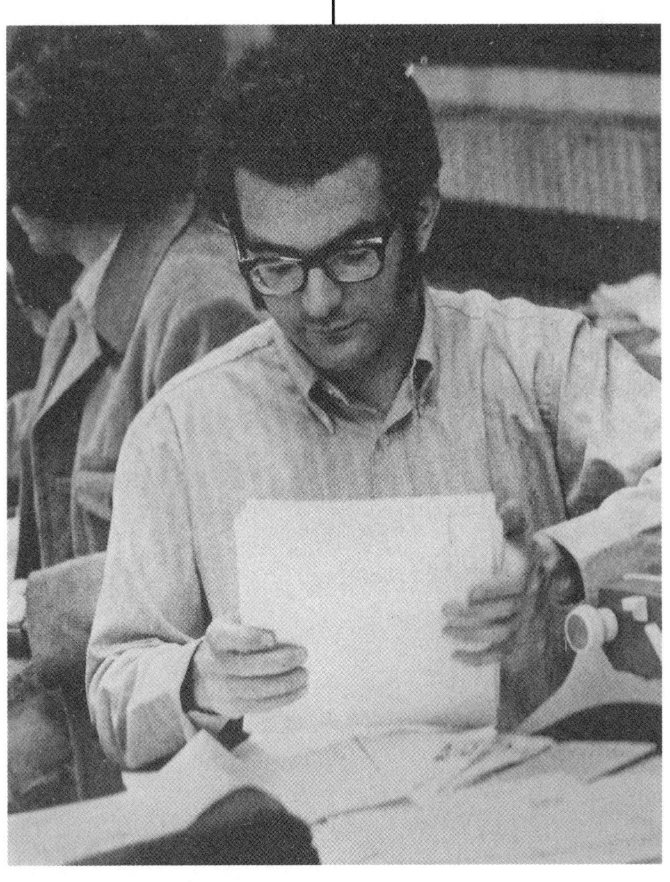

Figure 18: The Author as a college journalist at *The Michigan Daily* in Ann Arbor, Michigan.

My first major decision in 1968 was where to attend college. I received expected rejection letters from Harvard and Yale, but was happy to receive acceptances from the University of Wisconsin, the University of Michigan, and Michigan State University. I felt that, academically, Wisconsin and Michigan were better than MSU, so the choice was between those two.

In 1968 there was a lot of social upheaval, including bombings and violent demonstrations by radical elements against the Vietnam War, affecting the University of Wisconsin campus. Although I had family ties to Wisconsin (my parents both went to college there and I had relatives in Madison) and it was situated in a beautiful campus on Lake Mendota, I decided not to accept this offer.

The University of Michigan was also anti-war, but the protests there appeared to be less militant and more thoughtful. I saw the academic environment in Ann Arbor as being more conducive to learning, so I accepted admission there to begin as a freshman in August 1968.

In the spring of 1968 I started volunteering for the McCarthy presidential campaign. Eugene McCarthy was a US Senator from Minnesota running on an anti-war platform for the Democratic Party nomination for US President. I admired his courage in speaking out against the war and in opposing the Democratic Party establishment.

I did door-to-door pre-election canvassing in nearby Indiana, organized some of my fellow high school students to also do campaigning for McCarthy, and occasionally went to the McCarthy headquarters in downtown Chicago. The local newspaper covered a fundraising barbeque event held at my house that more than 100 people attended.

The national Democratic Convention to choose the party's nominee to run for president was held at the end of August 1968 in Chicago. I was disappointed at the time because Michigan had a trimester schedule, which meant that I couldn't attend the convention since I had to be in Ann Arbor to start at the university. From newspaper and television reports, I later found out that people with whom I worked on the McCarthy campaign were beaten and arrested during the Chicago 'police riot' that occurred. I was shocked and angry at the police brutality and concerned about the arrests and injuries. Had I not left for Ann Arbor, I could have been one of them.

In the meantime, I finished high school, graduating from Rich Central, and got a summer job on the maintenance crew at Allied Steel, a factory that made steel tubing and pipes. It was a dirty and dusty job that gave me appreciation for the relatively easy life of a student. The full-time workers, who thought I was soft (they were right), told me to slow down my work, which was difficult for a Type A person such as myself. My eagerness was not appreciated, and I eventually took the hint.

As NASA feverishly re-engineered the Apollo Command Module, I packed for college and my parents drove me to Ann Arbor the third week of August 1968. This wonderful small college town in Michigan was to be my home for the next eight years (I also went to medical school there). I moved into Alice Lloyd Hall, a newly coed dorm. I was the only one from my high school entering the University of Michigan so I had to make new friends.

For new freshmen students, social life revolved at first around dormitory activities. At the first wild dorm party,

I got terribly drunk and threw up. It was not a pretty sight, me sitting dizzily on a toilet with my head between my knees and barfing on the floor! I learned my lesson (drink moderately) and started to look for other activities on campus.

With my positive experience on the high school newspaper, I investigated *The Michigan Daily*, the independent campus paper founded back in 1890. There was no formal journalism department at the University of Michigan at that time, but generations of young, prospective journalists had learned the profession at *The Daily*. It was (and still is) an organization dedicated to the truth, irreverent but never irrelevant, and almost fraternity-like in its customs and rituals.

The headquarters of *The Daily*, at 420 Maynard Street, was a two-story brick building from the 1920s. It has recently been renovated and renamed, but the structure remains almost the same.

In 1968, the ground floor had printing presses and hot-type linotype machines run by skilled, veteran tradesmen. The upstairs was the newsroom, a large open space filled with old desks and typewriters, an Associated Press wire machine, an office for the senior editors, and a library filled with old bound volumes of the paper dating back to the turn of the 20th century. A key feature was a Coca-Cola machine that dispensed glass bottles of Coke for a nickel (subsidized by the newspaper). The desks and floors were strewn with old newspapers, empty Coke bottles and greasy pizza boxes from the nearby Cottage Inn Pizza restaurant – it was a mess.

The Daily was a subculture dominated by the senior editors, who actually took office in March of their junior years.

To trainees, these 'grizzled' 21-year-old campus paper veterans had godlike status as they critically edited articles, fought about the correct placement of the stories and argued politics, especially with regard to editorials. They seemed smart, confident and totally committed to *The Daily*, staying up to eat pizza and play bridge at 420 Maynard after the 2 a.m. deadline to put the paper to bed. This was the 'latest deadline in the state', which was a proud claim of *The Daily*.

After going to a recruitment meeting, I decided to sign up for the news staff – other departments were sports, photography and business. When I worked at The Daily as a trainee, I realized that I was different from my fellow freshmen. I was one of very, very few students planning to major in a science (zoology) and considering a scientific or medical career. Almost everyone else was either in the humanities or did not have the faintest idea what they would do with their college degree. I was pleased to have some preliminary plans for my future instead of just pursuing general studies (see Figure 18 page 65).

I can also say with certitude that in 1968 I was the ONLY person at the time at *The Daily* headquarters who had any serious interest in space. Attempts at discussions about the value of the space program were met with disinterest and disagreement.

The Apollo 7 mission in October 1968 marked the return to space by the US after the Apollo fire the year before; it was the first manned Apollo flight. The new redesigned Apollo CSM carried Wally Schirra, Donn Eisele and Walt Cunningham into Earth orbit for an 11-day flight to test the Apollo spacecraft.

Since no one else volunteered, I asked if I could write an article for the editorial page about the flight. I was only a freshman, but because I was the only volunteer, I was given the assignment.

I wrote an editorial, *A case for going to outer space*, in which I summarized the rationale for manned spaceflight. My main arguments were that the space program paid off in economic and practical applications, in scientific knowledge and in technological leadership. As for the NASA budget, I noted: "The war in Vietnam and pork barrel projects cost far more than space exploration and yield far fewer benefits, both actual and potential, than the space program. A sensible stable space program is an investment in the future, an investment this country should make".

The editorial was published in *The Daily* on 23 October 1968. Fifty years on from this editorial – my first but not the last for the paper – I would note that it sounds pretty good for an 18-year-old freshman. With just minor updating, it could be published again today.

My first trimester at the University of Michigan in the fall and early winter of 1968 was exciting and busy, between adjusting to campus life, my course load and my time at *The Daily*.

While at Michigan, I frequently passed the corner of University Avenue that had been named in 1965 in honour of astronauts Jim McDivitt and Ed White. They had received their bachelor's (McDivitt) and master's (White) degrees in 1959 from the university's famed aeronautical engineering department. The corner, near the Engineering Arch, was later turned into a plaza. Coincidentally, the Apollo 15 crew also all attended U of M for parts of their education.

I went home at the end of December 1968, pleased that I had decided to become a 'Michigan man' and looking forward to 1969. It was good to be back with my parents and brothers for the holidays. However, NASA had plans afoot to end 1968 with a bang.

Originally NASA had planned to test the Lunar Module on an early flight of the mammoth Saturn V Moon rocket, whereas Apollo 7 had used the smaller Saturn 1B rocket. However, Lunar Module development was delayed by several months due to engineering and manufacturing issues. So, the space agency faced the dilemma of having a Saturn V rocket ready for its first crewed launch, but with no Lunar Module to test.

In the spring of 1968, the brilliant Apollo spacecraft program manager George Low and some associates in Houston came up with the audacious plan of sending the first crewed Saturn V Apollo flight to orbit the Moon. Astronauts had never ridden aboard a Saturn V before, or ever even left Earth's orbit, and it was to be only the second manned Apollo mission.

After some reluctance, Dr George Mueller, the head of manned spaceflight, and NASA Administrator James Webb signed off on the plan. Astronauts Frank Borman and Jim Lovell (crew mates on Gemini 7) were named to the crew, as well as rookie Bill Anders.

Apollo 8 was launched 21 December 1968 by a 363-foot-high, three-stage Saturn V rocket from the Kennedy Space Center in Florida. I was travelling back home from Ann Arbor and missed seeing the launch live on television.

Borman, Lovell and Anders became the first human beings to leave Earth's orbit as they sped towards the Moon. "You are go for TLI," came the decidedly non-dramatic yet historic call from Mission Control in Houston by capsule communicator (CAPCOM) astronaut Mike Collins. The CAPCOM is the astronaut on the ground who communicates with the crew in space. 'TLI', trans-lunar injection in NASA jargon, is the rocket firing to send Apollo from Earth's orbit towards the Moon. Overall, this trip to the Moon was expected to take three days.

The Apollo 8 CSM went into lunar orbit on 24 December 1968. I watched the TV coverage at home. As Apollo 8 flew around the Moon, radio contact was lost on the far side, so there was no way to know whether the burning of the engine to slow the spacecraft down into a successful lunar orbit had worked or not. There was nail-biting apprehension because if the engines did not fire correctly, the spacecraft could have crashed into the Moon or been sent into a fatal trajectory into space that would have prevented its return to Earth.

At exactly the right moment, radio signals were received again as Apollo 8 came around the Moon, indicating that the spacecraft was in the correct orbit. There was applause from the floor of Mission Control in Houston. The three men radioed descriptions of the lunar surface, with its craters, valleys and mountains. They also took dozens of photographs.

As they completed their third orbit around the Moon, the men noticed Earth starting to appear just above the lunar surface. Realizing they were seeing 'Earthrise' for the first time, Anders took a series of black-and-white and colour pictures.

The colour picture taken by Anders of 'Earthrise' is perhaps the most influential photograph taken during this Apollo 8 flight. It showed Earth as a small blue globe in the infinity of the dark cosmos, without political borders and with a fragile, thin layer of air (Figure 19).

There had been several short television broadcasts from Apollo 8, but the most anticipated was one planned for Christmas Eve. No one knew what the astronauts would say, but their broadcast location from lunar orbit brought them an audience of hundreds of millions of people around the world.

The broadcast began with them showing ghostly pictures of the Moon below from their spacecraft windows. Borman introduced each of the three crew members, and they each described their impressions of the landmarks and terrain below. Then, as they approached lunar darkness, Bill Anders began their special Christmas message to Earth:

BILL ANDERS

"We are now approaching lunar sunrise, and for all the people back on Earth, the crew of Apollo 8 has a message that we would like to send to you."

'In the beginning God created the heaven and the earth.

'And the earth was without form, and void; and darkness was upon the face of the deep.

'And the Spirit of God moved upon the face of the waters. And God said, Let there be light: and there was light.

'And God saw the light, that it was good: and God divided the light from the darkness.'

Figure 19: Astronaut Bill Anders took this historic picture of 'Earthrise' from the Apollo 8 spacecraft as it orbited the Moon on 24 December 1968.

© NASA/David Chudwin

JIM LOVELL

'And God called the light Day, and the darkness he called Night. And the evening and the morning were the first day.

'And God said, let there be a firmament in the midst of the waters, and let it divide the waters from the waters.

'And God made the firmament, and divided the waters which were under the firmament from the waters which were above the firmament: and it was so.

'And God called the firmament Heaven. And the evening and the morning were the second day.'

FRANK BORMAN

'And God said, Let the waters under the heaven be gathered together unto one place, and let the dry land appear: and it was so.

'And God called the dry land Earth; and the gathering together of the waters called the Seas: and God saw that it was good.'

"And from the crew of Apollo 8, we close with good night, good luck, a Merry Christmas – and God bless all of you, all of you on the good Earth."

The crew had chosen to read the first ten verses of the Book of Genesis. It was perfect. Because the reading was from the Bible, there was a religious connotation to the broadcast relating to the Christmas season. However, there was no denomination mentioned, and most religions had a creation tradition. Moreover, the description of the creation of the 'heavens and Earth' jibed with the scenes of the barren Moon and black sky shown on the television screens.

Along with many people at the time, I had tears in my eyes as Frank Borman ended with his salutation of, "good night, good luck, a Merry Christmas – and God bless all of you, all of you on the good Earth." The Christmas reading from the Moon provoked a strong emotional reaction, overwhelmingly positive. It was, to that time, the most-watched television event in history.

The year 1968 had been an *annus horribilis*; a terrible year. Robert Kennedy and Martin Luther King, Jr, had been assassinated. Yuri Gagarin tragically died too young in an air crash. There had been race riots. The Vietnam War was raging with increasing casualties. Amongst all of this turmoil, the highly successful Apollo 8 flight, with its 'Earthrise' photo and its Christmas broadcast, was a rare bright spot for the United States and the world overall. So much so that when *Time* magazine selected its 1968 'Man of the Year', Borman, Lovell and Anders were selected to share the honour.

CHAPTER 6

A PIVOTAL YEAR: 1969

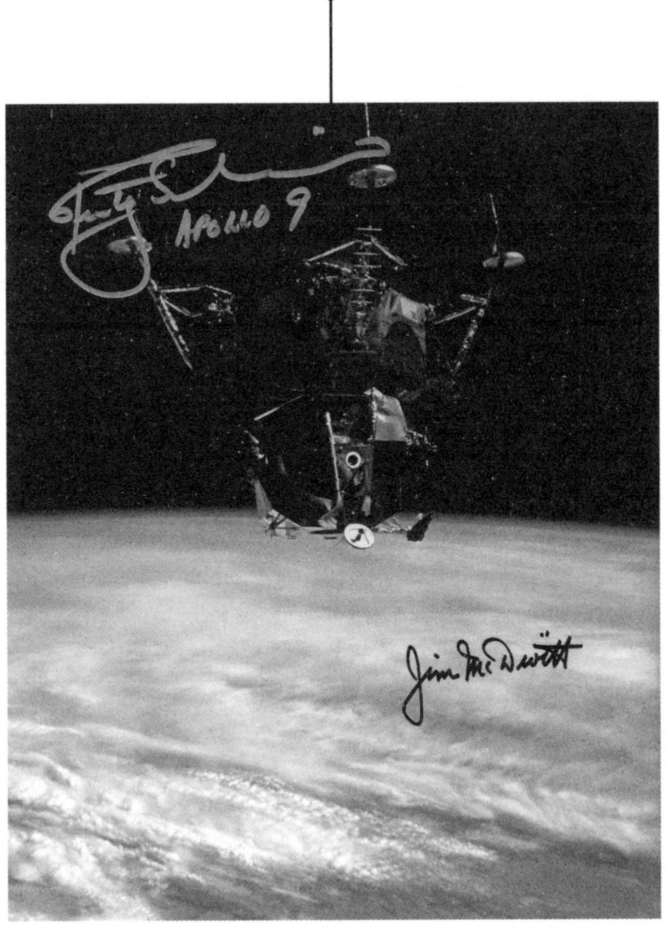

Figure 20: The Lunar Module, shown in Earth orbit during the Apollo 9 mission, was the pacing spacecraft in the Apollo program. Astronauts James McDivitt and Russell Schweickart tested it in March 1969.

The year 1969 was special in many fields of human endeavour; even January at the year's beginning brought important new developments.

In politics, Richard Nixon was sworn in as US president, and Spiro Agnew as vice president, on 20 January 1969. Both would leave office, disgraced, within the next five years. Nixon, along with advisers Henry Kissinger and Melvin Laird, came up with a plan to 'Vietnamize' the war there by placing more responsibility on the South Vietnamese troops and start bringing US forces back home.

In sports, the New York Jets football team defeated the Baltimore Colts 16-7 on 12 January 1969, in Super Bowl III. Later in the same year, the Boston Celtics were the 1968-69 National Basketball Association champs, defeating the Los Angeles Lakers 4-3 in a seven-game series. The Montreal Canadiens won hockey's Stanley Cup in 1969 by defeating the St Louis Blues in four straight matches.

In music, Elvis Presley returned to recording studios in Memphis in January 1969, and started working on songs in the albums *From Elvis In Memphis* and *Back in Memphis*. These songs marked a comeback for the rock 'n roll singer and included *Kentucky Rain* and *Suspicious Minds*. The Billboard Top Hit Single for January 1969 was *I Heard It Through the Grapevine* by Marvin Gaye, still popular today. *Crimson & Clover* by Tommy James & the Shondels took over as the Top Hit Single afterwards. And, of course, later in the summer, the Woodstock festival brought 'three days of peace and music' to upstate New York.

In the bookstores, *Portnoy's Complaint* by Phillip Roth and *The Salzburg Connection* by Helen MacInnes were the top fiction sellers during the first half of 1969.

A 'counterculture' had developed across the US by 1969, especially on college campuses and in college towns. The clothing was informal, with tattered and torn blue jeans both for men and women. Tie-dyed t-shirts or blue work shirts were standard, as were army-style coats. Bras were optional for women. Gone were the suits or sport coats and ties for men, and the short dresses for women, which had prevailed in the early- and mid-'60s.

Long hair was one of the badges of the counterculture, so much so that the musical *Hair* became one of the hit plays of the time. I had thick, bushy hair in 1969 but had to occasionally cut it to prevent it from frizzing out into an 'afro'. For men, beards were the rage. I grew one but found it to be too scratchy and it made me look really old.

Drug use was rampant, especially marijuana, otherwise known as 'pot'. Yes, I did inhale, although usually at parties where I bummed hits from others. I shied away from other popular drugs of the day, which included LSD, cocaine, quaaludes and amphetamines.

The politics of those years were self-described as 'revolutionary', although there was a remarkable conformity in thought, dress and culture. Much of the culture from 1969 seems either hopelessly misguided or romantic to us now, five decades later, but the music endures. Some of the old rockers from that time are still around – groups such as the Rolling Stones and individual artists like Bob Dylan, Judy Collins, Joan Baez, Peter and Paul (without the late Mary Travers), and Grace Slick. Many more were lost to drugs, Jim Morrison, Jimi Hendrix, Keith Moon and Janis Joplin among them.

The NASA and contractor engineers and scientists working on the space program in 1969 were at the other end of the cultural divide. The stereotype of the clean-shaven white male engineer with crew-cut hair, white short-sleeve shirt, thin black tie, plastic pocket protector with pens and pencils, and thick horned-rimmed glasses was, like many stereotypes, not that far from the truth.

The politics of NASA and contractor employees were generally conservative. The drug of choice was alcohol. Women were either disregarded or objects of sexual desires. Hippies were looked down on as lazy, dirty, unpatriotic and non-productive young people who rejected advanced technology yet took advantage of its fruits.

The focus of NASA management in early 1969 was to complete the construction of the first Lunar Module, the spider-like craft that was to actually land men on the Moon. But delays with Lunar Module development meant that President Kennedy's goal of landing before the end of the decade was becoming increasingly doubtful. A successful test of the Lunar Module in Earth's orbit was the first hurdle that needed to be passed.

Apollo 9, scheduled to be launched in March 1969, was to be the first complete Apollo/Saturn mission, with a Saturn V rocket, Apollo CSM and, for the first time, a manned Lunar Module. (There had been two previous flights of unmanned Lunar Modules.) The crew, which had been training together since 1966 as backups to the ill-fated Apollo 1 crew, consisted of veteran commander Jim McDivitt, Command Module pilot Dave Scott and rookie Lunar Module pilot Rusty Schweickart.

Apollo 9 was finally launched into Earth orbit on 3 March 1969, and the crew tested the Lunar Module's systems and successfully manoeuvred it. The Lunar Module had the radio call sign 'Spider' for this mission.

McDivitt and Schweickart fired both the descent and ascent engines of the Lunar Module, flying a round trip of 110 miles to and from the CSM, which had the radio call sign 'Gumdrop' because of its shape. This mimicked the lunar landing, using the descent engine to fly away from the CSM, jettisoning the descent stage, and flying back to the CSM using the ascent stage engine (see **Figure 20** page 77).

Schweickart was scheduled to perform an extensive spacewalk and test the new spacesuit that was due to be worn by the astronauts on the Moon, but he developed 'space sickness'. Soon after launch, he was overcome by dizziness, nausea and vomiting. Schweickart was a victim of what we now know as 'space adaptation syndrome' (SAS), caused by a delay in adaptation of the inner ear's vestibular apparatus to microgravity. It affects about half of astronauts, but in 10%, such as Schweickart, it is more severe, and in fact he never flew again.

Years later, at a Spacefest luncheon, Schweickart became increasingly irritated with me as I questioned him about SAS while he was trying to eat. Apparently even the memories of the experience made him queasy.

The success of Apollo 9 in 1969 paved the way for NASA to try to reach the Moon with only nine months to go until the end of the decade.

CHAPTER 7

CAPE KENNEDY OR BUST: APRIL-MAY 1969

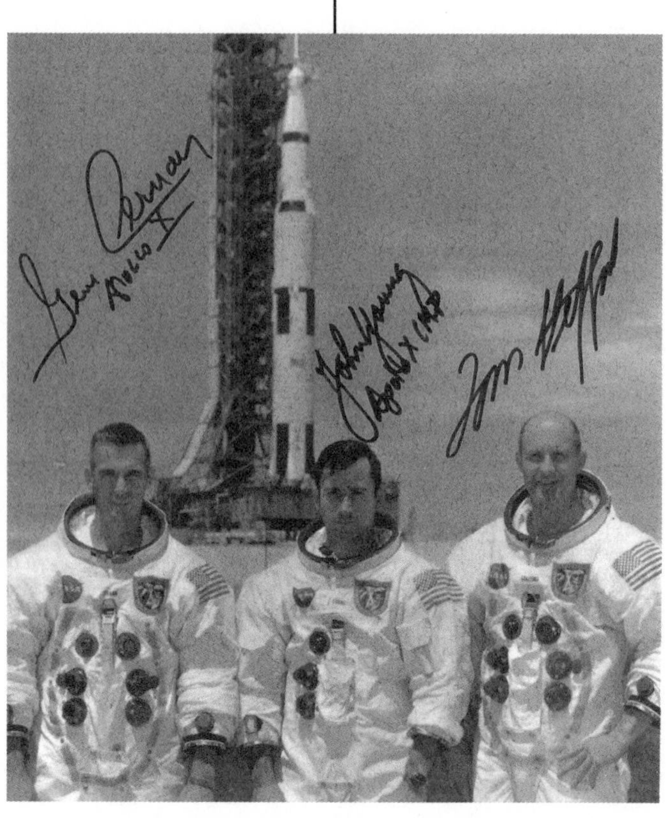

Figure 21: The Apollo 10 flight with astronauts Eugene Cernan, John Young and Thomas Stafford was the "dress rehearsal" for the Moon landing. The Author waited until this flight was accomplished to make reservations to go to Florida for Apollo 11.

After the success of Apollo 9, NASA began to prepare for the next Apollo flight (Apollo 10), a full rehearsal, in orbit around the Moon, of the rocket firings and manoeuvres required for a lunar landing.

Back in Ann Arbor, I was working hard, trying to balance my classes with my time at *The Michigan Daily*, where I had been promoted to the still-lowly rank of assistant night editor. This involved coming in 1-2 evenings a week and helping to produce the paper, which was published Tuesday through Sunday mornings. I edited Associated Press wire copy and also articles by our own reporters, wrote headlines and made phone calls. All this was under the watchful eye of the particular night editor for that issue, who oversaw the next edition of the paper. I also started to do some news reporting, assigned at first to cover university events.

Meanwhile, I had been in contact periodically with Marv, my old friend and fellow space enthusiast. He was going to college at the University of Illinois campus in Chicago while I was at Michigan. We talked mainly when I went back to Chicago for holidays and over winter breaks.

Marv was the one who first suggested in the spring that we travel down to Florida during the summer of 1969 to see a launch. Neither of us had viewed a launch in person, and now that we were men, at 18 years old, we could travel more easily.

We decided to put the idea on hold until we saw how Apollo 10, the next flight, would play out. This would determine whether there would be any launches during our summer break from college (June through August).

I was fortunate, through a friend of the family, to get a summer job working at a clothing store on fashionable Michigan Avenue in downtown Chicago. Murray Smikler's was a purveyor of fancy men's clothing. This job appeared to be ideal after my previous dirty one, the summer before, working at Allied Tube. (I'd had a summer job the year before that as a maintenance worker at a US Gypsum Corporation factory, where I was exposed to coal soot, paint fumes and lots of dust and grime.) Compared to coming home with a face blackened with soot and filthy work clothes, a summer on genteel Michigan Avenue seemed like it would be almost a vacation. I did insist on being able to take a week off during the summer, however.

In Ann Arbor, I started studying for trimester finals, as NASA quickly began to assemble the components for Apollo 10. The flight crew was one of NASA's most experienced ever. The commander was Tom Stafford, who had flown Gemini 6, commanded Gemini 9, and who was an expert in spacecraft rendezvous. The Command Module pilot was John Young, who had piloted Gemini 3 and commanded Gemini 10. The Lunar Module pilot was Gene Cernan, who had been the pilot aboard Gemini 9 (**Figure 21**).

The plan was to launch the combined CSM and Lunar Module to the Moon in May. The docked spacecraft would go into orbit around the Moon and then Stafford and Cernan would fly the Lunar Module to within 50,000 feet of the lunar surface. There, barely above the Moon's surface, the descent stage would be jettisoned and the ascent stage ignited to bring the two men back to rendezvous and dock with John Young in the orbiting CSM. The Lunar Module for Apollo 10 was too heavy to actually land on the Moon and take off again, lest Stafford and Cernan had any second thoughts about disobeying orders and trying to land.

Around this time, Marv and I discussed the feasibility of going to see the Apollo 11 launch. Assuming that Apollo 10 went well, the earliest Apollo 11 could launch would be mid-July. NASA wanted the option of either Apollo 11 or Apollo 12 achieving a landing before the end of 1969 – meeting Kennedy's goal of 'before this decade is out'. The time frame for Apollo 11 in July was perfect with regard to our summer breaks from college.

I suggested that I try to get us official NASA press accreditation for Apollo 11. From my work on *The Daily*, I knew that a press pass would open up all kinds of doors and allow us closer access to view the launch. I hoped that I could first get approval from the campus paper for us to cover the launch in person and that NASA would recognize us as journalists. Failing that, Marv noted that we could always go to Florida without press passes to see the launch as mere spectators.

By the beginning of May 1969, the end of my freshman year, I was still an assistant night editor at *The Daily* – a position way down on the totem pole. The newspaper had a long and honourable tradition of sending reporters to cover national political stories, but those choice 'away' assignments usually went to juniors or seniors. My ace in the hole was that I was practically still the only person in that politically left-leaning building at 420 Maynard Street who had an interest in science and space.

So, when I talked to the senior editors about covering Apollo 11, they agreed – provided I cover all my own expenses. *The Daily* only had a limited travel budget and sending a sophomore to cover a rocket launch was not high on their priority list.

With an assignment letter in hand from *The Michigan Daily* to cover Apollo 11, I approached NASA's Public Affairs Office about press credentials. I ran into a roadblock. NASA had more than 3,500 requests for credentials for the launch and could not fill all of them. More importantly, NASA had a policy not to accredit college reporters; they were considered students and not professional journalists. So, the answer was no. I was devastated, but Marv and I decided we would not give up on our dream to see a Saturn V launch – we would go anyway.

I knew it was essential to make hotel and airline reservations as early as possible, but this would have to wait until after the Apollo 10 mission was completed. It would not be until then that a firm launch date would be known for Apollo 11.

A Saturn V rocket launched Apollo 10 to the Moon on 18 May 1969. With a nod to the *Peanuts* comic strip, the CSM, with the radio call sign 'Charlie Brown', and the attached Lunar Module, radio call sign 'Snoopy', went into lunar orbit three days later.

On 22 May Stafford and Cernan entered the Lunar Module, separated from the CSM and fired the descent engine to place the Lunar Module in an orbit with a low point of about 50,000 feet above the Moon's surface. The pair tested the Lunar Module's engines, radar and other systems and inspected the prospective Apollo 11 landing spot on the Sea of Tranquility, which is found in the Tranquillitatis basin of the Moon.

The descent engine was jettisoned, as planned, but after the ascent engine was fired the Lunar Module suddenly began to rotate. Cernan famously swore "son of a bitch!" into an open microphone. The crew had improperly entered commands into the primitive Lunar Module computer. Along with Mission Control in Houston, Stafford and Cernan did some fast troubleshooting and the problem was fixed. Firing of the ascent engine raised the Lunar Module's orbit so it could rendezvous and dock with John Young in the CSM orbiting overhead.

This manoeuvre was successful and the three astronauts reunited aboard 'Charlie Brown'. The Service Module engine later fired to change the path of Apollo 10 to send it back towards Earth. The crew reached a speed of 24,791 mph during its return trajectory to Earth, making Stafford, Young and Cernan the fastest humans ever in history – a record that still stands. The men and their spacecraft were recovered from the Pacific Ocean by a US Navy ship, the USS Princeton, on 26 May.

So, the moment of truth concerning my summer plans had arrived. I could only take one week off from my summer job. One option was to go down to Cape Canaveral for the Apollo 11 launch without press credentials, as one of the hundreds of thousands of people expected there. Or, there was another option. I had heard of plans for a huge rock music festival to be held near White Lake, New York, in August. The Woodstock festival was to feature some of the greatest popular musical artists of the time.

So, it came down to a choice for me, whereas Marv was entirely focused on Apollo 11. Because of my work schedule and limited savings, I could not go to both events; it was either one or the other. As I considered my choice of space (Apollo 11) or rock 'n roll (Woodstock), I reviewed my interests in music and in space travel.

Like young kids of the time, I had my transistor radio and listened to rock, folk, blues and other pop music on it. I played piano in a short-lived seventh grade band. I saw the Beatles live in Chicago at Comiskey Park in August 1965. But my interest in space ran even deeper and had developed from a much earlier age.

In the end, I chose to go to the Apollo 11 launch. I figured that the first launch leading to humans landing on the Moon was a once-in-a-lifetime experience while there would be other music festivals – although in retrospect none as unique as Woodstock.

Now my travel planning escalated into high gear. The first task was to find a place to stay because the Cape Canaveral area was going to be inundated by hundreds of thousands of visitors and lodging would be at a premium. I reserved by phone a room at the Sea Missile Motel in Cocoa Beach for 13-18 July, sending them a $10 deposit (remember, this was pre-inflationary 1969). I received back a postcard, postmarked 31 May 1969, showing the motel and confirming the reservation. This was how reservations were made in the days before the internet (Figure 22).

SEA MISSILE MOTEL COCOA BEACH, FLORIDA
Corner of Cocoa Beach Causeway and A1A
Individual heat, air conditioning in every room, Hi-Fi, swimming pool. Deluxe rooms and suites. Restaurant next door. Telephone in every room.
For reservation phone SU. 3-2442

Dear Mr. Chudwin,
This acknowledges receipt of your 10.00 Deposit and guarantees you a room for the period of July 13 thru 18. This room is not subject to a 6 PM arrival rule. We will hold it all night pending your arrival. See you in July.
Sincerely, Steve Megregian

New Color Card Technique, R. A. Lasater, Apopka, Florida

62255

POST CARD

Address

Mr. David Chudwin
1031 Elliot Ct.
Olympia Fields, Ill
60461

Figure 22: Reservation acknowledgement card from the Sea Missile Motel in Cocoa Beach, Florida, for 13 through 18 July 1969 (the stay was later extended).

CHAPTER 8

GET READY, GET SET: JUNE 1969

APOLLO

11

Dave Chudwin

NAME

CPS Wire Network

ORGANIZATION

KENNEDY SPACE CENTER MANNED SPACECRAFT CENTE

PRESS

Figure 23: The Author's official NASA press pass for coverage of Apollo 11 for the College Press Service (CPS) Wire Network.

The next step was to get airplane tickets. On 2 June 1969 I bought my tickets to fly to Florida on 13 July, three days before the scheduled launch. Marv and I would fly from Chicago to Tampa, Florida, and then to the small Melbourne, Florida, airport. The round-trip ticket cost $94.50, which is equivalent to about $642 in 2018. For a college student at the time this was a big investment, but I had ideas about how to earn my way. With an airline ticket and a motel reservation, my friend Marv and I were all 'go' for Apollo 11!

Deus ex machina is an ancient literary plot device where a 'seemingly unsolvable problem is suddenly and abruptly resolved by the contrived and unexpected intervention of some new event, [or] character...' The *deus ex machina* of my Apollo 11 story was a senior editor of *The Michigan Daily*, Jim Heck. Jim was two years ahead of me, but was friendly and took an interest in helping trainees. I heard that Jim had been appointed editor of the College Press Service Wire Network in Washington, DC. The service was an association of college newspapers and its wire network was a means of exchanging stories among its members prior to the internet.

Jim was going to Washington for the summer and I asked him to plead my case in person before NASA's Public Affairs department – I would cover Apollo 11 not just for *The Michigan Daily*, but also for the College Press Service, effectively representing all US colleges. Good guy that he was, Jim agreed to try.

While waiting to hear about NASA credentials for Apollo 11, I prepared to leave Ann Arbor at the end of May to return to my parents' home near Chicago for my summer job at the clothing store. I knew I would have to get a haircut and get cleaned up for my work on Michigan Avenue. My hair had grown out, thick and bushy, and I had long sideburns.

The preparations for Apollo 11 occurred during a time in 1969 of great political and cultural unrest. As I went to work in Chicago and looked forward to my trip to Cape Canaveral for the launch, the summer of 1969 saw much more happening in the world besides space exploration. The Vietnam War was still raging and there was increasingly strong opposition to American involvement in that Southeast Asian civil war. Planning had started in the summer of '69 for a massive 'Moratorium to End the War' march in Washington, scheduled for 15 November 1969. I later covered this in DC as part of a *Michigan Daily* team.

Political changes in 1969 had a profound effect on the future of NASA and the space program. President Johnson, the 'godfather' of the space program, left office on 20 January 1969. As the powerful US Senate Majority Leader, he'd worked to establish NASA, to set up and head an influential Senate committee to oversee it, and to shepherd large budget increases for NASA through Congress. Heading the National Space Council was Johnson's most visible assignment as John F. Kennedy's vice president. During Johnson's presidency, from November 1963 through January 1969, Project Gemini had been successfully completed, as well as Apollo missions through Apollo 8. It is no coincidence that he was invited to, and attended, the Apollo 11 launch.

However, his successor, President Richard Nixon, saw space exploration as a tool for political advantage and international prestige. Nixon and the Congress would later cancel Apollo 18-20 and in 1972 approve plans for a scaled-down space shuttle that would be only partially reusable, the design of which would lead to many problems later on.

As I worked at the clothing store and listened to music like any other teenager, I impatiently waited to hear whether Jim Heck had any success in Washington getting the Apollo 11 press passes from NASA for Marv and me.

Music fans in 1969 listened to songs on either AM radio or on vinyl discs. The top song for 7 June 1969 illustrates that tunes from that era have held up pretty well. The Number 1 hit that week was Creedence Clearwater Revival's classic tune *Bad Moon Rising*, which they would later play at Woodstock in August and which is still popular today with over 59 million YouTube views in 2019.

Soon it was the middle of June 1969, and with no news from NASA about our press passes I figured the odds were not in our favour and I was disappointed about the situation. However, Marv and I were determined to see the launch, press passes or not. We had closely followed the space program and wanted to view a Saturn V launch in person, though we knew the experience would be so much better with press credentials. We were not going to give up.

Then, one day I received a thin envelope from the College Press Service in the mail. I opened it with much anticipation. In a letter dated 17 June 1969, Jim Heck informed me, "I'm now editor of the College Press Service wire network and it is only after this, and two weeks of red tape, talking to high NASA officials, etc., that I have finally gotten you and your friend some press credentials" (**Figure 24**).

SUCCESS! This was the news I had been waiting for – my friend Marv and I were going to cover Apollo 11 for the College Press Service, as well as *The Michigan Daily*, with full NASA press credentials. As Jim wrote, "You will be the only ungraduated people there" with press passes.

I was very excited we were getting official Apollo 11 press credentials because I knew press passes would give us unparalleled access. Jim informed me that NASA was

CPS wire network

1779 CHURCH STREET, N. W., WASHINGTON, D. C. 20036 • 202-387-7575 • TELEX 89-2618 • CABLE USSPA

June 17, 1969

Dear Dave,

I'm now editor of College Press Service wire network and it is only after this, and two weeks of red tape, talking to high NASA officials, etc. that I have finally gotten you and your friend some press credentials. They will be sent your way as soon as I confirm them here in Washington.

A few notes: 1) Please realize that your authorization for the Cape Kennedy press group is extremely important. NASA has never authorized any scholastic, non-scientific or other people for press credentials. It took a two-page letter informing the public relations man of our importance and impact to get the OK. Therefore, it is essential that you conduct yourselves as reporters -- and good ones.

2) I expect a good lenghty (say 40 inch) analysis of the space program and the relevance of a lunar landing. Though I disagree with your priorities on space programs please send me a good analysis using your bias after you have been in Florida. Also, right after the launch, if you could call me or special-air me some type of analytic story it would be nice. We have to send NASA your releases and it has to look genuine. Besides, you're not a bad writer and CPS can use that kind of coverage.

Figure 24: The good news from Jim Heck in a 17 June 1969 letter that he obtained press credentials to cover Apollo 11 from NASA for the Author and his friend.

going to be mailing me the press passes. He wrote that I needed my *Michigan Daily* press card with a photo as well as regular identification. He also included a courtesy letter stating that, "David Chudwin is a bonafide reporter for the College Press Service and its 500 subscribers throughout the world. All courtesies extended him during the Apollo 11 lunar landing will be appreciated."

I then checked the mailbox every day because I would not be sure it was really true until I had the actual NASA press pass in my eager hands. Not long after, I received in the mail my NASA press badge accrediting me for Apollo 11, representing the College Press Service Wire Network. (see Figure 23 page 90) I was thrilled! I still have that press pass; it is one of my prized possessions.

Along with my friend Marv, I was the only college journalist as such to receive approval by NASA to cover the first attempt to land on the Moon. We were also among the very youngest. The badge was stapled inside a plastic badge holder and was accompanied by instructions from NASA's Public Affairs Office. It allowed in-person coverage at both the Kennedy Space Center in Florida and the Manned Spacecraft Center in Houston.

I needed to figure out a budget and see if also going to Houston was a realistic possibility since I was paying for this low budget operation myself and funds were limited. I called around and found that I could rent a car as a 19-year-old for $16 a day. I already had my $94.50 return air flight and my $10 per night motel. Marv and I would split the car and motel expenses. These and other items, such as meals, brought the total estimated basic expenses to $200 plus airfare. Conservatively, I knew I had to come up with over $300 to cover those costs and contingencies.

That doesn't sound like much, however it was about $2,000 in 2018 dollars.

I had some money saved up from working previous summer jobs, but I would barely be able to pay to go to Cape Canaveral. So, Houston was out – I would watch the launch from Cape Canaveral and, with luck, cover the landing from there as well.

Besides the press badge, NASA Public Affairs also sent a six-page Press Advisory detailing plans for media coverage. Because over 3,500 journalists were expected, NASA was setting up an Apollo 11 News Center in a two-story industrial building in Cape Canaveral. The News Center was on Route A1A, on the opposite corner from the Cape Kennedy Hilton. Press badges also allowed unescorted car access to certain areas of Kennedy Space Center itself – Press Site 39, the Main Cafeteria and the Public Information Office (**Figure 25**).

At the end of June 1969, with less than three weeks remaining until my departure for Cape Canaveral, I still needed an idea to pay for part of the trip. I had savings from my summer jobs, but not enough for the estimated $300 that I needed.

Both my mom and my aunt Riss had been writing freelance magazine articles for years. While freelancers weren't highly paid, I thought that selling an article might help me earn some of the funds needed. I realized that my Apollo 11 coverage as a teenage journalist might provide a unique perspective. With that in mind, I borrowed my mom's Writer's Digest book and went to work to find magazines that might be interested. I sent off query letters to *Highlights for Children, Boys Life, Senior Science* and the *American Junior Red Cross News*. Then I waited to hear from them.

JOHN F. KENNEDY SPACE CENTER, NASA
KENNEDY SPACE CENTER, FLORIDA 32899

IN REPLY REFER TO PA-PIB

June 1969

TO ALL NEWS MEDIA:

The NASA Apollo 11 News Center is located in a two story building at 8810 N. Astronaut Boulevard (Route A1A), in the City of Cape Canaveral, Florida. The facility, which becomes operational July 1, is adjacent to the Chrysler Building and diagonally across A1A from the Cape Kennedy Hilton Motel (see attached map).

This temporary location will be the focal point for news operations concerned with the Apollo 11 mission thru liftoff. The Office phone number is AC 305 783-7781.

Updated status reports on Apollo 11 are available by calling a recorder phone at 784-2380 (please give the recorder time to rewind between calls). To receive or leave messages, please call the message center at 784-0771.

The KSC Public Information Office, physically located in the KSC Industrial Area on Avenue E, will be available as a work area only. None of the news operations will be conducted from that facility after July 1.

ACCREDITATION AND BADGING

Badges are valid for access to KSC and to the Manned Spacecraft Center, Houston, Texas, for the Apollo 11 mission. Badges are not transferable. (NOTE: NASA regulations do not permit accreditation of any person under 16 years of age).

UNESCORTED PRESS ACCESS TO KSC

Newsmen badged for the Apollo 11 mission may drive unescorted by the shortest route to Press Site 39, the KSC Main Cafeteria, and to the KSC Public Information Office via Gate 1, Cape Kennedy Air Force Station, or KSC Gates 2 and 3. Access

Figure 25: NASA press instructions for Apollo 11 issued in June 1969.

CHAPTER 9
'GO!': 11-13 JULY 1969

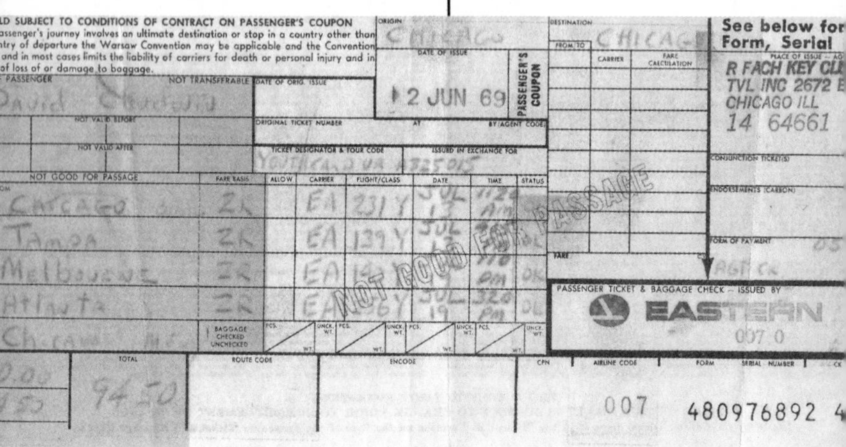

LD SUBJECT TO CONDITIONS OF CONTRACT ON PASSENGER'S COUPON
assenger's journey involves an ultimate destination or stop in a country other than
ntry of departure the Warsaw Convention may be applicable and the Convention
and in most cases limits the liability of carriers for death or personal injury and in
of loss of or damage to baggage.

PASSENGER | NOT TRANSFERABLE | DATE OF ORIG. ISSUE | ORIGIN | DATE OF ISSUE 2 JUN 69 | PASSENGER'S COUPON | DESTINATION | FROM/TO | CARRIER | FARE CALCULATION

See below for Form, Serial

PLACE OF ISSUE — AG
R FACH KEY CL
TVL INC 2672 E
CHICAGO ILL
14 64661

NOT VALID BEFORE | NOT VALID AFTER | ORIGINAL TICKET NUMBER | AT | BY/AGENT CODE | TICKET DESIGNATOR & TOUR CODE | ISSUED IN EXCHANGE FOR | CONJUNCTION TICKET(S) | ENDORSEMENTS (CARBON) | FORM OF PAYMENT

NOT GOOD FOR PASSAGE

FROM	FARE BASIS	ALLOW	CARRIER	FLIGHT/CLASS	DATE	TIME	STATUS
Chicago			EA	231 Y	JUL 13		
Tampa			EA	139 Y	JUL 13		
Melbourne			EA		JUL	PM	OK
Atlanta			EA	96 Y	JUL 19	320 PM	OK

NOT GOOD FOR PASSAGE

BAGGAGE CHECKED UNCHECKED | PCS. | UNCK. WT. | WT. | FARE

PASSENGER TICKET & BAGGAGE CHECK — ISSUED BY EASTERN 007 0

TOTAL 94.50 | ROUTE CODE | ENCODE | CPN | AIRLINE CODE 007 | FORM | SERIAL NUMBER 480976892 4

Figure 26: Airline ticket issued 2 June 1969 for the Author to fly from Chicago to Melbourne, Florida, on 13 July to cover the Apollo 11 launch. The round-trip fare was $94.50.

© David Chudwin

Fast forward to 11 July 1969. It was my 19th birthday and I was leaving in two days for Cape Kennedy to cover the first attempt to land humans on the Moon. There were so many details to remember, and so I typed out a to-do list. I didn't want to forget to bring important items such as airline tickets, NASA badges, College Press Service badge and letter, motel reservation confirmation, NASA instructions and a road map. I also reminded myself to check in with NASA News Center, see about interviews and get a Complex 39 Parking Pass from NASA. In addition, I included a schedule of possible news stories.

The next couple of days I was busy packing. I went out to the drugstore to buy three rolls of colour slide film (36 exposures each) for the old camera my father was lending me. I also bought a pocket spiral notebook to scribble notes during the rapidly approaching adventure.

I got up early on Sunday 13 July, excited and eager to be leaving for Florida to cover the Apollo 11 launch, scheduled for three days later. I met Marv at O'Hare Airport; we congratulated each other on the start of our own voyage.

Standing in line next to us at the check-in counter was an older lady who looked vaguely familiar. I glanced at her ticket and saw the name 'Rose Cernan' – mother of astronaut Eugene Cernan! I recognized Mrs Cernan because three years earlier Marv and I had attended the celebration in Bellwood, Illinois, for Cernan and Tom Stafford after Gemini 9, where we had seen the Cernan family.

At O'Hare, we talked to Mrs Cernan, learning that she too was going to Cape Canaveral to see the Apollo 11 launch. We took off from O'Hare for Tampa where we and Mrs Cernan switched planes to head to the Melbourne airport and an unforgettable experience (**Figure 26**).

On arrival at the Melbourne airport I saw Mrs Cernan being greeted by a few men, including one in a blue NASA jumpsuit, whom I recognized as astronaut Jim Irwin. As I went to the reservations counter to change my return flight, Mrs Cernan came and asked where Marv and I went to school. She then personally introduced us to astronauts Irwin, Alan Bean, Charlie Duke and Bruce McCandless. They were at the airport to pick up wives or family members arriving for the Apollo 11 launch (see Figure 35 page 114).

I knew that Bean had already been assigned to the next mission, Apollo 12, and I asked for his autograph on a magazine. Jim Irwin then took a photo with my camera of Bean and me at my request – unfortunately it was the first image on the roll and later became partially exposed to light. Bean said that this was the right time to come to Cape Canaveral. "I'm next," he said (Figure 27).

We exited the small Melbourne airport terminal to the outdoor stand where suitcases were delivered, as there were no baggage carousels there. Marv and I just missed the bus and had to wait for the next one, which was not scheduled to come for 45 minutes. While outside, we again saw astronauts Bean, Irwin, Duke and McCandless. Apparently, their flights were also delayed. We said hello again and took some pictures of them conversing.

Marv and I had barely stepped off the plane and were thrilled to be already meeting four NASA astronauts, three of whom would later walk on the Moon (Bean, Irwin and Duke) and one who would first fly the Manned Maneuvering Unit backpack in space while unattached to the space shuttle (McCandless).

The airport shuttle bus eventually arrived and for $3.50 each it took us to the Sea Missile Motel in Cocoa Beach.

Figure 27: Astronaut Alan Bean (left) and the Author on 13 July 1969. The picture was taken by astronaut Jim Irwin. It was the first frame of a roll of colour film and was partially exposed to light. The image has been converted to black and white and processed to equalize the exposure.

© David Chudwin, processing courtesy of Mark Usciak

Marv and I checked into the motel, which was clean but was clearly an aging property. The street sign in front of the building noted that the rooms were air-conditioned and each had a TV. After unpacking our suitcases, we looked around the motel grounds and then took a quick swim in the outdoor pool. It was warm and humid outside, typical for Florida in July, so the cool pool was refreshing.

We then dressed and strolled to the beach, where we could see the gantry towers of the Eastern Test Range in the distance. "Beautiful sun, sand, surf and space," I noted in my small spiral notebook. I was thrilled to be there.

We headed back to Highway A1A and took a very long walk north to the Hilton Hotel since we were not picking up our rental car until the next day. There we saw CBS television broadcaster Walter Cronkite holding court at the swimming pool. We also signed up at a booth in the hotel lobby for 'reservations' to go to the Moon with Trans International Airlines – a clever PR gimmick by this now defunct airline.

On the way back to the motel we stopped at the Mousetrap bar for a drink; we encountered astronauts McCandless and Curt Michel (a scientist-astronaut who later resigned and never flew in space) who were having a few drinks together as well. This was a time when 18 years and above was the drinking age.

We returned to the motel, got some dinner, and turned in early for an exciting day ahead. I shook my head in disbelief as I realized that our own Apollo expedition to cover the launch had started so auspiciously. I thought it was a good omen for the rest of the trip that we had met Mrs Cernan and then four NASA astronauts within a half-hour of landing in Florida. As with so much of this journey, luck and good timing were in our favour.

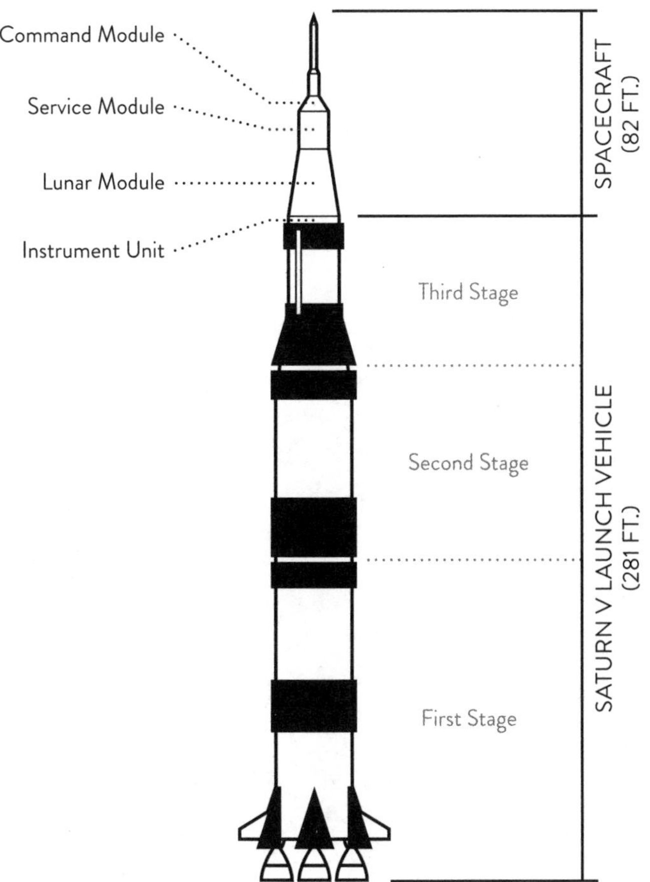

Figure 28: Saturn V launch vehicle.

CHAPTER 10

T-MINUS 2 DAYS AND COUNTING: 14 JULY 1969

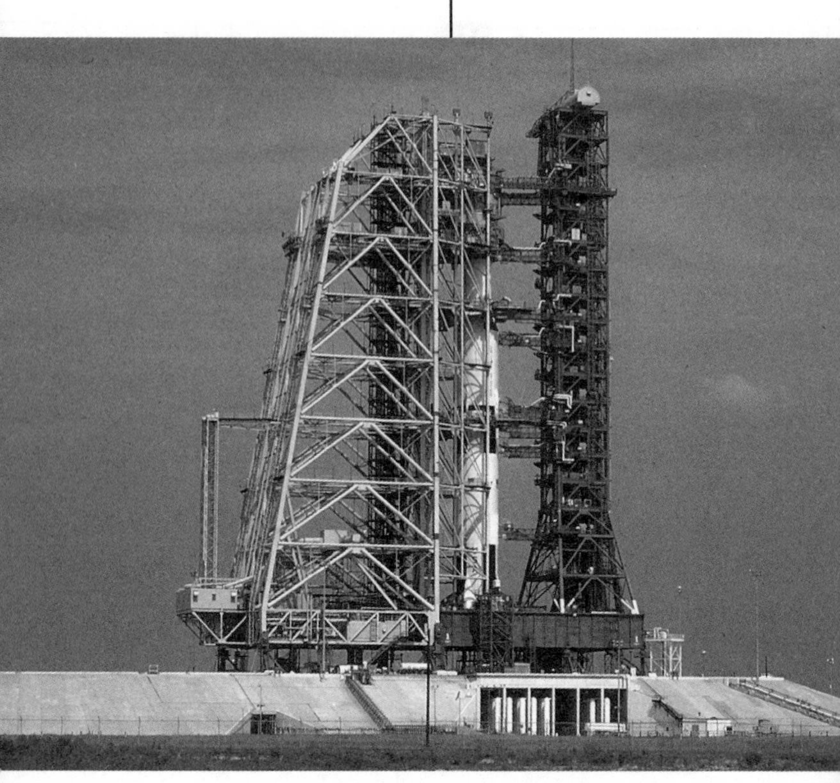

Figure 29: The Apollo 11 Saturn V was approached within three-quarters of a mile during a special press mini-bus tour on 14 July 1969.

Fourteen July was two days before the scheduled launch, with the launch time designated as 'T' and the time to launch called 'T-minus xx days or minutes'.

Early on that Monday Marv and I picked up our rental car and headed to the NASA Apollo 11 News Center located in Cape Canaveral – a complete madhouse, full of journalists from all over the world. There were long tables in the large pressroom on the second floor with telephones for reporters to call in stories, other tables with NASA press releases and flight plans, and industrial exhibits where companies were touting their contributions to Apollo. On the first floor there was a large room with a stage for press briefings. Loudspeakers brought messages and mission updates from NASA Public Affairs.

There was the babble of languages from around the world, reinforcing the fact that this was an international event. Indeed, some of the interest overseas was as strong as, if not stronger than, in the United States.

We grabbed copies of the press materials, including the Apollo 11 flight plan book and the NASA press kit. Another of the big advantages of having a press pass was access to these free materials. On purpose, I had packed my suitcase for Florida only half full so that I would have room to bring such 'goodies' back home.

We signed up with NASA for a four-hour tour that day of the Kennedy Space Center and its surroundings. Nine of us, including journalists from Spain, Switzerland and Belgium, headed out in a minibus. Our guide was a knowledgeable volunteer contractor employee. We started off at a space museum where we saw examples of rockets, including Redstone and Atlas, which had boosted the Mercury astronauts into space (**Figure 30**).

Figure 30: A Redstone rocket surrounded by its gantry and the base of an Atlas rocket are visible in this 14 July 1969 picture taken at the Space Museum at the Kennedy Space Center.

© David Chudwin

We then visited inside the Project Mercury control center and drove by the sites of Mercury, Gemini and unmanned launches. With sadness, we paused near Launch Complex 34, where the Apollo 1 crew had lost their lives 2 ½ years earlier. The red gantry remained standing above the abandoned concrete launch pad, but has since been dismantled.

I thought to myself at the time that space exploration was a risky business. This was especially the case with Apollo 11 because there were so many unknowns about landing on and lifting off from the Moon. In two days we would see the culmination of the efforts of over 400,000 workers across the country. Some experts had put the chance of success for the first attempt to land and return at only 50-50.

Our tour guide then drove the minibus to within three-fourths of a mile from the Saturn V, which was parked on Pad 39A, and we stopped to take some pictures. The rocket soared 363 feet (110 m) above a huge concrete base structure see (Figure 28). The giant rocket was surrounded by a grey Mobile Service Structure framework and was attached to a red Launch Umbilical Tower (see Figure 36 page 115). I could not believe how big the launch pad was, and how tall the Saturn V was towering above it. "God, it is huge!" was my diary comment (Figure 29).

We drove to another vantage point, only 2,000 feet from the Saturn V, where we saw a wire escape system and an emergency escape vehicle.

Our press tour continued, stopping at the incredible crawler-transporter that hauled the Saturn V from the Vehicle Assembly Building (VAB) out to the pad. We walked around the base of the crawler, touching the huge treads. The gigantic transporter weighed six million pounds, was adjustable from 20 to 26 feet in height, and had eight giant tracks (see Figure 39 page 117).

We then went to the VAB where we took an elevator to the top level and looked down some 500 feet below. We saw rocket stages in different points of assembly.

Our tour ended at the modernistic Launch Control Center where we were allowed from observation booths inside to see three control rooms, also called 'firing rooms', including the one where Apollo 11 was being prepared for launch in two days time (Figure 31).

We were also briefly permitted on the periphery of the floor of another firing room where the next mission, Apollo 12, was already being worked on. After the Kennedy Space Center tour, we hurried back to the Apollo 11 News Center in Cape Canaveral for an important news conference.

We went to the 'Center Director's Briefing', scheduled for 2:30 p.m., where the heads of NASA's field centers involved with Apollo 11 were to take questions from the assembled press corps, Marv and me included.

The speakers were Wernher von Braun (director of the Marshall Space Flight Center in Alabama), Kurt Debus (Kennedy Space Center, Florida), Robert Gilruth (Manned Spacecraft Center, Texas), George Mueller (NASA Associate Administrator for Manned Space Flight), and John Clark (Goddard Space Flight Center, Maryland) (see Figure 41 page 118).

I was in awe to be in the presence of these great space leaders. They were the men, along with Sam Phillips (Apollo Program Manager), George Low (Apollo Spacecraft Program Manager) and Chris Kraft (Manned Spacecraft

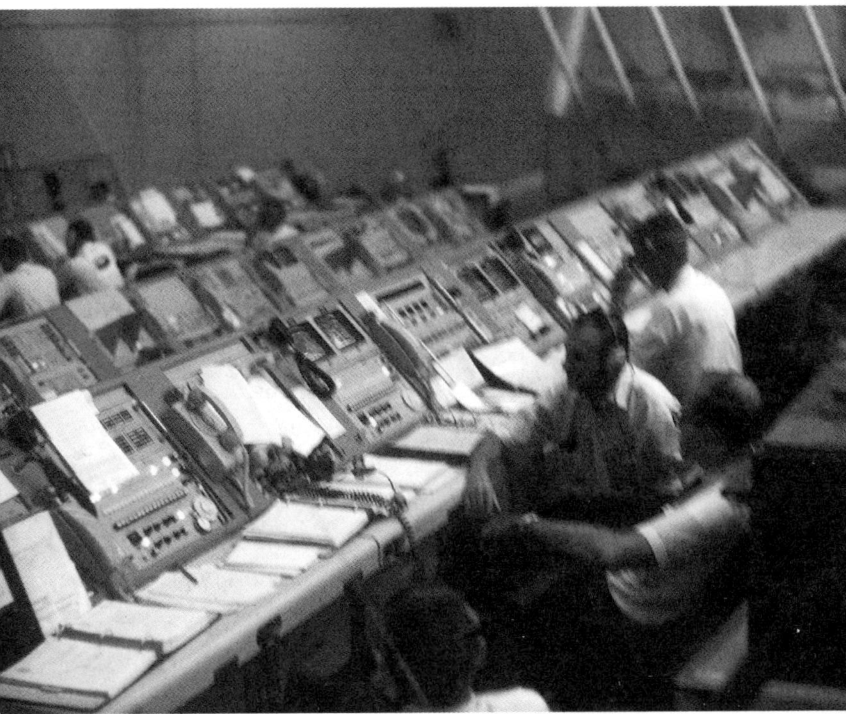

Figure 31: Launch controllers for Apollo 11 on 14 July 1969 at T-2 days in the Launch Control Center. The photo was taken from one of the glass observation booths behind and above the firing room.

Center Director of Flight Operations), who were going to be directly responsible for getting us to the Moon. There was a great sense of anticipation in the room with the launch in only two days hence.

I took pictures and notes as the men spoke. Von Braun, as usual, was the most quotable. When asked about the significance of the upcoming flight, von Braun compared it to "aquatic life crawling on land for the first time."

Marv and I then ate dinner at the nearby Cape Kennedy Hilton. Afterwards, we headed back to the Apollo 11 News Center to watch a 7 p.m. live television interview with the Apollo 11 crew. They were in quarantine, to prevent them from catching infections, and spoke to us by closed circuit TV from their crew quarters in the MSOB. We were present in the audience with the interviewers at the News Center. Asking the questions were CBS anchorman Walter Cronkite, UPI space reporter Al Rossiter, Jr, and science writers Evert Clark and Joel Shurkin. Jack King of NASA's Public Affairs Office was the moderator (Figure 32).

During the interview, Mike Collins, who was to orbit the Moon while Armstrong and Aldrin landed, joked, "I am one of the few Americans who will not be able to see the extra-vehicular activity. Please save the tapes for me." During the interview, Neil Armstrong was his usual reserved but confident self, answering questions tersely, with an engineer's precision.

After the Apollo 11 crew press conference, we took a NASA bus to a vantage point to photograph the Saturn V on Pad 39A at dusk, and then spectacularly at night under high-intensity xenon lights. We took some pictures of ourselves in front of the rocket and then waited for dusk (see Figure 34 page 114). As the evening sky

Figure 32: Panel of journalists interview the Apollo 11 crew by remote broadcast on 14 July 1969. The journalists were (left to right) Walter Cronkite (CBS News), Al Rossiter, Jr (UPI), Evert Clark and Joel Shurkin.

started to darken, we saw round shining lights at various levels of the grey Mobile Service Structure and the red Launch Umbilical Tower.

Then, with the sky fully black, the bright xenon lights were turned on in a magnificent display illuminating the Saturn V. The primitive manual camera I had did not fully capture the beauty of the scene. I did not have the photographic expertise to properly expose both the xenon light trails in the dark sky and the details of the Saturn V itself. However, I did get a few shots of the Saturn V bathed in the spotlights. In my diary, I described the Saturn V as 'a jewel in the night' with beacons of light shooting out on all sides. It was one of the most remarkable sights of a remarkable trip (see **Figure 47** page 121).

We got back to the Sea Missile Motel completely exhausted, but what a day it had been!

Highlights included:

- Getting within 2,000 feet of the Saturn V
- Going to the top of the VAB
- Walking on a Launch Control Center 'firing room' floor
- Seeing the 'architects' of Apollo at the 'Center Director's Briefing'
- Attending the live television interview with the Apollo 11 crew
- Ending with the magnificent display of lights focused on the Saturn V at night

Full of adrenaline, Marv and I stayed up until 1:30 a.m. going through the stacks of NASA press releases and contractor publications we had picked up at the News Center much earlier that day. Good thing I had brought that half-empty suitcase!

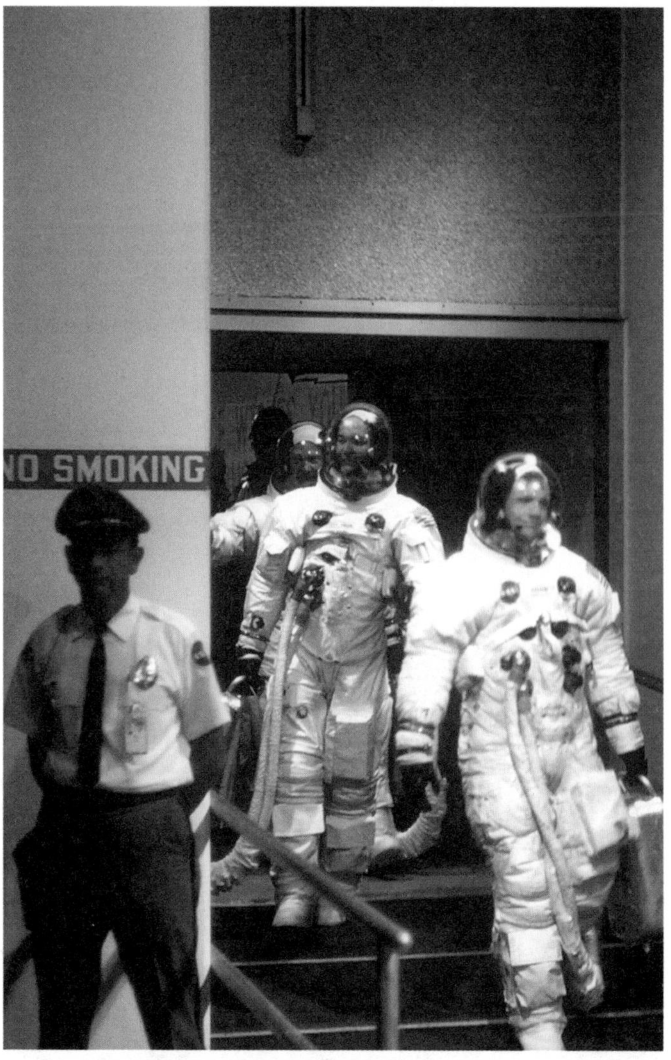

Figure 33: Apollo 11 Astronauts Neil Armstrong, Michael Collins and Buzz Aldrin leave the Manned Spacecraft Operations Building at the Kennedy Space Center on 16 July 1969 on their way to the first landing on the Moon.

© David Chudwin

Figure 34: The Author in front of the Apollo 11 Saturn V at dusk on 14 July 1969.

© David Chudwin

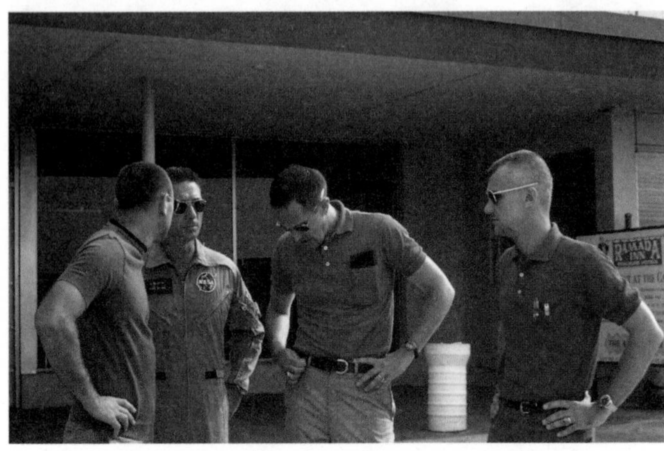

Figure 35: Astronauts Alan Bean, James Irwin, Charles Duke, and Bruce McCandless at the Melbourne, Florida airport on 13 July 1969. Bean, Irwin and Duke would later walk on the Moon.

© David Chudwin

Figure 36: The Apollo 11 Saturn V on Pad 39A on 14 July 1969. The three-stage rocket stands 363 feet above its launch platform. The rocket is surrounded by the Mobile Service Structure (grey) and attached to the Launch Umbilical Tower (red).

Figure 37: The first stage of the Saturn V rocket later used to launch Apollo 12, viewed in the Vehicle Assembly Building on 15 July 1969. Note the technicians under the rocket.

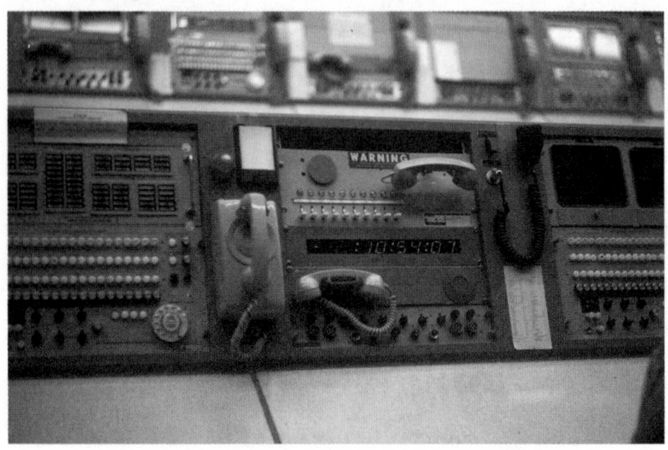

Figure 38: Launch Director's console in the Launch Control Center at the Kennedy Space Center.

Figure 39: The NASA crawler-transporter with the Vehicle Assembly Building in background at the Kennedy Space Center.

© David Chudwin

Figure 40: The Apollo 11 Saturn V on 15 July 1969, the day before launch. The liquid hydrogen fuel tank is visible at right. Note the "No Smoking" warning.

© David Chudwin

Figure 41: The "architects" of Project Apollo with (left to right) Wernher von Braun, Kurt Debus, George Mueller, Robert Gilruth, and John Clark at a press briefing 15 July 1969.

Figure 42: Apollo 11 Press Site grandstand on 16 July 1969 just before the Apollo 11 launch.

Figure 43: Former President Lyndon B. Johnson in the VIP grandstand at the Kennedy Space Center just prior to the Apollo 11 launch. US Army Chief of Staff General William Westmoreland is in the dark green unifrom above him.

© David Chudwin

Figure 44: Apollo 11 Astronauts Neil Armstrong, Michael Collins and Buzz Aldrin lift off aboard a Saturn V rocket to begin their journey to the Moon on 16 July 1969.

© David Chudwin

Figure 45: Apollo 11 Astronauts Buzz Aldrin, Neil Armstrong, and Michael Collins (left to right) visit Chicago 13 August 1969 following the Apollo 11 flight. The Chicago Water Tower pumping station is behind them.

Figure 46: Astronauts Neil Armstrong (right) and Buzz Aldrin, the first humans to land on the Moon, in a parade in Chicago, Illinois on 13 August 1969.

Figure 47: Xenon lights illuminate the Apollo 11 Saturn V at night on 14 July 1969.

CHAPTER 11

T-MINUS 1 DAY AND COUNTING: 15 JULY 1969

Figure 48: The Mobile Service Structure gantry is slowly pulled away from the Apollo 11 Saturn V on Pad 39A on 15 July 1969.

© David Chudwin

We had another jam-packed day scheduled for Tuesday 15 July, the day before the planned Apollo 11 launch:

- Press tour of the VAB and Launch Control Center
- Rollback of the Mobile Service Structure from Launch Pad 39A, exposing the Saturn V to view.
- Pre-launch press briefing with NASA officials
- Personal interview of NASA's head of manned spaceflight, Dr George Mueller

In the morning, Marv and I took another NASA press tour to return first to the VAB and then to the Launch Control Center for a more detailed visit. We started the day by boarding a NASA bus at the News Center in Cape Canaveral. Seated near us was noted author Norman Mailer, who the following year published the book *Of a Fire on the Moon*, about his experiences covering the launch.

We drove again to the VAB where we were permitted to walk right next to the base of the 363-foot-tall Apollo 12 Saturn V, being prepared for the next Apollo flight. All three stages of the rocket were already stacked atop each other. Two of the huge F-1 engines and swing-arms of the first stage were visible, dwarfing the technicians working inside (see Figure 37 page 116).

Then we were able to see all three individual stages of the Apollo 13 Saturn V, which had not yet been stacked atop each other.

The NASA press bus then took us from the VAB to the nearby Launch Control Center, where we went to the top of the building and had a spectacular view from the roof of Pad 39A in the distance. The Apollo 11 Saturn V was still encased in the Mobile Service Structure framework, which was scheduled to be rolled back later that afternoon.

The crushed-rock roadway leading from the VAB to the pad was clearly visible, as was the large white round tank used to store the liquid hydrogen rocket fuel.

We went inside the Launch Control Center where there were three control rooms that processed the Saturn V rockets.

Firing Room 1, which was preparing Apollo 11, was off-limits to us, but from the glass-enclosed observation gallery above we were able to see rows of the launch controllers working their electronic workstation consoles. The mood appeared relaxed, although there were less than 24 hours remaining before launch (see Figure 31 page 109).

We were then escorted to the floor of the then-unoccupied Firing Room 3. Here, the journalists could walk right up to the launch director's console as well as all the other positions (see Figure 38 page 116). It all seemed very high tech – by 1969 standards. There were long rows of electronic workstations, each console dedicated to one aspect of the launch. There were telephones, cathode ray screens and a myriad of lights and toggle switches (Figure 49).

The Launch Control Center had large mainframe computers, each taking up practically a whole room.

Admission to the floor of the Firing Rooms was usually highly restricted. Our ability to walk around next to the control consoles was another example of the access our press credentials provided. Marv and I would never have been this close if we had just travelled down to Cape Canaveral without NASA press passes.

We were then escorted to observe Firing Room 2, which had just a few launch controllers who were monitoring preparations for the next Apollo mission, Apollo 12. As we looked up from the floor, we could see the glassed-in

Figure 49: Rows of electronic consoles in Firing Room 3 of the Launch Control Center where flight controllers monitor each rocket system.

observation area reserved for VIPs during the launch. We went up to that observation booth and looked back down on Firing Room 2, where controllers and other personnel were working.

Later that afternoon we boarded another NASA tour bus to observe the rollback of the Mobile Service Structure that had been protectively surrounding the Saturn V rocket on Pad 39A. Our bus stopped just before a road-block manned by policemen (see Figure 48 page 122). We were excited to take photos as the huge grey metal framework gradually pulled back from the pad, exposing the mammoth rocket and its Launch Umbilical Tower. Unfortunately, clouds rolled in and it was hazy, so our view was partially obstructed.

Afterwards, the bus transported us to a different vantage point where we had a beautiful view of the 'naked' Saturn V, free of its framework. (The clouds had lifted a little by then). The large spherical liquid hydrogen tank used to fuel the rocket was also in our field of view, draped with the ominous 'Liquid Hydrogen, No Smoking' notice in red lettering (see Figure 40 page 117).

Our NASA bus then headed back to the Kennedy Space Center Pad 39 Press Site for a news conference called the 'Prelaunch Briefing'. At the Press Site, the top operational officials for Apollo 11 were on a stage facing the press grandstands, where several hundred reporters were seated (Figure 50).

The officials included astronaut Deke Slayton (Manned Spacecraft Center flight crew operations), Dr Charles Berry (Manned Spacecraft Center medical operations), George Low (Apollo Program Manager), George Hage (Apollo Mission Director), Rocco Petrone (Kennedy Space Center

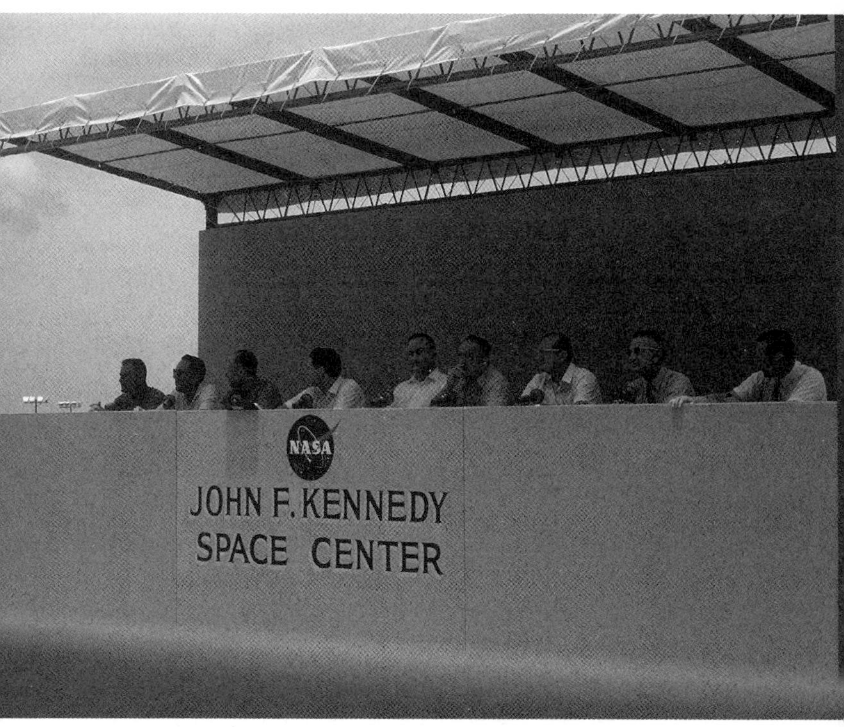

Figure 50: The Apollo 11 "Pre-Launch Briefing" on 15 July 1969 at the KSC Press Site. NASA officials discuss preparation for the Apollo 11 launch scheduled for the next morning. (Left to right) Deke Slayton, Dr Charles Berry, George Low, George Hage, Rocco Petrone, Lee James, Ozro Covington, Royce Olson and PAO Jack King.

Launch Operations Director), Lee James (Saturn V Program Manager), Ozro Covington (Goddard Space Flight Center support) and Col Royce Olson (Department of Defense space flight support). NASA's Jack King was the moderator.

Hage reported that all was proceeding well toward the planned launch the next day at 9:32 a.m. Eastern Daylight Time. Petrone stated the weather looked very good as far as launch conditions were concerned. Then the members of the media went on to ask a series of mostly uninformed questions, such as whether the astronauts were ready. We briefly talked afterwards with Deke Slayton and Dr Berry, exchanging pleasantries.

When we had first arrived at the Apollo 11 News Center a couple of days before, we had an opportunity to sign up for individual interviews with NASA officials. We were able to land a 3:15 p.m. appointment for that afternoon with Dr George Mueller, Associate Administrator for Manned Space Flight. As noted before, Mueller was the head of the manned space program for NASA. He was responsible for many key decisions in the Apollo program, most notably the concept of 'all up testing' in which rocket systems were tested all together rather than component by component. Later, he became known as the 'father' of the Skylab (the space station launched and operated by NASA) and Space Shuttle programs.

We drove back to the News Center to talk to Mueller but found, to our disappointment, that he was not there but at his hotel. We rushed to the Holiday Inn where he was talking to a series of journalists in his hotel room, accompanied by a NASA Public Affairs Officer.

When we arrived, Mueller was finishing an interview with two Japanese journalists. I was excited to talk one-on-one with one of the 'architects' of the space program. I had a fascinating 20-minute personal interview with Mueller in which he laid out a bold future plan for space exploration beyond Apollo. I recorded the interview and realized that it would make a perfect magazine article. The interview was in fact the basis of a later 1969 article I wrote about the Apollo 11 launch and the future of space exploration.

Marv and I had dinner at the Holiday Inn after I had finished the interview, then I went back to the News Center to use their typewriters to write a story for *The Michigan Daily* and the College Press Service. On 15 July, *The Daily* published a preview story about Apollo 11 that I had written before leaving for Cape Canaveral; the article had also been sent out on the College Press Service Wire Network.

I worked for a couple of hours on a lengthy story about the preparations for tomorrow's launch using a typewriter on tables in the second-floor newsroom. I then dictated the text via a pay phone to *The Daily* for the next day's edition. Because I did not have access to a teletype, then the only way to transmit text, I had to read it slowly on the telephone so that the person on the other end in Ann Arbor could transcribe it by manually typing out the words.

The article appeared the next morning, on the front page of the 16 July 1969 edition of the paper. I couldn't reach the College Press Service by phone that night because no one there answered my call.

I drove back to the Sea Missile Motel in the warm and humid Florida heat to try to get some sleep. I hoped tomorrow would be the big day we had been anticipating, but I knew that weather and mechanical problems could intervene. I set the alarm for 4.30 a.m. and hoped for the best. Exhausted, I had no problems falling asleep.

CHAPTER 12

LAUNCH: 16 JULY 1969

Figure 51: Apollo 11 with Neil Armstrong, Michael Collins, and Buzz Aldrin aboard blasts off towards the Moon from the Kennedy Space Center on 16 July 1969.

After seeing the Apollo 11 crew walk-out in their white spacesuits at dawn on 16 July from the Manned Spacecraft Operations Building (see **Prologue**), Marv and I re-boarded our NASA bus. Full of adrenaline from viewing the Apollo 11 crew take their last steps on Earth before heading to the Moon, we headed out on the slow-moving bus, caught in heavy bumper-to-bumper pre-launch traffic, to the Kennedy Space Center Pad 39 Press Site. Our NASA bus was in a major traffic jam. We later learned that more than a million people were gathering to watch the launch.

The Pad 39 Press Site was a large grandstand about 3.5 miles from the Saturn V rocket sitting on Pad 39A. That early morning it was already packed with journalists setting up photographic equipment in front of the bleachers and claiming spots in the grandstand for their portable manual typewriters. There were large old-fashioned television cameras on platforms to the side of the grandstand (see Figure 42 page 118).

We climbed to the top of the grandstand and I took a picture of the scene in the early morning light. We saw reporters and cameramen filling the grandstand below us and hundreds more in the grassy area in front and along the edge of the water. The Saturn V rocket was bathed in the hazy dawn light in the distance (Figure 52).

There was an air of great anticipation as the journalists prepared to watch and photograph the historic launch, which had been scheduled weeks ago for 9:32 a.m. Eastern Daylight Time – celestial mechanics dictated the optimum launch times.

We looked around the Press Site but then decided to view the launch from a different location – the VIP Site

Figure 52: View from the KSC Press site grandstand of the Apollo 11 Saturn V in the distance just after dawn on 16 July 1969. Photographers and cameramen are visible setting up at the water's edge.

© David Chudwin

where hundreds of dignitaries NASA had invited for the occasion were gathering. Politicians, military leaders, former NASA brass, ambassadors and entertainers were among those who were scheduled to attend. The advantage of the VIP Site was that we could 'people watch' all these individuals while waiting to 'bird watch' the rocket launch.

Marv and I took a NASA bus over to the VIP Site. We had to show our press passes a couple of times but security was not that tight by current standards. There were several low grandstands for the invited Apollo 11 guests. Marv and I milled around on the grassy area in front as the VIP guests gradually arrived.

We had a brief talk with Australian-born scientist-astronaut Phil Chapman, one of the 'Excess Eleven' who never flew in space. Former President Lyndon Johnson and his wife Lady Bird then appeared with a Secret Service escort. The tall Texan, dressed in a dark suit, stood up to acknowledge the applause of the crowd. Former NASA Administrator James Webb sat to the right of Johnson, and not too far away was former Peace Corps Director Sargent Shriver. Gen. William Westmoreland, former US commander in Vietnam and Army Chief of Staff at the time, was also in the grandstand (see **Figure 43** page 119).

In a different section, I noticed American television entertainers Johnny Carson and Ed McMahon. Even Hermann Oberth, one of the fathers of rocketry, was there – we had briefly encountered him earlier at the hotel. We also saw Senators Barry Goldwater and William Proxmire – an opponent of the space program, but still attending the launch. Vice President Agnew was in the Launch Control Center while President Nixon was at the White House.

Marv and I staked out a spot on the grass a few hundred feet in front of the VIP grandstands to watch the final countdown for Apollo 11. The sun had risen and there was a bright blue sky with just some scattered clouds and not much wind. The temperature was warm and mildly humid, but not uncomfortable for a Florida summer morning. There was a strong sense of expectation on the part of the observers who were eagerly awaiting the liftoff.

I was overwhelmed by a sense of history, reinforced by the presence of so many notables. The event seemed like the 'Super Bowl' of space. Many of the people responsible for Apollo were present – political leaders, engineers, scientists, astronauts, journalists and, outside the Kennedy Space Center, hundreds of thousands of space enthusiasts. They were all gathered to see the culmination of their efforts to fulfill President Kennedy's dream of landing humans on the Moon and returning them to Earth before the end of the decade.

A big question mark, though, was whether Apollo 11 with its precious crew was going to launch on time. The space program had a long history of 'scrubs' – cancellations of launches, usually due to mechanical or weather problems. Indeed, it was unusual for rockets to launch on the targeted day and time set weeks before. Too many things could go wrong.

This troubled me because we could only stay in Florida for a limited time, perhaps for one scrub, which would result in at least a two-day delay before another attempt could be made. However, we remained optimistic that the scheduled 16 July launch date would be accomplished.

Meanwhile, Jack King – the distinctive voice of Launch Control – could be heard on loudspeakers giving authoritative commentary about the progress of the countdown. I had a new roll of film in my camera and resolved to take a quick series of pictures of the launch itself. The camera was manual without automatic focusing or controls.

The countdown went smoothly, with no unexpected holds. The anticipation was mixed with trepidation. So much could go wrong that could delay the launch, or even worse, endanger the crew. We were kept 3.5 miles away, which was the closest spectators could come without certain injury in case of an explosion of the rocket. However, everything continued to be nominal, the strange NASA term for 'normal', as the countdown progressed to under the T–minus two minutes mark. There was good weather, no engineering problems, and the astronauts were reporting they were well.

As the countdown progressed to T–minus nine seconds I started taking pictures every few seconds, watching the scene through the viewfinder of the camera. The Saturn V was over three miles away but so huge that it was clearly visible.

At ignition we saw a small ball of yellow flame at the base of the Saturn V, but all was silent – at least for that moment. Flames and smoke then quickly shot out hundreds of feet from either side of Pad 39A, but the Apollo 11 Saturn V just seemed to silently sit there for several seconds (**Figure 53**).

The silence was powerful. Then, as we continued to wait with growing concern, it happened – lift-off! There was a slight, slow upward movement of the huge rocket stack with Armstrong, Collins and Aldrin riding on top (see **Figure 51** page 130). The rocket yawed slightly to

Figure 53: Flames shoot out from the base of the Apollo 11 Saturn V as the five first stage engines reach maximum thrust.

avoid hitting the Launch Umbilical Tower (see **Figure 44** page 119). We started to hear a rumble and then an increasingly louder, crackling roar. Waves of sound assaulted my ears and physically battered my chest – I felt the sound as well as heard it. The physical sensation of the pounding of the launch, as well as the loud, deafening roar accompanying it, was all-encompassing. I could actually feel heat from the five first-stage rocket engines putting out 7.5 million pounds of thrust. Observers were completely engrossed in the noise, heat and light emanating from the Saturn V.

The rocket rose agonizingly slowly above the launch tower (**Figure 54**). It then very gradually gained speed and flew through the scattered, sparse clouds. Meanwhile, as the crowd cheered the spectacle, I had been furiously snapping pictures of the lift-off. I was surprised both by how slowly the Saturn V rose from the pad and by how violently the delayed, deafening sound waves attacked us. The crowd was excited by the spectacle and grateful that the launch had been on time and so far successful.

The huge rocket soared into the blue sky and seemed to speed up even more, and gradually became a point of light among the scattered clouds. I continued to take photos until I was out of film. There was silence again except for the final cheers and applause of the onlookers.

Marv and I walked back to the VIP grandstand to get some quotes. There were several hundred people milling around the area in front of the grandstand. We circulated in the crowd looking for familiar faces to interview.

We talked briefly to TV personalities Johnny Carson and Ed McMahon, and then to astronauts Bill Anders and Fred Haise, the backup Lunar Module pilot who saw

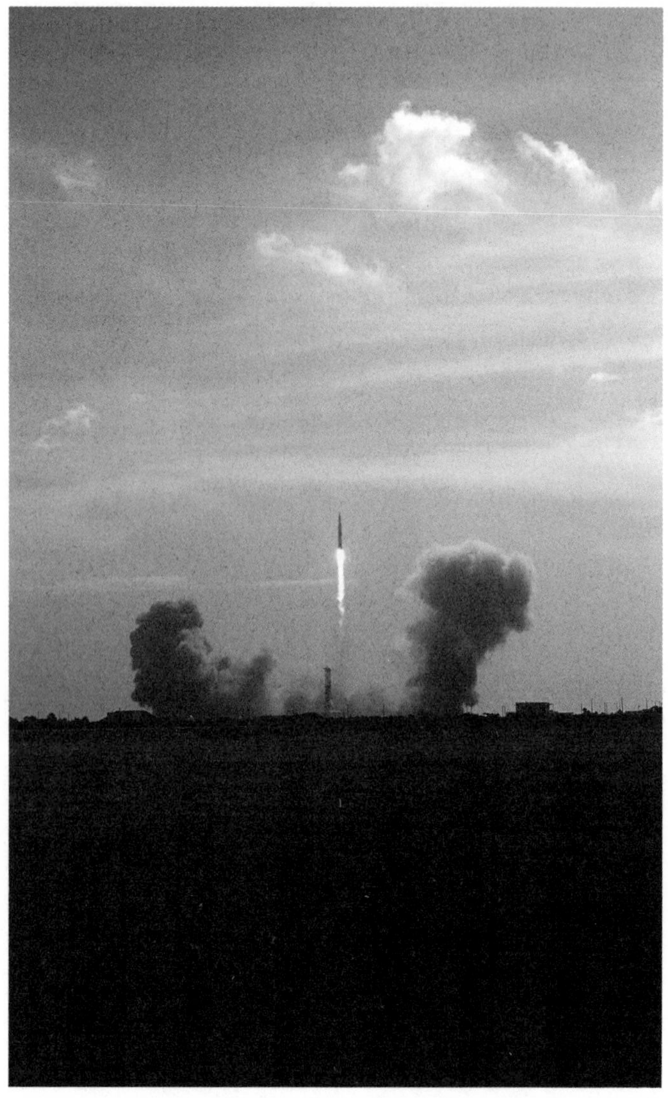

Figure 54: The Apollo 11 Saturn V clears the tower as a thunderous roar from the rocket hits spectators.

the crew off in the White Room. "Their spirits were very good, just like anyone who's waited a long time and worked very hard for something like this – looking forward to it," Haise told us. We also saw Tom Stafford and Gene Cernan in the crowd but didn't get a chance to talk to them.

We stuck around for a while but then headed back to the Press Site for the T-plus one hour (one hour after launch) official NASA news briefing. During that press conference, NASA and the Department of Defense officials informed us that all was OK with the flight. They made a point that the Apollo 11 launch was accomplished exactly on time, at 9:32 a.m. on the day and time set months before.

Marv and I were extremely grateful that weather, mechanical errors or other problems had not led to any launch postponements. We only had a limited time window we could stay at Cape Canaveral and the on-time launch was in no way assured. Fate was on our side for the launch, but what about the scheduled landing on the Moon?

I had decided that I wanted to remain at Cape Canaveral for the landing, and planned to extend my reservation at the Sea Missile. In contrast, Marv wanted to watch it at home so he made arrangements to return to Chicago on Saturday 19 July, the day before the landing.

I had a feeling of wonderful exhilaration that afternoon following the launch. The enormity of what we had seen over the three previous days was just starting to sink in, and I knew the experience had been one of the high points of my life.

We got up close to the Apollo 11 Saturn V on the pad – to within 2,000 feet – and even closer to the Apollo 12 Saturn V in the VAB. We went inside the VAB and Launch Control Center and then to their roofs. We were able to touch the mobile transporter and walk along its path. We had the chance to stand on Pad 39B.

We had gone to press conferences with space pioneers such as Wernher von Braun, Robert Gilruth, George Mueller and Kurt Debus. We had met and talked to astronauts including future Moonwalkers Al Bean, Jim Irwin, Charlie Duke and Gene Cernan, as well as Moon voyagers Tom Stafford, Bill Anders and Fred Haise. We were eyewitnesses to the Apollo 11 crew's last steps on Earth during their walk-out, and then saw them launched on their way to the Moon.

Without press credentials, we would not have been able to do any of this. As noted, it is estimated that up to one million people saw the launch in person there on 16 July 1969. However, most of them were many miles away. We, among about 6,000 journalists and invited guests, saw it from just over three miles away, the closest that civilians were allowed.

I thought about this as we headed back to the motel for a short rest. Today had been one of the most exciting days of my young life, a truly life-changing event for me. While I had been fascinated by space exploration since a young age, the topic became almost an obsession after Apollo 11.

In addition to the news stories I would file, I made up my mind to tell my story in the future to others who were not fortunate enough to have been there in person on that historic launch day. The first launch to land on the Moon was a watershed event in human history, and I was privileged to be there.

CHAPTER 13

MOON LANDING: 20 JULY 1969

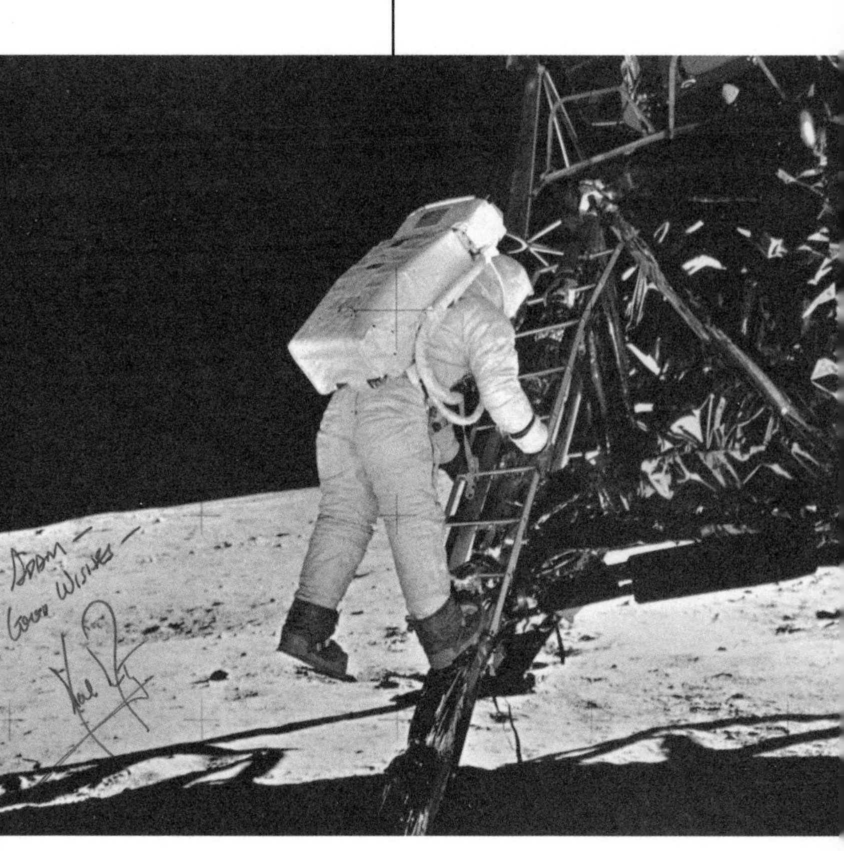

Figure 55: Buzz Aldrin descending down the ladder of the Lunar Module to the Moon's surface on 20 July 1969. The image was taken by Neil Armstrong, who in 1987 inscribed the lithograph to the Author's son Adam.

After their successful launch, the Apollo 11 crew went into a preliminary Earth orbit to check out the spacecraft systems before heading towards the Moon. The rocket firing that sent Armstrong, Collins and Aldrin on their way was called the TLI, or 'trans-lunar injection'. The rocket burn was successful two hours and 20 minutes after launch, and the Apollo 11 crew was on a trajectory to the Moon.

Coming down from the emotional high of the launch, Marv and I returned to the Sea Missile Motel in Cocoa Beach. While the astronauts headed towards the Moon, I took a swim at the motel pool. I thought about them floating weightlessly in the microgravity of space as I attempted less successfully to float in the warm pool water. I was envious of them floating so easily on their way to the Moon.

Shortly after, I got ready and returned to the NASA Apollo 11 Press Center in Cape Canaveral while Marv stayed at the motel. The first thing I did was to pick up the latest transcripts of the pre-launch commentary and the air-to-ground voice communications since launch. NASA stenographers recorded on a real-time basis every word spoken on the public communications voice channel; copies for reporters were laid out on tables at the Press Center. These voice transcripts were highly useful because it was impossible for busy reporters to pay much attention to the loudspeakers that constantly relayed voice messages and commentary.

I then reviewed my notes from the day so far in the small notebook that I'd brought from Chicago. These invaluable notes formed the basis of my stories for *The Daily*, future articles about my Apollo 11 experiences, and this book.

I started to write my story of the launch for the next morning's issue of *The Daily* on a portable typewriter at the NASA Apollo 11 Press Center. "The Apollo 11 astronauts are streaking towards the Moon after a spectacular blast-off viewed by more than a million people in the Cape Kennedy area," read the lead paragraph. I tried to include my own personal observations as well as quotations I had obtained. I saved the original typed copy from that night.

Marv and I then had dinner at the nearby Holiday Inn. I went back to the News Center and dictated my story on a pay telephone to *The Daily*. It was to be ten days until I saw the actual layout of the article, lacking the fax machines and computers of today. The story received first page placement and was accompanied by two wire copy photographs showing the astronauts and the Saturn V rocket.

After having been up since 4:30 a.m. to catch the Apollo 11 crew walk-out, Marv and I went to bed early that night.

After the launch on Wednesday 16 July, most of the 3,500 journalists left for Houston to cover the rest of the flight. However, a couple hundred of us, mainly foreigners, stayed at Cape Canaveral to follow the mission. The next three days there, Thursday through Saturday, were uneventful. I slept in late at the motel each morning, grabbed a quick breakfast, and then headed out to the News Center.

The heretofore bustling place was largely deserted after the launch day. The newsroom still had loudspeakers that relayed the Public Affairs Office voice loop from Houston; there were also a couple of colour television consoles to huddle around. The long tables with typewriters were still present, as well as the stacks of voice transcripts. The contractor tables were unoccupied, with just a few brochures and fact sheets left behind. What was missing were most of the journalists, who had migrated to Houston, home of Mission Control.

Marv left for Chicago on Friday 18 July. We had shared some great adventures together on the trip, as well as going together to previous space events. Marv had come up with the idea of going down to Cape Canaveral to see a launch, while I had obtained the press credentials and organized the trip. It was a team effort.

We were already old friends by 1969 and knew each other's strengths and weaknesses. At that point, very little of the friendly competitiveness that was later a part of the relationship was apparent. I was sad to see him leave but I looked forward to some 'alone time', necessary for introverts like myself. I checked in at the News Center every day but then I left for the beach, the swimming pool at the motel, or local shops. It was a relaxing vacation time for me, allowing me to unwind after the excitement of the pre-launch press activities and the launch itself.

However, I did write stories for *The Daily* and the College Press Service. I was back again at the News Center on Thursday 18 July, for a longer period of time, to write an article previewing the Moon landing. It was going to be published in *The Daily* on Saturday morning, the day before the scheduled Sunday landing.

The article's lead paragraph stated, "Speeding towards the moon, the three Apollo 11 astronauts checked out their lunar lander in preparation for breaking into lunar orbit this afternoon." I summarized the preparations for going into lunar orbit and later the departure of the Lunar Module, radio call sign 'Eagle', with Armstrong and Aldrin aboard for the landing.

As I wrote the story, I realized the complexity of the upcoming landing activities. The Lunar Module descent engine had to fire just right to change its orbit to intersect with the Moon's surface. Armstrong needed to find a level area on which to land because their maps did not have the resolution to detect boulders or small craters that could damage the Lunar Module. The pressurization and oxygen supply of the Lunar Module needed to be maintained because the Moon has no atmosphere. The lunar surface where they were to land had to be 'walkable' so that the Lunar Module or men did not sink into Moon dust.

Later, the Lunar Module ascent engine had to fire correctly to get them off the lunar surface and to rendezvous with Mike Collins in the orbiting CSM, radio call sign 'Columbia'. Finally, the Service Module engines would need to burn exactly right to get Apollo 11 out of lunar orbit and back to Earth, otherwise they would be flung into a fatal pathway that would either crash into the Moon or that would miss Earth.

All this needed to go perfectly for a successful mission. The astronauts themselves put the chance of success at only about 50-50. In fact, before the launch, new NASA Administrator Thomas Paine privately told the astronauts not to take any unnecessary risks. He promised them that they could have the next mission if they had to return due to problems. This was an unprecedented, confidential promise.

On Sunday 20 July, I got to the Apollo 11 News Center in Cape Canaveral around 1 p.m., in time for the Lunar Module Eagle's undocking from the commandship Columbia. There were maybe three dozen reporters there at the time, the majority having left for Houston.

There were a couple of colour televisions, the old-fashioned console types, which showed network coverage of events. However, instead of listening to network TV, I preferred to follow the NASA Public Affairs Office commentary and live broadcasts from the spacecraft from the loudspeakers in the News Center. These were supplemented by the written voice transcripts that were laid out approximately hourly on the tables in the second-floor newsroom.

I sat at one of those long tables in the newsroom, taking notes in my small spiral notebook. The first manoeuvre was the separation of the Lunar Module from Columbia at 11.44 a.m. “The Eagle has wings,” Armstrong reported.

Following the Lunar Module separation, there were a series of rocket engine burns by the Lunar Module descent stage to lower the orbit of the landing vehicle to bring it down a prescribed pathway to the lunar surface. “Right down US 1, Mike” Armstrong radioed Collins.

At 2:49 p.m. Mission Control gave the OK for DOI (descent orbit initiation), the main descent rocket burn, which occurred at 3:07 p.m. “Off to a good start, keep it cool” came the call, after Eagle was lowered into a 57.2 by 9.1 nautical-mile-high orbit.

At 4:01 p.m. Mission Control gave a ‘go’ for PDI (power descent initiation), or the final approach to the lunar surface. I felt a sense of anticipation, but also worry. All the previous manoeuvres had been carried out before by Tom Stafford and Gene Cernan during the Apollo 10 flight. However, this last descent would be something never attempted before, and definitely risky.

Armstrong had to fly the Lunar Module to a smooth spot on the surface and he had a limited amount of time and fuel to accomplish this. If the Lunar Module landed on one of the large boulders, it could be destroyed on hard impact. If the Lunar Module landed on a steep slope, it could tip over so that no return to orbit would be possible, dooming Armstrong and Aldrin. Finally, a successful firing of the Lunar Module's ascent engine would later be necessary to return the men to the CSM in orbit above – their only ticket to return to Earth.

The final descent to the Moon's surface started at about 4:05 p.m. Mission Control gave out a series of calls to the men. "Everything looking good," at 4:07 p.m. "Better than in the simulator" at 4:10 p.m (**Figure 56**).

I listened intently as Mission Control radioed the final approval for landing. Straining to hear the voice communications, I was struck by the enormity of the moment as humans were about to attempt the first landing on another celestial body, an historic event that will be remembered for thousands of years. I also had a sense of fear, based on background information from NASA and my own study of the landing procedures, because so many things could still go wrong. Armstrong's piloting skills would be put to the ultimate test.

I recorded the different milestones in my notebook, including the final "You are go for landing" at 4:15 p.m. Aldrin started to call out readings to Armstrong of their height, speed and direction. On the ground in Houston, astronaut Charles Duke was serving as CAPCOM, the radio link between Mission Control and the astronauts; he had played the same role for Apollo 10 (see **Figure 57** page 151).

Aldrin read out a series of numbers punctuated by a 1201 systems alarm. These alarms frightened listeners, who thought there might be a need for an abort. We did not know it at the time, but these alarms were due to

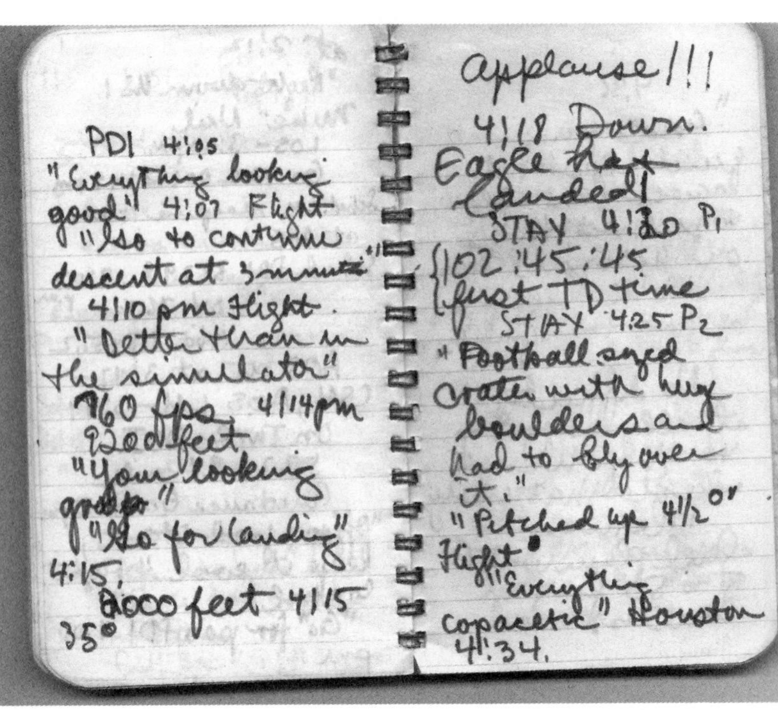

PDI 4:05
"Everything looking good" 4:07 Flight
"Go to continue descent at 3 minutes"
4:10 pm Flight.
"Better than in the simulator"
760 fps 4:14pm
"Your looking good"
"Go for landing"
4:15
feet 4:15
35°

applause!!!
4:18 Down.
Eagle has landed!
STAY 4:20 P1
102:45:45
first TD time
STAY 4:25 P2
"Football sized crater with huge boulders and had to fly over it."
"Pitched up 4 1/2°"
Flight
"Everything copacetic" Houston
4:34.

Figure 56: Author's contemporaneous notes of the touchdown of Apollo 11 on the Moon.

overloading of the primitive computer Eagle used to guide its descent. Steve Bales, a young flight controller, recognized these particular alarms from previous simulations and gave a 'go' to Flight Director Eugene Kranz.

Mission Control flight teams were designated by colours. Known as 'White Flight', Kranz was head of the Flight Control Division and lead flight director for the mission. He was known for being tough as nails, demanding as much from himself as those who worked for him in Mission Control. 'Tough and competent' was the motto of this extraordinary ex-military man, who wore his trademark white vest for the occasion.

Piloting the Lunar Module towards the Moon, Armstrong found that the designated landing spot was rough, with dangerous boulders. He saw a smooth area ahead beyond a small crater and flew the Lunar Module further and longer than planned. This consumed fuel, which became dangerously low and triggered a warning light.

"Thirty seconds," Charlie Duke called out to Armstrong, signalling the amount of time he had left to land before running out of fuel and crashing

After a perilous descent expertly flown by Armstrong, he and Aldrin landed at 4:17:40 p.m. Eastern Daylight Time (EDT) on 20 July 1969. Applause and cheers rang out in the News Center at the Cape where I had been nerv-ously listening.

I had a few tears of joy in my eyes as I become momentarily emotional. I thought of the Apollo 1 crew and the sacrifice Grissom, White and Chaffee made with their lives on Pad 34 nearby. I thought of President Kennedy, who had the boldness to set the country on the way to this moment. I thought of the over 400,000 American engineers, craftsmen, technicians and scientists who had worked on Apollo. And I thought of Neil Armstrong, Mike Collins and Buzz Aldrin, who understood the risks yet volunteered for this dangerous assignment.

"Houston, Tranquility base here. The Eagle has landed," Armstrong reported after a few brief technical readouts. An overwhelmed Charlie Duke, the CAPCOM, responded "Roger, Tranquility. We copy you on the ground. You've got a bunch of guys about to turn blue. We're breathing again. Thanks a lot." Duke, in his excitement and relief, actually said "Twank" and had to correct himself (Figure 57).

Humans had landed on the Moon! The first part of the Apollo 11 mission – the landing – was a success. I had been much more excited about the landing itself, rather than the first steps on the Moon, because getting safely to the surface was the greatest challenge. The first steps were more symbolic.

The two men walking on the Moon was not scheduled to happen until late at night. So, I went to eat dinner alone at the Camelot Inn. I missed Marv's company, although in some ways it was easier to plan just for myself.

Since the hatch opening and first steps on the Moon were scheduled for around 9:30 p.m., I made sure that I arrived back at the NASA Apollo 11 News Center a little before 9 p.m., but the astronauts were running late. The few reporters still there, myself included, huddled around the television consoles to see the ghostly pictures from the Moon. Loudspeakers in the newsroom relayed the live voice communication. While there was some static, the astronauts sounded like they were down the block rather than a quarter-million miles away.

CAPCOM Roger, copy.
PAO Altitude 4200.
CAPCOM Houston. You're go for landing. Over.
EAGLE Roger, understand. Go for landing. 3000 feet.
CAPCOM Copy.
EAGLE 12 alarm. 1201.
EAGLE 1201.
CAPCOM Roger. 1201 alarm.
EAGLE We're go. Hang tight. We're go. 2,000 feet. 2,000 feet into the AGS. 47 degrees.
CAPCOM Roger.
EAGLE 47 degrees.
CAPCOM Eagle looking great. You're go.
PAO Altitude 1600. 1400 feet. Still looking very good.
CAPCOM Roger. 1202. We copy it.
EAGLE 35 degrees. 35 degrees. 750, coming down at 23. 700 feet, 21 down. 33 degrees. 600 feet, down at 19. 540 feet, down at 30 - down at 15. 400 feet, down at 9. (garbled) 8 forward. 350, down at 4. 330, 3-1/2 down. We're pegged on horizontal velocity. 300 feet, down 3-1/2. 47 forward. (garbled) Down 1 a minute. 1-1/2 down. 70. Got the shadow out there. 50, down at 2-1/2. 19 forward. Altitude-velocity lights. 3-1/2 down, 220 feet. 13 forward. 11 forward, coming down nicely. 200 feet, 4-1/2 down. 5-1/2 down. 160, 6-1/2 down, 5-1/2 down, 9 forward. 5 percent. Quantity light. 75 feet, things looking good. Down a half. 6 forward.
CAPCOM 60 seconds.
EAGLE Lights on. Down 2-1/2. Forward. Forward. Good. 40 feet, down 2-1/2. Picking up some dust. 30 feet, 2-1/2 down. Faint shadow. 4 forward. 4 forward, drifting to the right a little. 6 (garbled) down a half.
CAPCOM 30 seconds.
EAGLE (garbled) forward. Drifting right. (garbled) Contact light. Okay, engine stop. ACA out of detent. Modes control both auto, descent engine command override, off. Engine arm, off. 413 is in.
CAPCOM We copy you down, Eagle.
EAGLE (Armstrong) Houston, Tranquility base here. The Eagle has landed.
CAPCOM Roger, Tranquility, we copy you on the ground. You've got a bunch of guys about to turn blue. We're breathing again. Thanks a lot.

Figure 57: Real-time voice transcript of the Apollo 11 lunar landing with communications between Armstrong and Aldrin in Lunar Module Eagle and CAPCOM Charles Duke in Houston.

I marvelled in the News Center at the communications technology that made this possible.

As the preparations for depressurizing the Lunar Module and then opening of the hatch proceeded, I took notes in my small pocket notebook of some of the time milestones. Armstrong stepped off the Lunar Module footpad and set foot on the lunar surface at about 10:56 p.m. EDT. His famous first words were, "That's one small step for (a) man, one giant leap for mankind" according to the NASA voice transcript. The sound was a little garbled at the News Center. I strained to hear each word. "I'm taking a small step for man and a giant leap for mankind" was how I transcribed it at the time.

To me the 'first step' was at best a small milestone, and I have agreed with Buzz Aldrin that their accomplishment should have been described as 'First Men on the Moon'.

I monitored the Moonwalk from the News Center, listening to the voice communications and trying to understand the duo's progress from 240,000 miles away (see Figure 55 page 141). Meanwhile, Michael Collins was circling above in the command module Columbia. He was perhaps the only human totally unable to see the events on TV, and observers at the time described him as the loneliest man in the universe. (Collins later stated that he did not feel that way.)

The lunar extra-vehicular activity was completed about 1:15 a.m. EDT with the men back inside the Lunar Module and the hatch sealed. I headed back to the Sea Missile Motel to crash. It had been a very long but eventful day. Although I would have preferred to cover the landing from Mission Control in Houston where all the flight controllers and NASA officials were now located, that would have been too costly. Certainly, being at the NASA Apollo 11 News Center at Cape Canaveral was better than watching it at home. I was exhausted and fell into a deep sleep.

The next morning, 21 July 1969, I slept until 10:30 a.m. I had brunch at the Astrodine restaurant and headed for the News Center. After arriving, I started to write a final story for *The Daily* about the return to Earth.

While there, I listened to the critical lift-off of Armstrong and Aldrin aboard the Eagle's ascent stage back to lunar orbit and a rendezvous with Collins in Columbia. After dictating the story to *The Daily* on a pay phone, I returned to the hotel to pack (**Figure 58**).

This was no easy task because I had collected piles of flight plans, NASA and contractor press kits, news releases and a complete set of voice transcripts for 16-20 July. The voice transcripts alone were at least eight inches thick. Despite having planned for this with my half-empty large suitcase, it was still difficult to shoehorn everything in. (Today, almost five decades later, these items have been carefully saved in my study.) I left the motel room and paid my motel bill, which was $8 per night single occupancy after Marv left, because I was scheduled to leave the next day.

I returned to Chicago on Tuesday 22 July. I had mixed emotions as I flew off from the Melbourne airport. I knew I had just completed the experience of a lifetime, yet I was also looking forward to getting back to the 'real world' of my family, friends and my summer job on Michigan Avenue. I knew that when I returned to Ann Arbor at the end of August, I would have some extraordinary stories to tell my classmates, as we always asked each other what we had done over the summer. The summer of 1969 indeed had been very special for me.

LEAVE LUNAR ORBIT

Astronauts start return to Earth

By DAVE CHUDWIN
Special To The Daily

CAPE KENNEDY—The Apollo 11 astronauts are heading back to earth after a triumphant 21 hr., 36 minute visit to the moon. The moonmen, back in their command ship Columbia, fired their engines at 12:57 a.m. today to put themselves on a homeward path.

Earlier, lunar explorers Neil Armstrong and Edwin (Buzz) Aldrin, blasted off from the Sea of Tranquility to rejoin crewmate Michael Collins, orbiting in Columbia overhead.

"You're right down the track," reported Mission Control following the 1:54 p.m. lift-off.

After a series of intricate maneuvers, Armstrong and Aldrin linked up Eagle, their lunar module, with Columbia at 5:35 p.m. Eagle, was jettisoned about four hours later.

There were some brief unexplained troubles in the docking and Collins reported that Eagle was jerking during the maneuvers. But the two space vehicles became locked together three minutes later than planned.

Docking was critical to the safe return of Armstrong and Aldrin because Eagle is not designed to withstand the heat of re-entry into the earth's atmosphere.

The lift-off from the moon came after some monumental moments in the history of exploration. For the first time a human being set foot on another celestial object.

The astronauts' longest day began at 7:02 a.m. Sunday, when the Apollo 11 crew woke up and ate breakfast. After several hours of systems checks, Armstrong and Aldrin separated

See APOLLO, Page 3

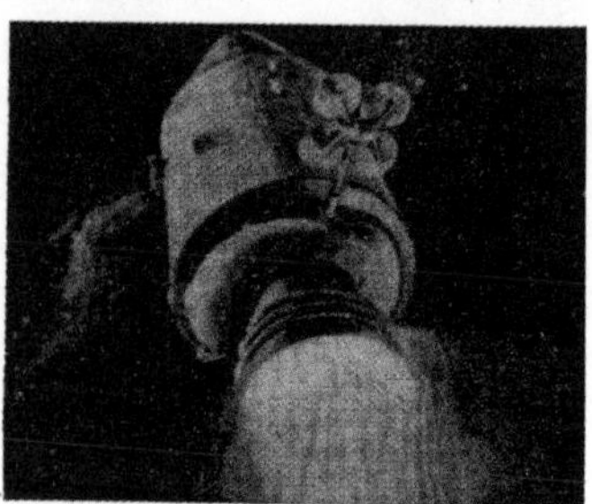

—Associated Press

Heading back home to Earth

Apollo 11 crew starts return trip to Earth

(Continued from Page 1)

Eagle from Columbia and headed for the moon.

A series of engine burns then lowered Eagle to the lunar surface at 4:18 p.m. "Houston, Tranquility Base here," Armstrong radioed. "The Eagle has landed." Immediately the astronauts began testing Eagle's systems in case an emergency take-off would have been necessary. When all appeared well, they reported details of the landing.

"The auto-targeting was taking us right into a football field-sized crater with a large number of big boulders," said Armstrong. "It required flying manually over the rock field to find a reasonably good area (to land)."

About 6 p.m., after performing a simulated count-down and eating, the astronauts requested permission, quickly granted, from Mission Control to begin their moon-walk five hours early.

Finally, after several minor delays, Armstrong and Aldrin began depressurizing the cabin about 10:25 p.m. Soon after, Armstrong went through Eagle's hatch and began climbing down the ladder.

Reaching the last rung, Armstrong jumped to the footpad of

a telephone call from President Nixon.

Running a half-hour behind schedule, the astronauts had to cut short further rock gathering.

At 12:30 a.m. yesterday, Aldrin re-entered Eagle. Forty-six minutes later, Armstrong left the surface, ending America's first moon-walk.

Figure 58: *The Michigan Daily* article by the Author recapping the Moonwalk and the return to Earth. The report was published on 22 July 1969.

CHAPTER 14

THE APOLLO 11 CREW VISITS CHICAGO

Figure 59: Buzz Aldrin, Michael Collins and Neil Armstrong receive a hero's welcome during a parade in Chicago on 13 August 1969. They ride in an open car on State Street near the iconic bronze clocks on the Marshall Fields store (upper right).

© David Chudwin

Although my trip to Cape Canaveral was over, my Apollo 11 reportage was not. Back in Illinois, I unpacked my suitcase containing my Apollo 'treasures', and went back to work at the clothing store.

I followed on television the landing of the Apollo 11 Command Module Columbia in the Pacific Ocean on 24 July. The crew was retrieved from Columbia by personnel from a US Navy aircraft carrier, the USS Hornet. While Columbia was still in the water, the astronauts changed into Biological Isolation Garments that were deemed necessary to protect the world from any possible dangerous Moon organisms.

Armstrong, Collins and Aldrin were taken by helicopter to the ship, where they were put in a trailer-size isolation unit. While this quarantine may seem ridiculous now, at the time it was considered a required precaution.

President Nixon had flown to the USS Hornet to greet the men, and he talked to them through the window of the isolation unit, congratulating them on the mission's success. Although not a strong supporter of the space program, Nixon intended to milk the glory of Apollo 11 for as much political capital as possible.

The isolation unit, with Armstrong, Collins and Aldrin aboard, was flown from the USS Hornet to Houston, where the men finished a total of three weeks of biological isolation in the Lunar Receiving Laboratory. The crew was released from isolation on 10 August to be physically reunited with their wives, children and friends.

Meanwhile, NASA and the White House were planning a long public relations campaign featuring the men and their wives that would take them around the world. This 45-day 'Great Leap' tour would take them to 25 countries, where they would be feted by foreign leaders, including Queen Elizabeth II of England. The start of this marathon was to be a cross-country US tour by Armstrong, Collins, Aldrin and their wives on Wednesday 13 August 1969.

The Nixon White House orchestrated parades honouring the Apollo 11 crew in New York in the morning, Chicago in the afternoon, and Los Angeles in the evening. A state dinner was planned for that night in Los Angeles, at which Nixon would present the men with the Presidential Medal of Freedom, the nation's highest civilian honour.

When I learned that Armstrong, Collins and Aldrin would be coming to Chicago on 13 August, I swung into action. I retrieved my NASA Apollo 11 press pass, bought more colour slide film, and resolved to cover the event. Chicago had a long tradition of ticker tape parades, but this was to be one of the largest.

It was a bright, sunny and warm Wednesday afternoon when the Apollo 11 crew arrived in Chicago after the earlier parade in New York City. Tens of thousands of people jammed the Chicago parade route waiting for the astronauts. The crew rode together standing in an open car, as did their wives sitting in another, escorted by a phalanx of policemen. Despite the heat, the men wore suits and ties, with long sleeve shirts (see **Figure 45** page 120).

The Chicago parade route started at the north end of Michigan Avenue near the Drake Hotel. Escorted by police vehicles, the procession made its way south, slowly driving down Michigan Avenue to the cheers of thousands of people lined up along either side of the 'Magnificent Mile'. They passed such landmarks as the old Chicago Water Tower, the iconic Tribune Tower and the Wrigley Building on this first part of their route.

Meanwhile, I was doing my best to run along with the astronauts' motorcade, flashing my NASA press pass to the police and snapping pictures as best I could. I ran along the street curb where the first line of police officers was stationed. I knew if I tried to approach too close to the car I would be stopped, so I was careful to keep some distance. I took almost two dozen pictures of the parade, many of them close-up shots of the three astronauts.

The parade route turned west to Wacker Drive, just across the Chicago River from the Chicago Sun-Times building (later demolished to construct Trump Towers). I followed, running beside the astronauts' car, taking pictures of them with the Sun-Times building as the backdrop (see Figure 46 page 120). As the motorcade drove adjacent to the Chicago River, fireboats sprayed arcs of water coloured red, white and blue in tribute to Armstrong, Collins and Aldrin (Figure 60).

Confetti began to fly as the men turned south on to State Street; it was as if there was a snowstorm in August. The motorcade inched up State Street, which was lined with cheering spectators standing ten-deep on either side. The enthusiastic crowd greeted the Apollo 11 crew with cheers, shouts of welcome, applause and big smiles.

The astronauts returned the enthusiasm of the crowd with broad smiles and waves. The parade route went past the venerable Marshall Fields store (now Macy's), with its fabled bronze clocks, where I took more pictures (see Figure 59 page 155).

As the crew slowly snaked up State Street, and then over to LaSalle, the astronauts were met by hundreds of thousands of people in the Loop area, including those hanging out of buildings and skyscrapers. The astronauts

Figure 60: Neil Armstrong and Buzz Aldrin (rear) wave to spectators as in the background jets of coloured water sprayed from fire boats on the Chicago River pay tribute to the astronauts. The Apollo 11 astronauts visited Chicago 13 August 1969.

made a point to look up and wave to the spectators hundreds of feet above. I was surprised by the size of the turnout and the spectators' excitement.

By the time the motorcade reached the 'canyon' of LaSalle Street, I was out of film and the security people told me in no uncertain terms to back off from my pursuit, press pass or not. "Get back on the sidewalk, now!" was the order from one policeman in a blue uniform. And by this time, I was sweating and exhausted and so I decided to call it a day. I was satisfied I had gotten close to the astronauts and knew I had some good photographs.

The astronauts continued down LaSalle Street where tons of confetti and ticker tape were thrown down from the towering buildings. I could see the blizzard of confetti from afar while quickly leaving the Loop area to avoid getting stuck in the departing crowds. I was excited to see Armstrong, Collins and Aldrin again less than a month after watching them begin their journey to the Moon on 16 July.

Meanwhile, I was working on a freelance magazine article to help pay for my trip. I began by transcribing the tape-recorded interview I had on 15 July with Dr George Mueller, NASA's head of manned spaceflight.

There were two main themes in the 20-minute private interview. The first concerned the opposition by some young people, especially anti-war protesters and those on the Left, to space exploration. Some saw it as part of the military-industrial complex that was waging the hated Vietnam War (even though NASA was a civilian agency), and others were frightened about future technology they thought could enslave them. Having just turned 19, I presented a few questions to Mueller as a devil's advocate, reflecting some of these negative views of my young peers at the time.

The second theme concerned a blueprint for our future in space. It was July 1969 and humans had landed on the Moon. What was the next step? Mueller presented a bold plan for an architecture to set up a base on the Moon. His plans included space stations around the Earth and the Moon, a shuttle between those two stations, a lunar lander and a shuttle to the Earth-orbiting station.

Of these, only the Earth-orbiting space station and space shuttle to Earth orbit were ever realized. It was inconceivable then that almost 50 years later, the US would not even have the capability to launch people into space following retirement of the space shuttle. The International Space Station is the only remnant of Mueller's visionary plan.

Mueller cogently discussed both of these issues, and I prepared a verbatim transcript from our tape-recorded interview. I then wrote an article draft using my description of the walk-out of the Apollo 11 astronauts as an introduction, followed by excerpts from the Mueller interview, and ending with my description of the Apollo 11 launch. I sent an edited draft to five publications and awaited their verdicts. I included with the manuscript some crude photographic copies of my best colour slides.

One of the first rejection letters I received was from *Reader's Digest*. However, this was not a surprise to me because it was certainly a long shot to be accepted by the popular, big-circulation magazine. However, as more rejections came back, I despaired about the chances of my Apollo 11 article ever being published. Rejections are a fact of life for any writer, but I still found them depressing to receive. However, I did not give up hope.

In September 1969, I received a letter from Edgar Good from the *American Red Cross Youth Journal* offering me $125 for the article and first publication rights – equivalent to $839 in 2018. This would cover my $94.50 airfare and a little more, so I quickly accepted. Then I waited to see how the first article about my trip would turn out.

My Apollo 11 article appeared with the title 'New Worlds for Tomorrow' in the November 1969 issue of the *American Red Cross Youth Journal* (vol. 46, pg. 22-25). The first two pages had the title over an 'Earthrise' image, and there were five other photo illustrations, including my own picture of the Apollo 11 crew walkout and NASA images of Mueller, the launch and the Moonwalk.

The article began with an editor's note: "David S. Chudwin officially covered the flight of Apollo 11 for several college publications and for the JOURNAL. He is 19 years old, a sophomore at the University of Michigan, and one of the editors of *The Michigan Daily*, the student newspaper. Writing is one of his hobbies. He has been interested in the space program for over 10 years. His recollection of the flight of Apollo 11, and an interview he conducted with an official of the space program, seem appropriate in these last days before the flight of Apollo 12."

Though the magazine was not a high profile one, I felt proud that I had received a cheque for my first freelance article and that I was a bona fide paid author. Although I had been published in my high school newspaper and in *The Michigan Daily*, this was my first magazine publication.

While at Cape Canaveral, I had a keen sense of the historic nature of what I had seen and vowed to be a messenger to others about the promise of the space program. So, with publication of that article, I felt a sense of satisfaction that my promise to tell the story of Apollo 11 from my unique perspective had now begun.

CHAPTER 15

SPACE MEMORABILIA

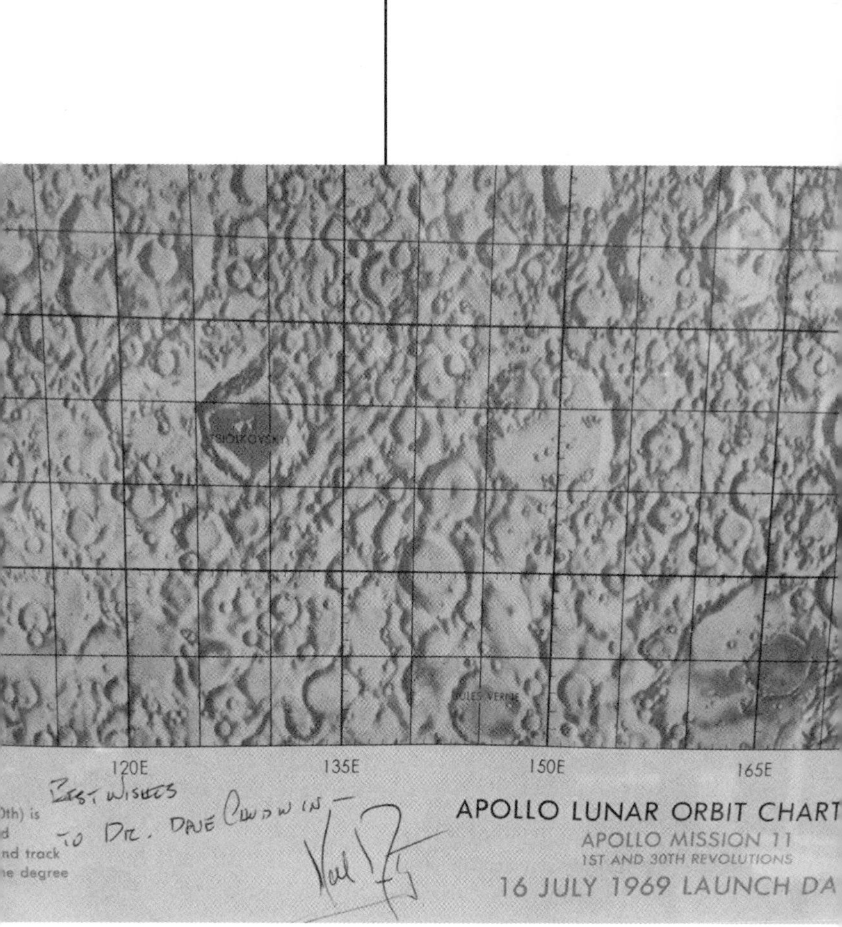

Figure 61: Apollo 11 Lunar Orbit chart inscribed to the Author in 1994 by Neil Armstrong.

© NASA / David Chudwin

After returning home from Cape Canaveral, I went through a thick stack of papers containing a NASA flight plan, press kit, public relations plan, lunar orbit maps, hundreds of pages of transcripts, industrial folders and press releases. I also brought back some envelopes I had postmarked at the Cape Canaveral Post Office on the 20 July landing date.

This memorabilia reminded me of my remarkable experiences covering Apollo 11 and were tangible souvenirs of the events I had witnessed. I had a sense of history as I organized the various papers and documents. In the back of my mind I thought they might be useful if I ever wrote about my Apollo 11 coverage.

I had collected autographed space memorabilia since Gemini 4 in 1965 so I decided that, over time, I would try to get the Apollo 11 crew to autograph some of these items. I felt a special kinship with them, having seen for myself their lift-off on 16 July 1969 and the Chicago parade on 13 August.

A few months after Apollo 11 came back, I wrote to Mike Collins, sending him some of the walk-out and parade pictures that I had taken. I requested an autograph on two stamped envelopes, one having the Kennedy Space Center postmark for the launch and the other an official NASA cachet on a recovery envelope from the USS Hornet. It took a while, but not only did Collins personally sign the two envelopes, he also sent a NASA colour lithograph depicting the crew that he inscribed to me (see Figure 72 page 210). This is one of my favourite Apollo 11 souvenirs.

The early astronauts received thousands of requests for autographs from space enthusiasts around the world.

With their busy training schedules, it was hard for them to find time to sign all of them. So most autograph requests were signed with an autopen – a mechanical device that uses a moving pen over a template to replicate a signature. Every autopen autograph is the same as the other so veteran collectors quickly began to recognize the characteristic autopen patterns for each astronaut. Other telltale clues included a dot at the end of each word, uniform thickness of the lines and use of a felt-tip pen. The signatures of Armstrong and Aldrin on the lithograph from Collins were autopen autographs.

I also sent launch and recovery envelopes to Buzz Aldrin, but as expected I received back autopen signatures. Almost 20 years later, in 1987, Buzz was kind enough to inscribe for free an Apollo 11 crew lithograph to my then young son Adam. However, he soon started charging increasing autograph fees for signatures.

Astronauts while on duty at NASA always gave autographs for free; it was up to their own discretion whether to sign or not. Retired astronauts saw that their autographs had become commercial commodities. Memorabilia they had signed for free were being offered at auctions or later on eBay. There were some unscrupulous individuals who would obtain dozens of signatures, either under false names themselves or even by paying students to request them.

Most of the astronauts felt that some people had taken advantage of their generosity in signing autographs for free. A market had developed for astronaut memorabilia, with the astronauts providing the commodities for free and not seeing any of the profits.

The first astronaut to charge any fee was Jim Irwin, who in the mid-1980s asked for $3 for a signed lithograph of him on the Moon. It was pre-printed with the phrase 'His Love From the Moon', and Irwin would inscribe it and personally sign it.

Since then, most retired astronauts have started charging for their signatures as the commercialization of space memorabilia has exploded. These fees have steeply escalated, with Aldrin ($600) and Gene Cernan ($500) the highest of the Apollo astronauts in 2016, before Cernan's death. An exception was John Glenn, who never charged for his autograph.

The situation with Neil Armstrong's autograph is more complex. While a genuine autograph of the first man on the Moon may now cost $1,000 or more, until 1994 Armstrong was among the most generous of signers among the astronauts. He estimated that he signed over 100,000 autographs up until the 25th anniversary of the Moon landing, in July 1994, when he stopped giving any autographs (with very rare exceptions).

Thereafter, he would be happy to pose for pictures with dignitaries, space workers and ordinary space enthusiasts, but was adamant about not signing. He reminisced that Charles Lindbergh, the great aviator, advised him not to give autographs. Some later collectors groused about his policy, noting that his no-autograph stance made his signature scarcer, but there were no shortages of his autographs for sale from the thousands he had signed previously.

I obtained my first Armstrong autograph after Gemini 8 in 1966 when I sent him a NASA colour photo of the Agena lift-off. A few weeks later I received the photo back from Houston, inscribed to me – years later crewmate Dave Scott's signature was added to complete the Gemini 8 crew (see Figure 14 page 52). I was thrilled to get

Armstrong's signature, but I also sent requests to many of the other Apollo astronauts. Collecting space memorabilia had become a hobby of mine.

One of my most prized Armstrong autographs is a rare Apollo 11 'insurance cover' signed by the crew when the three were in quarantine at the Kennedy Space Center before the launch. The envelopes were then postmarked in Houston for the 20 July landing date (Figure 62).

Insurance covers were envelopes produced to help the astronauts' families in case the astronauts were killed in a tragedy during their flights. They could not get standard commercial life insurance because of the risks their jobs involved. Though they did have some insurance through their *Life* magazine contracts, sales of the insurance covers were designed to supplement those funds in case of a tragedy. Several hundred of these philatelic envelopes, with Manned Spacecraft Center Stamp Club or Dow Unicover cachets designs, were produced, autographed by the crew before the flight, and then postmarked on the date of their launch or Moon landing.

I was able to buy an insurance cover for $350 in the 1980s from noted space collector and space cover dealer Ken Havekotte. The price was reduced due to the poor quality of the Houston postmark on this one. These rare covers go for as much as $5,000 now. (Thanks, Ken!) As forged Apollo 11 crew signatures have proliferated, these insurance covers have the best possible provenance as to their authenticity.

Perhaps the most sentimental of my Neil Armstrong autographs is a scarce NASA lithograph showing Apollo 11 on the Moon that he personally inscribed to my son Adam in 1987. That year, when Adam was 2, I sent

Figure 62: Apollo 11 'insurance cover' envelope signed by the crew before launch, intended to be sold to help their families in case they perished during the mission. The envelope was postmarked in Houston on 20 July 1969.

© David Chudwin

Figure 63: Apollo 11 stamp First Day Cover signed by all four flight directors – Eugene Kranz, Gerald Griffin, Glynn Lunney and Cliff Charlesworth.

© David Chudwin

individual pictures of the 12 US Moonwalkers to each of them and asked them to inscribe the photo to Adam. I also included a snapshot of Adam so they could see to whom they were writing. I was successful with everyone but John Young and Dave Scott (who were added later).

Armstrong wrote, "To Adam – All Good Wishes" and then signed his autograph on a NASA lithograph of a picture Armstrong had taken of Buzz Aldrin exiting the Lunar Module (see Figure 55 page 141). While Armstrong signed thousands of autographs, very few of them were of scenes on the Moon, as opposed to those of him posing in his spacesuit or crew portraits. This rare complete set of 12 signed and inscribed Moonwalker photos belongs to my son, who is now in his early 30s, although they are safely stored in a bank safe deposit box.

The story of the most amazing, and last, autograph I obtained from Armstrong begins back in 1969 at the NASA Apollo 11 News Center. I snagged two copies of a large Apollo 11 colour lunar orbit map there. In 1993, I realized I had nothing to lose by writing to Armstrong again to see if he would sign the map; I had not requested anything in many years. By this time, Armstrong had retired to a farm near Lebanon, Ohio, a small rural town near Cincinnati, and was only sporadically responding to autograph requests.

I sent out the lunar orbit map to his Ohio address and a few weeks later received the intact envelope back, marked 'REFUSED' on the front. Not willing to give up, I remembered that the Astronaut Office at the Johnson Space Center in Houston could forward mail to former astronauts, although this is no longer the case today.

So, in 1994 I sent the map addressed to Armstrong at the Houston address.

I knew this was risky because there were no assurances that Armstrong would receive the map, let alone sign it, but I thought it was worth a chance. Many weeks went by and I thought it was lost.

But then on 20 July 1994, the 25th Anniversary of the Moon Landing, I went out to my mailbox and saw a large envelope with a Cincinnati postmark. My hands were shaking as I opened it. Inside was my lunar orbit map, inscribed "Best Wishes to Dr Dave Chudwin – Neil Armstrong" in ballpoint pen at the bottom of the map (see Figure 61 page 163).

I was surprised and thrilled. I later learned that he decided to stop signing as of 20 July so my map was one of the last items autographed by him.

Of all the space memorabilia I own, this is the most precious to me, not only because I have not seen elsewhere such a map autographed by Armstrong, but also the eerie circumstance of it arriving in my mailbox on the 25th Anniversary of the landing. This is a keepsake that will always remain in our family.

So, in my space memorabilia collection I have a half-dozen signed items by the 'First Man' – three philatelic covers, two photos and a lunar orbit map. These were obtained over 28 years, between 1966 and 1994, so I do not think they represent an excessive number of requests.

I also wanted to obtain signed Apollo envelopes from some others who played key roles in the success of Apollo 11. I list them here not as a catalogue of my collection, but as a tribute in recognition of their contribution to the first Moon landing. These included

Apollo 11 flight directors, capsule communicators and NASA program and center directors.

While most of the public attention focused on the three Apollo 11 astronauts, they stood at the top of a pyramid of over 400,000 people who worked on Project Apollo.

Armstrong and Aldrin would not have safely landed on and returned from the Moon without the staff of Mission Control in Houston. There were four flight directors assigned to Apollo 11 who were directly responsible for different phases of the mission. Working along with each of them were four astronauts serving as CAPCOMs, who served as the verbal link between the crew in space and the flight controllers on the ground.

The team for the Apollo 11 launch and extra-vehicular activity was Flight Director Cliff Charlesworth and CAPCOM astronaut Bruce McCandless. The team for the lunar landing was Gene Kranz and astronaut Charlie Duke. The team for the lunar ascent was Glynn Lunney and astronaut Ron Evans. The final team for night periods was Gerry Griffin and astronaut Dr Owen Garriott.

The flight directors were the men who, during their shifts, had ultimate authority over the vast numbers of engineers and scientists on the ground supporting Apollo 11. They headed the flight control team in Mission Control that was the 'brains' behind the astronauts. As such, they had unquestioned 'go/no go' authority over the mission proceeding or being aborted at any point.

Over a 40-year period I wrote to or met each of these four flight directors and asked them to sign an Apollo 11 'First Day Cover'. Unfortunately, Cliff Charlesworth died in 1991 and his signature is rarely seen. First Day Covers are envelopes with a special postmark on newly released stamps that show the date and location of the release. The First Day Covers for the 10-cent Apollo 11 stamp, designed by Paul Calle, had a Washington, D.C., postmark dated 9 September 1969 and text reading 'First Day of Issue' (see Figure 63 page 168).

I purchased a second envelope signed by some of the astronaut CAPCOMs for Apollo 11 and added further autographs to it. It is imperfect because Al Worden was not an official CAPCOM, and the autograph of Bruce McCandless appears both as an autopen and genuine signature. While the role of Charlie Duke during the landing is legendary – "You've got a bunch of guys about to turn blue" – the contributions to Apollo 11 of the other CAPCOMs, including Bruce McCandless, Ron Evans and Owen Garriott, have largely been ignored.

Besides the flight directors and CAPCOMs at the Manned Spacecraft Center in Houston, other key managers employed by NASA and contractors worked at NASA Headquarters in Washington, the Marshall Space Flight Center in Huntsville and the Kennedy Space Center in Florida to make Apollo 11 a success. The Apollo Program was a multi-billion-dollar enterprise and these were the men who directed it. (As noted earlier, it would take many more years for women to assume such roles due to the sexism of the times).

In the year following Apollo 11, I wrote to many of NASA's top brass to congratulate them on their achievement and to seek their autographs on identical First Day Covers bearing the Man on the Moon stamp released after the flight.

I wrote to NASA Administrator Tom Paine, Apollo Program Director General Sam Phillips and Apollo 11

Mission Director George Hage at NASA Headquarters in Washington. At the Manned Spacecraft Center, I sent covers to Director Robert Gilruth, Deputy Director Chris Kraft and Apollo Spacecraft Program Manager George Low. At the Kennedy Space Center, I wrote to Director Kurt Debus and Director of Launch Operations Rocco Petrone.

Each of these brilliant men played key, but different, roles in organizing the Apollo program to successfully land on and return men from the Moon. I was happy to receive the autographed envelopes from each of them and enjoyed the ritual of going to the mailbox each day to see if any of them had come back.

In addition, I have in my memorabilia collection a large number of different stamped envelopes postmarked for the Apollo 11 launch, lunar landing, and recovery aboard the USS Hornet from, respectively, the Cape Canaveral, Kennedy Space Center, Houston, USS Hornet and other post offices. With different designs, these un-autographed 'space covers' also remind me of my Apollo 11 experiences.

While collecting 'space covers' may not be as popular now with the end of the space shuttle program, these envelopes were postmarked on the day of important space events and serve as philatelic souvenirs of Apollo 11 and other space milestones. They are tangible commemorations of the 'who, what, where, why and when' of important space events.

CHAPTER 16

MEETING THE APOLLO 11 CREW IN LATER YEARS

Figure 64: Neil Armstrong in 2009 attending a celebration honouring Apollo 12's 40th Anniversary.

I saw the entire Apollo 11 crew in person twice in 1969, first during their walk-out on the way to the Moon on 16 July and then during their triumphant parade in Chicago on 13 August. It would be 40 years, however, until I saw all three again.

I had the pleasure of meeting Buzz Aldrin at a number of space events from 2005 through May 2015. Of the Apollo 11 crew, Aldrin was the most gregarious and publicly active. A special treat for me was to be at his dinner table for a Spacefest banquet in 2012. Spacefest is an annual event where astronauts, artists, scientists, autograph seekers and space enthusiasts gather for a weekend of talks, art shows, autograph sessions, and a banquet where each table features an astronaut or other space notable (Figure 65).

Aldrin was also the most complex and contradictory of the crew. While he could be at times abrupt, rude and even greedy about autograph fees (the 'bad Buzz'), he was often genial, approachable and friendly (the 'good Buzz'). Aldrin had great powers of concentration on areas in which he was interested, such as rendezvous techniques and travel to Mars, however he had little interest in other subjects. He could be socially awkward at times, but also gracious and engaging under other circumstances.

He was a tireless public advocate for the future of space exploration, championing advanced technology to get us to Mars and beyond. His activities included testifying before Congress, giving numerous speeches and appearances, and attending space events such as Spacefest and Astronaut Scholarship Foundation fundraisers. He popularized human Mars exploration with a campaign that featured t-shirts that read: 'Get Your Ass to Mars!'

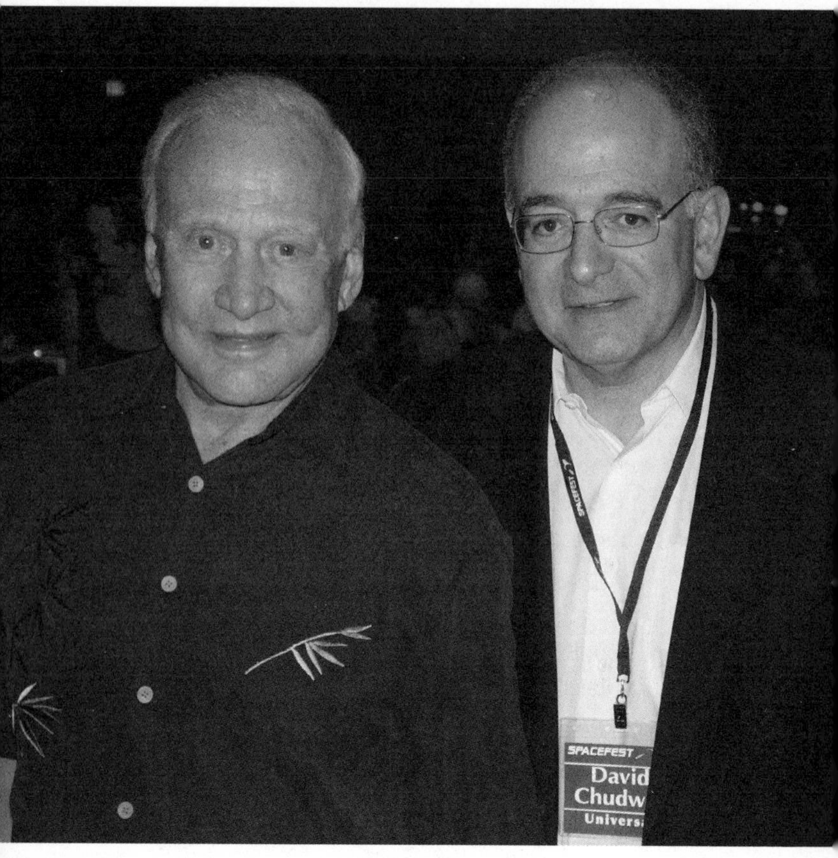

Figure 65: Buzz Aldrin and the Author
at a Spacefest banquet in 2012.

He also was involved in some sensational incidents, such as punching Bart Sibrel in the jaw in September 2002, after the Moon hoaxer provoked him (no charges were filed), and a messy divorce from his third wife Lois that was eventually settled in January 2013.

While critics denounced some of his activities as tasteless (such as appearing on *Dancing with the Stars*), no one could deny Buzz's energy, high intelligence and his passion for the future. Even in his late-80s, Aldrin barely slowed down.

Michael Collins led an active life after Apollo 11, but for a while avoided most public events except for meeting the US President every five years on the anniversary of the Moon landing.

One of his greatest achievements was overseeing the construction and opening of the new National Air & Space Museum (NASM) on time and on budget as its director from 1971-78. The NASM was wildly popular, quickly becoming the most visited museum in Washington and by 2014 the fifth most visited museum in the world. His leadership in supervising the building and operating of the NASM won him widespread praise.

Collins was also an accomplished writer. His book *Carrying the Fire*, published in 1974, has been widely acclaimed as one of the best astronaut autobiographies. An updated version of the book was released in 2009, for the 40th anniversary of the Apollo 11 mission.

He also penned *Liftoff: The Story of America's Adventure in Space* (1988), a history of the space program;

Mission to Mars (1990), a non-fiction book concerning future spaceflight to Mars; and the children's book *Flying to the Moon and Other Strange Places* (1976), which was later re-released as *Flying to the Moon: An Astronaut's Story* (1994), about his NASA experiences.

In later years, he took up watercolour art. As a favour to fellow artist Kim Poor, the co-founder of Spacefest, Collins and his late wife Pat did appear at Spacefest II in San Diego in 2009. When I got the chance to meet him there, I introduced myself, and to my astonishment he said, "I know who you are" (Figure 66).

I was honoured but puzzled as to how he knew my name. It turns out that he was an anonymous member of the astro-philatelic group Space Unit in the 1980s when I was editor of its newsletter, *Astrophile*.

Collins was in many ways a renaissance man – test pilot, astronaut, writer, museum director and artist. I always had said that if I could have dinner with any astronaut, past or present, Mike Collins would be my first choice.

My wish was granted at Spacefest VII in June 2016 where I was seated to Collins' left at the banquet. Collins had come to this event with his daughters Kate and Ann. Many of us at his table knew each other from prior Spacefests or other space events, and we'd all registered for that year's Spacefest in the first minutes after registration had opened since that determined priority in seating at the banquet.

It was a magical evening for those at the table, as Collins quoted poetry, talked about the importance of the arts and answered questions from his table partners. One of the highlights was his dramatic recitation from memory of an excerpt from John Milton's book, *Paradise Lost.*

Figure 66: Michael Collins and the Author at Spacefest in 2009. Collins and his late wife Pat attended for the first time.

© David Chudwin

At the dinner, I showed Collins on my mobile phone my Apollo 11 walk-out close-up picture of him in his spacesuit (see Figure 3 page 12). He pointed to the paper bag he was carrying next to his portable air-conditioner unit and asked if I knew what it was. He was surprised that I knew it contained the gag gift to be given to Pad Leader Guenter Wendt.

As noted earlier, Wendt held a long tradition of exchanging humorous gifts with astronaut crews as his team inserted them into their spacecraft in the White Room. It was a way of relieving tension at a very tense moment. Collins had remembered that Wendt liked fishing but did not have time for it, so Collins proposed giving him a fish trophy. Collins recounted that he arranged to get a fish from the Banana River and nailed the dead fish to a wooden plaque inscribed to Wendt the night before the launch.

Wendt enjoyed the gift but had to freeze the plaque because it was an actual fresh, but dead, fish. The plaque remained in Wendt's freezer for years until he had the fish preserved by a taxidermist. The plaque was on display at the Kansas Cosmosphere museum for several years, but after Wendt's death it passed into the hands of a Canadian space enthusiast and memorabilia collector.

Collins continued to reside in Florida where he painted regularly and enjoyed his retirement. The loss of his beloved wife Pat was a big blow, but he made frequent trips to Boston to be with family members. In my opinion, Collins was one of the most educated and well-rounded of the astronauts; he was comfortable with himself and wore his fame well.

The next time I saw Neil Armstrong in person again was in 2009. By then, Armstrong had achieved almost mythic status and was only making a limited number of public appearances. He was shy and liked to avoid the limelight.

He gave several speeches per year, reportedly commanding a fee of over $100,000 per talk, but he also went gratis on several military missions to cheer up American troops overseas. One memorable trip sponsored by the USO was in 2010 with Apollo 17 commander Gene Cernan and Apollo 13 commander Jim Lovell.

Armstrong did make a point to go to anniversary dinners for the other Apollo missions. This was his homage to his comrades, the other Apollo astronauts, who had contributed so greatly to getting to the Moon but had not received the same recognition and fame as Armstrong, who would forever be known as the 'First Man'.

I attended the Apollo 12 40th Anniversary dinner in 2009 at Cape Canaveral. This event was sponsored by the Astronaut Scholarship Foundation, and when Armstrong arrived he was surrounded by security men wearing radio earpieces. I began to understand why he required extraordinary security when he was literally mobbed by well-wishers seeking a photo with him or to say hello. My hopes for a personal picture one-on-one with Armstrong were dashed because of the mob around him, but I was able to get some close-up shots of him by elbowing into the crowd (see Figure 64 page 174). However, I was pictured along with Armstrong, Cernan and NASA Administrator Charles Bolden in an image of the banquet room (Figure 67).

Figure 67: The Author standing at far upper right while Neil Armstrong, Gene Cernan, and NASA Administrator Charles Bolden are in the foreground. The photo was taken in 2009 at the Apollo 12 40th Anniversary dinner.

In 2010, Armstrong and I both attended the Apollo 13 40th Anniversary dinner at the Adler Planetarium in Chicago. I could not get close but was able to photograph him from a distance. This was the last time I saw Armstrong. He died on 25 August 2012, at age 82, in a hospital in Cincinnati due to complications after heart surgery. Per his wishes, his remains were cremated and his ashes were scattered at sea with full military honours on 14 September 2012, the day after a memorial service at Washington National Cathedral.

No one could have been a better choice for 'First Man' than Neil Armstrong. He was a brilliant pilot, an engineering professor, an intellectual fascinated by the intricacies of subjects ranging from aeronautics to chronometers, a quiet man who conducted himself with dignity, and a man who was comfortable with his place in history.

While some criticized him for not being more of a cheerleader for space, Armstrong did serve as vice-chairman of the commission investigating the 1986 space shuttle Challenger disaster and made appearances before Congress on the future of space exploration.

After his death, NASA honoured Armstrong's achievements by renaming the Dryden Flight Research Center in California for him, as it did with the Kennedy Space Center Operations & Checkout Building, the former MSOB that had been the location of the astronaut quarters where he stayed before Apollo 11.

Neil Armstrong's name will be remembered for thousands of years as the Marco Polo of the Space Age. I was privileged to have seen him in person as he walked out in his spacesuit to fly to the Moon, in the Chicago parade after his safe return, and at the Apollo 12 and 13 anniversary dinners. Rest in peace.

PART TWO

LESSONS FROM APOLLO

Figure 68: The "New Nine" astronauts selected in 1962 included (upper row) Elliot See, James McDivitt, James Lovell, Edward White, Thomas Stafford (bottom row) Charles Conrad, Frank Borman, Neil Armstrong and John Young. This second group of U.S. astronauts were the core of the Apollo Program.

CHAPTER 17

BE BOLD!

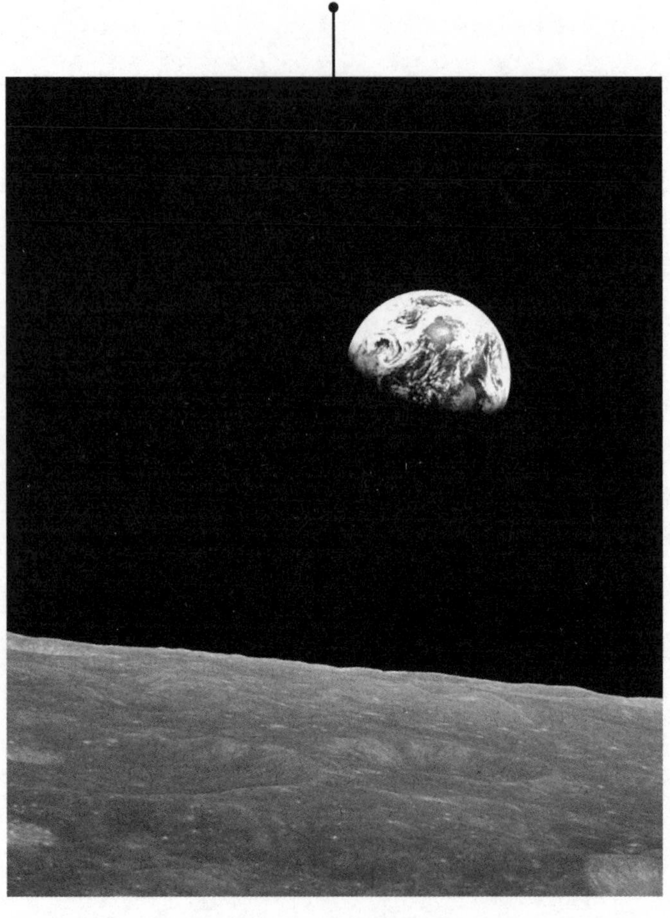

Figure 69: The flight plan for Apollo 8 to go into orbit around the Moon on the first crewed Saturn V flight was one of the bold decisions that allowed the U.S. to achieve the goal of landing on the Moon before the end of the decade. This photo by Bill Anders shows 'Earthrise' over the lunar surface.

© NASA

What are some of the lessons learned from the Apollo missions? In this second section of the book I will discuss some aspects of the Apollo program that have affected our thinking about space exploration

The first lesson is about the advantages of making bold decisions and not being timid in exploring the 'New Frontier' of space. These bold decisions included setting the Moon as a goal, choosing the scheme to get there, testing the Moon rocket and spacecraft all together, and sending astronauts to orbit the Moon on the first crewed Saturn V flight. I will explore each of these four examples.

On 5 May 1961, Alan Shepard made America's first manned spaceflight. As noted above, the suborbital mission consisted of just one person squeezed into a small space capsule riding aboard a modified Redstone ICBM for only 15 minutes. Yet with only this tip-toe into space, President John F. Kennedy three weeks later laid out an ambitious goal of landing humans on the Moon before 1970, only 8 ½ years hence. In a speech he gave to a joint session of Congress on 25 May 1961, Kennedy told the nation:

"I believe that this nation should commit itself to achieving the goal, before this decade is out, of landing a man on the moon and returning him safely to the Earth. No single space project in this period will be more impressive to mankind, or more important for the long-range exploration of space; and none will be so difficult or expensive to accomplish."

This was a bold, courageous and risky step, because in 1961 the United States had neither the rockets nor spacecraft to accomplish the goal.

At the time, I was only 10 years old and I did not understand the enormity of the task. However, flying to the Moon resonated with me because of some of the science fiction stories I had read. As mentioned earlier, I was especially captivated by author Robert Heinlein, who frequently used Moon bases and colonies as a setting in his short stories and novels.

What series of events led President Kennedy to aim for the Moon? As noted in Chapter 2, the Soviets set all the early records in spaceflight. The Russian rockets were larger, more powerful and more reliable than early US rockets.

President Eisenhower had responded almost reluctantly to public calls for the US to counter the Russians. Pushed by public opinion and the Democrats in the Senate, Eisenhower in 1958 agreed to establish NASA and modestly increase funding for unmanned satellites, Saturn rocket development and Project Mercury, the plan to put an American into Earth orbit.

After Kennedy was inaugurated as President in January 1961, he faced several crises with respect to the country's space ambitions and national security. The launch of Russian cosmonaut Yuri Gagarin into orbit on 12 April 1961 put the issue of US space inferiority on the front burner again. The first manned spaceflight by Gagarin was a propaganda victory for the Soviets, proving the superiority of Communism in their eyes. They portrayed the mission as an example of socialist technology defeating capitalism.

Just five days later there was another black eye for the United States, this time involving the Communist regime headed by Fidel Castro in Cuba, just 90 miles from the US. On 17 April 1961, Cuban paramilitary groups financed by the US Central Intelligence Agency unsuccessfully tried to invade Cuba in an attempt to topple Castro. The effort, known as the Bay of Pigs invasion, failed miserably, making the United States again look ineffectual.

We now know that three days later, on 20 April 1961, Kennedy sent a secret memo to then Vice President Johnson, who was head of the Space Council.

In the memo, Kennedy asked:

"Do we have a chance of beating the Soviets by putting a laboratory in space, or by a trip around the moon, or by a rocket to land on the moon, or by a rocket to go to the moon and back with a man? Is there any space program which promises dramatic results in which we could win?"

Kennedy ordered Johnson to submit a report, "at the earliest possible moment." Johnson was told to consult with NASA Administrator Webb, Defense Secretary Robert McNamara and White House science advisor Jerome Wiesner.

Over the next week there was a flurry of activity at the highest levels of NASA Headquarters and its field centers, the Department of Defense, the Bureau of the Budget and the White House. Johnson reported back to the President with a detailed six-page memo on 28 April 1961.

Johnson concluded that the Soviets already had rockets capable of launching a space laboratory, sending unmanned probes around the Moon and even soft-landing instruments on the Moon. He suggested that the first opportunity the United States had to beat the Russians would be manned circumnavigation or a landing on the Moon.

"However, with a strong effort, the United States could be conceivably first in those two accomplishments by 1966 or 1967," Johnson concluded.

The next day, 29 April 1961, Wernher von Braun sent an influential secret memo to Johnson. In it, he argued: "We have an excellent chance of beating the Soviets to first landing of a crew on the moon" and "With an all-out crash program I think we could accomplish this in 1967-68."

It is very clear from these documents that the focus of the policy debate was beating the Soviets in what had become a 'space race'. Kennedy wanted a long-range goal that the United States could accomplish ahead of the Russians, taking into account their lead at the time in rocket boosters.

Just a month later, on 25 May 1961, Kennedy announced the lunar landing objective and other space plans in his speech to Congress. It was audacious to commit the nation to a lunar landing when neither the rockets nor spacecraft had even been designed or built. While the goal was ambitious, Kennedy made his recommendation on the basis of a comprehensive review of American and Soviet technology by the US space, defense and intelligence agencies and advice from experts such as von Braun. The decision was risky, but it was not rash.

Determining how to best get to the Moon (and back) is another example of such a bold decision. There were three major competing schemes.

The first suggested approach was to develop a huge rocket booster to fly directly to the Moon, land there, and then return to Earth. This direct ascent method had the advantage of simplicity in that only a single rocket, however big, was required. This was initially favoured by NASA

Administrator Webb. However, the rocket would have been too expensive and so large that it would have been impossible to build with the technology available in 1961. And, importantly, there would not have been enough time to develop the rocket before Kennedy's 'end of this decade' goal.

Thus, the leading plan early in 1961 to get to the Moon was called Earth Orbit Rendezvous (EOR). This scheme called for one large rocket to launch a lunar lander and a second large rocket to launch a crewed spacecraft into Earth orbit. The two would rendezvous and dock around the Earth and then head together for the Moon. The two rockets required were smaller than the direct approach, but the launch failure of one of the rockets would prevent success.

A third way of going to the Moon, Lunar Orbit Rendezvous (LOR), was a latecomer to the table. A single rocket would carry the manned spacecraft and a small two-stage lunar lander into orbit around the Moon. Then the lunar lander would separate from the command ship and land on the Moon. The lower stage of the lander (descent module) would act as a launch pad for the upper stage (ascent module) to blast off from the Moon and rendezvous with the orbiting command ship. The lunar lander would be jettisoned and just the command ship would return to Earth.

The advantage of LOR was that it would take much less energy to send men to lunar orbit than directly to the Moon's surface. Unlike EOR, only one launch booster was required. The main downside was that it required rendezvous and docking in far-off lunar orbit rather than the closer, more friendly confines of Earth orbit.

Dr John Houbolt, of NASA's Langley Research Center, the major proponent of this scheme, made a presentation about LOR to NASA Associate Administrator Robert Seamans in December 1960. LOR also became the favourite approach of the Manned Spacecraft Center in Houston while EOR was championed by Wernher von Braun at the Marshall Space Flight Center.

As a ten-year-old, I was too young to understand the technical details of the debate. However, I was aware at the time that NASA had not yet decided exactly how to land on the Moon.

NASA set up study groups to investigate these pathways to a lunar landing, On 7 June 1962 a Lunar Module Decision Conference was held. After hours of long presentations, von Braun threw in the towel as far as EOR was concerned and came out in favour of LOR. On 22 June, the panel in charge of manned spaceflight headed by Seamans approved LOR and it was officially announced to the public on 11 July 1962 (my 12th birthday).

So, given the information and technical ability they had at the time, NASA took the risky decision to land on the Moon with a technique requiring astronauts to rendezvous and dock with a mother ship in lunar orbit, far away from Earth, in order to return home. This decision was made long before the US or any other country had performed this technique in Earth orbit, let alone around the Moon. However, technical studies suggested this was not only possible, but also the best way to proceed.

A third bold decision which insured that President Kennedy's goal would be met was to engage in 'all up testing' to reach the Moon sooner. As noted earlier, this refers to testing an entire rocket vehicle together instead of testing each component individually.

For many years, each stage, or section, of a rocket was tested one by one in a step-wise approach. For example, the first four flights of the Saturn 1 rocket developed by Wernher von Braun and his colleagues at the Marshall Space Flight Center just had an active first stage; the second stage and payload were dummies filled with water ballast. It was not until the fifth Saturn 1 flight, on 29 January 1964, that the second stage was added, which allowed the second stage to go into Earth orbit (a record heavy payload for a satellite at that time).

If this same traditional philosophy of step-wise testing was going to be embraced for the three-stage Saturn V Moon rocket, it would take months to sequentially start with the first stage, then add the second stage, then add the third stage, and finally add the payload components.

This was the approach always used by von Braun and his associates. They planned to order as many as 20 Saturn V Moon rockets for the Apollo program, and would conduct up to 10 Saturn V test flights before undertaking a manned mission.

Enter Dr George Mueller, an electrical and missile engineer. Mueller was chosen by NASA Administrator Webb to head the manned space program in November 1963. Mueller had just completed a study for Webb that suggested an organizational change requiring the NASA center heads, such as von Braun and Robert Gilruth, to report to an Associate Administrator instead of Webb himself. Webb accepted that recommendation and named Mueller to the post of Associate Administrator for Manned Space Flight.

While working on missile development for the military in prior years, Mueller had adopted the all up testing approach. Mueller's rationale was that in the space environment, the step-by-step approach might not reveal unexpected problems with the entire, integrated space vehicle. He was quoted as saying the following in a NASA oral history:

"You don't want to be testing piecewise in space. You want to test the entire system because who knows which one's going to fail, and you'd better have it all together so that whatever fails, you have a reasonable chance of finding the real failure mode, not just the one you were looking for."

After assuming his NASA position in 1963, Mueller proposed using all up testing for the Saturn V Moon rocket under development at the time. He believed that all up testing would accelerate the tight schedule to meet Kennedy's goal, reduce the number and expense of Saturn V rockets needed to accomplish the program, and would be a more realistic test of rocket performance than with dummy second and third stages.

This was anathema to von Braun and the Marshall Space Flight Center. But eventually they became convinced, primarily by the engineering arguments, that all up testing provided a greater opportunity to discover problems with the integrated vehicle in the space environment.

So, the first test of a Saturn V rocket (called Apollo 4) was the launch of a complete Saturn V rocket, with all three stages, on 9 November 1967. The payload was a complete Command and Service Module (CSM).

Instead of sending the CSM to the Moon, the third stage, before separating, sent the CSM into a highly elliptical orbit around the Earth. The Service Module rocket was fired to return the CSM to Earth, simulating a return from the Moon.

The Apollo 4 flight was highly successful and allowed the Apollo program to leapfrog to a manned Apollo flight after only one more unmanned Saturn V rocket test – Apollo 6 in April 1968. The Saturn V successfully launched a CSM and a test model of the Lunar Module into Earth orbit during the Apollo 6 flight.

Mueller's proposal to test all three stages of the Saturn V rocket together was controversial, but without it, chances were slim that the US would have landed on the Moon by the end of the decade.

The final bold decision to be discussed here was the decision to send Apollo 8, the first crewed Saturn V flight, to orbit the Moon. The original plan for Apollo 8 was to use the Saturn V to put the combined Lunar Module and CSM carrying Frank Borman, James Lovell and William Anders into a highly elliptical orbit of 3,500 miles above the Earth's surface. The astronauts would then perform the first tests of the Lunar Module in space. Finally, the three astronauts would practice the return to Earth, testing the heat shield and parachute recovery systems from a high Earth orbit.

Mission planners at the beginning of the Apollo program envisaged 10 different flight profiles would eventually be needed to accomplish the goals of the program. The original Apollo 8 flight was called an 'E Mission' in the sequence of Apollo flights (**Table 1**).

Table 1: Apollo mission types

20 September 1967
The Manned Spacecraft Center proposed to the NASA Office of Manned Space Flight a sequence of missions leading to a lunar landing mission. The sequence included the following basic missions:

A	Saturn V/unmanned CSM development
B	Saturn IB/unmanned lunar module development
C	Saturn IB/manned CSM evaluation
D	Saturn V/manned CSM and lunar module development (A dual Saturn IB mission would be an alternative to the Saturn V for mission D)
E	CSM/lunar module operations in high Earth orbit
F	Lunar orbit mission
G	Lunar landing mission (like Apollo 11)
H	Lunar landing mission (Apollo 12, 13, and 14)
I	Reserved for lunar survey missions (not used)
J	Lunar landing missions, upgraded hardware (Apollo 15, 16, and 17)

While the unmanned Apollo 4 and 6 flights validated the Saturn V launch vehicle, development of the Lunar Module dragged behind due to technical and budget issues. As the Lunar Module delays lengthened, the plan for Apollo 8 became unrealistic – there would be no Lunar Module to fly for months.

At that time, the brilliant engineer George Low was the Apollo Spacecraft Program Manager in Houston. Born in Austria, Low migrated with his family to the US at age 12. He studied aeronautical engineering at Rensselaer Polytechnic Institute, and when NASA was formed in 1958 he became its first head of manned spaceflight.

In 1964 he was named deputy director of the Manned Spacecraft Center, working closely with Robert Gilruth, who headed the Houston operation. After the Apollo 1 fire in 1967, Low was appointed to head the Apollo Spacecraft Program Office in Houston, charged with correcting the engineering problems with Apollo.

In planning exercises in 1967, Low and colleagues considered the possibility of an 'E prime mission' (**Table 1**) in which the combined CSM/Lunar Module would be sent to the vicinity of the Moon instead of an elliptical high Earth orbit as originally planned. However, it soon became apparent to Low and Gilruth that Lunar Module development was so far behind that it would not be ready in 1968, even though the Saturn V rocket and CSM were on track for a first crewed launch that year.

In July 1968 Low came up with the novel idea of sending the CSM – without the Lunar Module – to either loop around the Moon or to go into orbit around it. This was a bold proposal for the first crewed Saturn V flight, which to that point had not gone anywhere besides Earth orbit on previous unmanned missions. This scheme was called a 'C prime mission' (Table 1) because it did not involve the Lunar Module.

Low pursued the feasibility of such a flight plan and met with Director of Flight Operations Christopher Kraft on 7 August 1968, asking him to develop a plan for a lunar orbit mission. A frantic series of secret meetings followed (Figure 70).

They came up with a flight plan for a lunar orbital mission, which they proposed to NASA manned spaceflight chief Mueller, who was in Europe for a space meeting. While skeptical, Mueller eventually signed on to the concept. They had a harder time convincing NASA Administrator Webb, who thought the idea was too risky. Webb ordered that any approval for an Apollo 8 lunar orbit goal be delayed until after a successful flight of Apollo 7.

Finally, after Apollo 7's success in October, on 12 November 1968 it was announced publicly that Apollo 8 would go the Moon and enter lunar orbit. With only about six weeks until the scheduled launch, members of the NASA team worked overtime on many fronts, including crew training, trajectories, flight plans and hardware preparation of the Saturn V and CSM.

NASA had kept the debate about the goals of Apollo 8 tightly under wraps, so I was not aware of the plan to send Apollo 8 to the Moon until the official announcement on 12 November. I was 18 years old then and immediately understood both the risks and great opportunities of the audacious Apollo 8 lunar orbit plan. It was an exciting time for the space program, with skeptics wondering whether such an ambitious flight could be pulled together in time for a December launch.

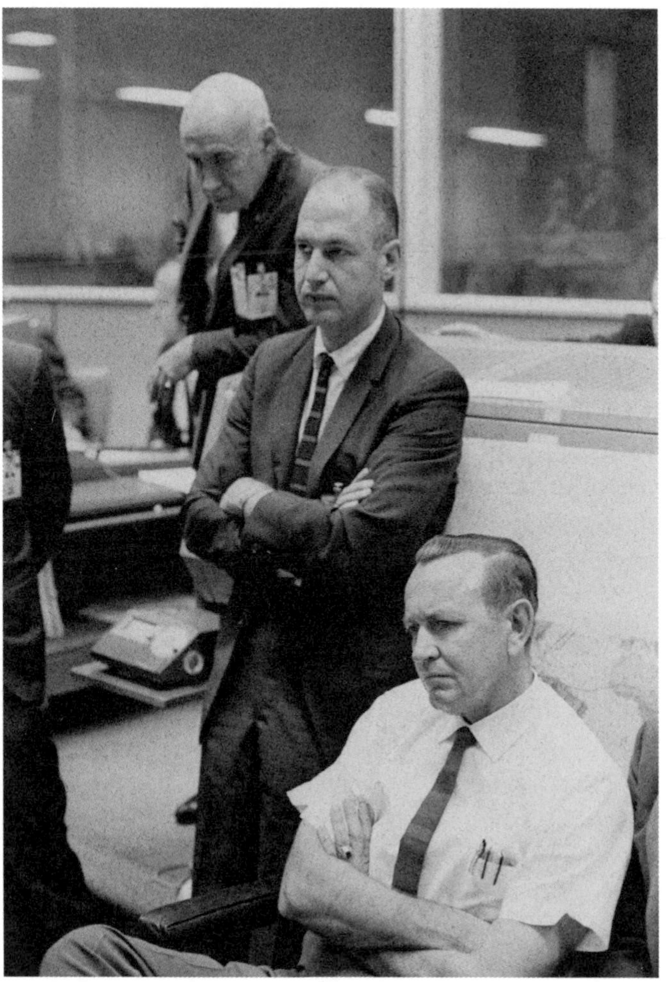

Figure 70: George Low (center) proposed sending Apollo 8 to orbit the Moon to Manned Spacecraft Center director of flight operations Christopher Kraft (right) and director Robert Gilruth (left) in August, 1968.

Apollo 8 was indeed launched on 21 December 1968, and the mission was a complete success. From an engineering point of view, there were no problems reaching the Moon, entering lunar orbit, heading back to Earth and safely landing.

Even more important were some of the intangible effects of the flight. As noted in Chapter 5, the crew's dramatic Christmas Eve television broadcast from lunar orbit, during which they read from the Book of Genesis, was seen by hundreds of millions of people around the world. The 'Earthrise' picture Anders took showing the blue Earth above the bleak lunar surface has been described as one of the most influential pictures of all time, showing the fragility of Earth and the lack of political boundaries as viewed from space (see **Figure 69** page 186).

Each of the four bold decisions discussed here had common characteristics.

First, in every case there was a strong, persuasive leader or administrator who was not afraid to push ahead against opposition. President Kennedy's decision to go for a Moon landing by the end of the decade was criticized by many as being overly ambitious and too expensive, but he forged ahead. Dr John Houbolt and his colleagues at Langley Research Center were at first voices in the wilderness concerning their LOR plan to go to the Moon. Houbolt was relentless in promoting LOR despite opposition from powerful figures such as von Braun. Dr George Mueller insisted on all up testing even though this was contrary to established practice espoused by von Braun and the other former German rocket engineers at Marshall Space Flight Center. Finally, George Low had to persuade skeptical NASA officials, especially Mueller and Webb, that flying Apollo 8 to lunar orbit could not only be done successfully but would speed up the program.

Each of these decisions was based on detailed planning or experience. The decision to set a goal of landing on the Moon was made after extensive studies and recommendations based on President Kennedy's 21 April 1961 memo asking how the US could beat the Soviets. The LOR concept arose as part of detailed engineering studies at Langley long before any definite plan to go to the Moon. Mueller's insistence on all up testing was the result of long experience testing military missiles. The Apollo 8 decision to orbit the Moon was made after studies ordered by Low and Kraft showed that such a mission was feasible.

Finally, these decisions all involved going beyond conventional wisdom. The US had a total of 15 minutes of manned space flight experience with Alan Shepard's suborbital mission when President Kennedy set sights on the Moon. The common expectation then was that the US would set goals in Earth orbit, especially since the US at that time had no reliable heavy-lift boosters. To land on the Moon and return was a great leap forward and a clear challenge to NASA and the space industry.

After that lunar goal had been enunciated, the stated preference of von Braun and his allies was to use the Earth Orbit Rendezvous approach. However, Houbolt and his colleagues at Langley showed that LOR would save on weight and schedule. They were met with skepticism until engineering studies showed that their unconventional approach was superior.

And as we've said, President Kennedy's goal of landing on the Moon before 1970 would not have been met without the all up testing demanded by Mueller.

Each of these bold decisions highlighted the benefits of unconventional wisdom – thinking outside the box – to progress in unexpected ways. It is fitting that an exploration enterprise such as NASA used such methods in the 1960s to reach for the Moon.

However, NASA became more risk-averse after astronauts were killed in the 1986 Challenger and 2003 Columbia space shuttle tragedies. Some NASA veterans have complained that the agency has lost its ability to think boldly and act quickly. For example, instead of putting men and women aboard the first flight of the Space Launch System (SLS) – NASA's advanced heavy-lift rocket under development – they plan to send the spacecraft without any humans aboard to lunar orbit. My own opinion is that a crewed flight would be preferable. Time will tell whether this decision was wise.

In the future, will NASA have the drive and imagination to boldly explore, and eventually inhabit, other parts of the Solar System? The young people of today will find the answer to that question in the decades ahead.

CHAPTER 18

NO BUCKS, NO BUCK ROGERS

Figure 71: To save development costs, the complicated design of the space shuttle led to more risks and higher operational costs. Over 30 years, 14 astronauts were killed in two accidents, and the shuttle never flew more than nine times in one year.

© NASA

Space exploration is expensive. Indeed, much of President Eisenhower's hesitancy about committing the US to space activities was due to the cost. Without enough funding (the 'bucks') there can be no rockets, spacecraft or space-walking astronauts (the 'Buck Rogers'). In this chapter I will discuss the rise and fall of NASA's budgets over the last 60 years, and lessons learned on the effects of funding limitations on safety and the pace of space exploration.

NASA's budget for calendar year 1959, its first full year of operation, was $145 million, or the equivalent of $1.23 billion in 2018 dollars. This represented about 0.2 % of the total federal budget in 1959, a relatively small amount, but consistent with Eisenhower's initial modest goals.

With the ramp-up of NASA's early activities, such as Project Mercury, development of the Saturn I rocket and the launch of unmanned probes such as Ranger, there was a five-fold increase in the space agency's budget between 1959 and 1961 – from $145 million to $744 million ($6.2 billion in 2018 dollars).

This significant increase happened as NASA added its large research centers and hired more contractors to do the actual construction of assembly buildings, launch pads, spacecraft and rocket boosters.

President Kennedy upped the ante when he announced the goal of landing on the Moon before 1970 by giving NASA the resources it needed for Saturn V and Apollo spacecraft design, manufacturing and testing. The 1962 NASA budget was $1.257 billion ($10.4 billion in 2018 dollars). However, over the next four years NASA's budget almost quadrupled, to $5.933 billion in 1966 ($45.6 billion in 2018 dollars, or more than twice the current NASA budget of $20.7 billion). This 1966 outlay represented the maximum budget NASA received in its history – an astounding 4.41% of the total federal budget.

However, faced with mounting US deficits and huge military costs due to the Vietnam War, NASA experienced budget cuts of a half-billion dollars in each of the years 1967, 1968, and 1970. The budget dropped from $5.993 billion in 1966 to $3.38 billion in 1971 – a decrease in 2018 dollars equivalent to $45.6 billion down to $20.8 billion.

These drastic 65% budget reductions led to the cancellation of Apollo flights 18, 19 and 20. There were also compromises in the design of the space shuttle that would make it more expensive and less safe to operate (**Chart 1**).

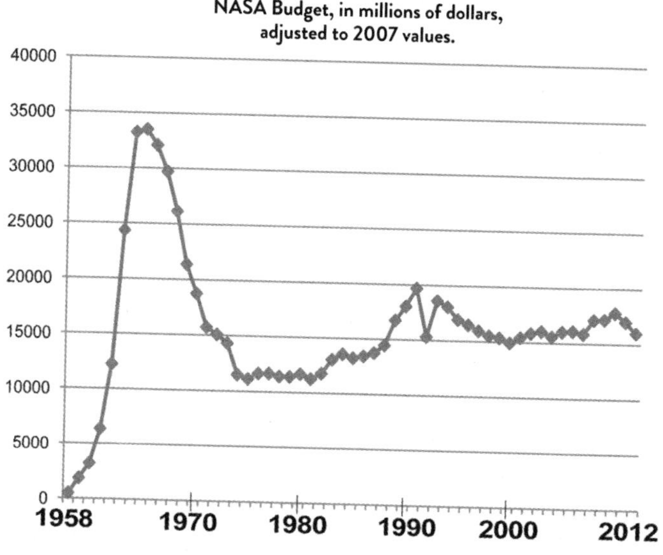

Chart 1: Chart showing the steep rise in the NASA budget during the early 1960s and a a precipitous drop in the early 1970s.

© NASA

Some of the money during NASA's budgetary heyday from 1962 to 1966 went for one-time-only construction costs, including the VAB, Launch Control Center, Pads 39A and 39B, rocket test stands at Marshall Space Flight Center and construction of the Manned Spacecraft Center in Houston. However, much of the money was for operational costs, including procurement of rockets and spacecraft, personnel budgets for NASA and its many contractors, and administrative costs.

It is ironic that the most drastic cuts were from 1967 to 1971, the period during which most of the Apollo missions flew. While Apollo was not affected directly, the budget cuts did lead to demoralization among some of the almost 400,000 Americans who worked on Apollo, mainly contractor personnel. It is a tribute to them that they remained committed to excellence and doing their jobs right, despite knowing that many of them would receive pink slips as Apollo wound down.

I remember some of the sarcastic humour by space workers in Florida during my trip there in 1969, who talked about getting laid off as their reward for successfully launching Apollo 11. There was some bitterness that the workers had given their hearts and souls to NASA by working long overtime hours, weekends and holidays, yet were facing unemployment as the Apollo program concluded.

While the hardware for Apollo 18, 19, and 20 was largely completed, one of the main reasons for cancelling them was to save on the operational costs of those missions. However, the decision was not entirely budgetary. There were some, like the Manned Spacecraft Center director Robert Gilruth, who did not believe the additional missions were worth the potential loss of human life if the flights went awry. They knew that space is a dangerous endeavour, and that NASA had been lucky to not yet lose anyone in space (the 1967 Apollo 1 fire having occurred during a ground test).

The biggest 'victim' of the budget cuts was Skylab, which was originally called the Apollo Applications Project (AAP). As championed by Dr George Mueller, a series of orbiting workshops was envisaged. With reduced funding, AAP was 'downgraded' to what would be called Skylab, with only one orbiting workshop. There would be three scheduled manned launches to Skylab in 1973-74.

Skylab was very successful, and if it had remained in orbit, follow-on missions would have given the US a rudimentary space station long before the International Space Station was operable. However, due to budget stringency, Skylab had no reboost capability and delays in the space shuttle made it impossible to save the craft; it crashed to Earth in July 1979. The US thereby lost a great opportunity to have had a functioning space station in the late 1970s and 1980s. It was another case of the US government being 'penny wise and pound foolish'.

As NASA began in 1970-71 to plan a space shuttle as a replacement for Apollo, budget considerations directed the design of the shuttle. Original proposals suggested that the entire first stage of the shuttle be flown back to Earth, reducing replacement times and reducing operational costs. Because such a reusable first stage increased weight, development time and development costs, a compromise design called for just the shuttle main engines, which were attached to the orbiter, to be reusable (**Figure 1**).

For budgetary reasons, the shuttle was proposed as a 'space truck' that would be utilized by both NASA and the Defense Department. This was a trade-off in return for the Defense Department chipping in part of the costs. It was a 'deal with the devil' because the Air Force dictated that the shuttle be capable of going into polar orbit and have a payload bay large enough to carry huge military satellites, including large 'spy satellites' that would conduct unmanned reconnaissance missions.

This larger shuttle had increased development costs. To lower these costs, twin solid rocket boosters (SRBs) were added as well as a throw-away fuel tank. The result was an unnecessarily complicated device with the main engines attached to the manned orbiter, but a disposable main fuel tank and SRBs (see Figure 71 page 203).

These decisions, made to reduce development costs, resulted in less reusability, higher operational costs, and a design with inherent safety risks. These risks included use of solid rockets (which could not be controlled once ignited), a larger orbiter because it had to have enough room for the main engines, and no abort capability for the astronauts just after launch.

The shuttle was optimistically promoted as a means of making travel into Earth orbit routine, with missions every two weeks. The shuttle would be used for virtually all US launches, including crewed missions, unmanned civilian satellites, planetary probes and military satellites.

The shuttle made economic sense only if it could fly frequently.

This notion was wildly unrealistic. It took weeks of work to prepare the orbiters and their main engines to return to space, and to attach new Solid Rocket Boosters and External Tanks. The maximum number of shuttle missions was nine in 1985, far fewer than the 26 that optimistic shuttle planners suggested might be possible.

The shuttle system would have been safer, quicker and more economical had it had a sufficient budget to start. Because of funding constraints, NASA in 1972 emphasized comparatively low developmental costs for the shuttle as a selling point. The space agency 'bought in' relatively cheaply (compared to a completely reusable architecture) at the price of higher operational and, ultimately, safety costs.

Forty-five years later, a **2017** space agency budget of $19.5 billion was the equivalent of only $2.87 billion back in 1969. Building rockets and spacecraft is expensive, especially with the ongoing infrastructure costs of NASA, including aging civil service employees and aging facilities.

The final NASA appropriation for fiscal year **2018** ended up being $20.74 billion, in the omnibus appropriation bill approved by Congress in March 2018. This was higher than what the administration of President Donald Trump had requested.

In February 2018 the Trump administration proposed a **2019** NASA budget of $19.9 billion. While the budget plan touted returning to the Moon, there were no additional funds towards that goal. The budget documents showed a nearly flat NASA budget over the next five years.

Any further significant increase in the NASA budget is not likely, so a re-thinking of the maximum that can be done realistically with current funding is in order. Since the pace of exploration depends on the money available, public-private and international partnerships to increase resources, as discussed below, may be the only possible way to provide more bucks for space exploration.

CHAPTER 19

THE ASTRONAUTS

Figure 72: Apollo 11 crew NASA lithograph inscribed to the Author by Michael Collins.

No one group has personified the space program more than the astronauts – the men and women who ride rockets and fly spacecraft. The Apollo program started with only male US military test pilots as astronauts, but one of the lessons of Apollo was the benefits of broadening that base to include scientists such as Apollo 17 geologist Harrison 'Jack' Schmitt, who walked on the Moon.

The 'Original Seven', who were named in 1959 – Alan Shepard, Gus Grissom, John Glenn, Scott Carpenter, Wally Schirra, Gordon Cooper and Deke Slayton – became national heroes overnight. I admired them as a child and had the privilege of meeting four of them in later years (see Figure 7 page 26).

Since then, NASA has named a total of 22 groups of astronauts to serve in its human spaceflight programs. In addition, the European Space Agency and Canadian Space Agency have named their own astronauts to fly on the space shuttle and to the International Space Station.

President Eisenhower wisely decided that the first American space pilots should be military men, and specifically only experimental test pilots. The selection process for the Original Seven began in January 1959 and culminated in the 9 April 1959 press conference in Washington where they were introduced to the public.

During the selection process, NASA had identified 110 military test pilots who might qualify and whittled that down to 18 finalists. The initial goal was to pick six, but it was difficult to pare down the candidates to fewer than seven. Each of these men would eventually fly in space, beginning with Shepard in 1961 through Slayton aboard ASTP in 1975; Glenn also later flew a second time on the space shuttle in 1998, at age 77, becoming the oldest person to fly in space.

Several of those who were rejected in the first selection were later accepted when NASA named an additional nine astronauts in September 1962 – Neil Armstrong, Frank Borman, Charles 'Pete' Conrad, James Lovell, James McDivitt, Elliot See, Thomas Stafford, Edward White and John Young (see Figure 68 page 184). These men, called the 'New Nine', were the core of the Apollo astronaut team, six of them flying to the Moon and three actually landing there (Armstrong, Conrad and Young).

The first astronauts brought test pilot culture to the space agency. They were all smart and curious, enjoyed taking calculated risks, were good observers as test engineers, loved speed and competition, and believed in working hard and playing hard – with alcohol and sex (including marital infidelity) important parts of the off-duty culture. NASA did not anticipate the adulation that the first groups of astronauts received, but quickly developed a public affairs policy to market the space program by taking advantage of the popularity of the astronauts.

These men, however, were all too human and did not always match up to the 'All American' image they were given. With the exception of John Glenn, extra-marital affairs were common among the Original Seven, to the point that Glenn, at a private meeting, told them to keep their zippers closed.

Although military marriages are often stressful because of long absences and the inherent risks, the astronauts were frequently sleeping away from home, flying around to different training sites. Their fame attracted women and provided an easy opportunity for straying from their wives. Divorce in that era was taboo in many circles, and was even considered a disqualification for space flight. One of the reasons that Donn Eisele did not fly after Apollo 7 was his divorce. The threat of a divorce was one reason scientist-astronaut Duane 'Doc' Graveline, MD, resigned under pressure after only three months.

While the NASA strategy of selecting only test pilots worked well for the first space flights, it quickly became apparent that test pilots did not have the scientific training or skills that would be needed for long-duration Earth orbital flights or missions that went to the Moon.

Later, in 1965, NASA began to look for qualified physicians and scientists to serve as scientist-astronauts for Apollo and Skylab flights (the space shuttle had not yet been approved). In June 1965, the six finalists were announced – Graveline and F. Curtis Michel resigned before flight assignments; Schmitt landed on the Moon during Apollo 17; physician Joseph Kerwin, electrical engineer Owen Garriott and physicist Edward Gibson flew on Skylab.

A second group of 11 scientist-astronauts was named in August 1967 when the elaborate plans for AAP were still on the table. This group came to be known as the 'Excess Eleven'. Because of the reduction of AAP to the Skylab program, the cancellation of Apollo 18-20 and delays in the space shuttle program, there were no flight opportunities for members of this group for as long as 18 years.

This happened despite the impressive credentials of some of these men. Dr Story Musgrave, for example, had graduate degrees in mathematics, chemistry, medicine, physiology, business and literature. In addition, he was a jet pilot, accomplished parachutist, surgeon and researcher in space physiology. While selected in 1967, he did not fly in space until 1983. He did subsequently fly a total of six shuttle missions.

Dr William Thornton was another Renaissance man from this group. He earned degrees in physics and medicine, flew jet planes, became a flight surgeon and was a physiology research principal investigator. He waited 16 years for his first mission and then made two space flights in his career, the first in 1983 and the second in 1985.

The first to fly of the 'Excess Eleven' was physicist Joseph Allen in 1982; the last two to launch were astronomer Karl Henize and geochemist Anthony England, together in 1985. In total, four of the 'Excess Eleven' resigned due to the lack of flight opportunities or for other personal reasons.

Through the 'Excess Eleven', NASA maintained a requirement that all astronauts had to be qualified as jet pilots (scientists who were not were required to take a year of jet flight training).

However, planning for the space shuttle in the 1970s led to a sea change in the philosophy of NASA's flight crew operations. The shuttle crew would have a commander and a pilot to act as traditional pilot astronauts and actually fly the spacecraft, but an additional three to five crew members would also go into Earth orbit on the shuttle. They were designated mission specialist or payload specialist astronauts, two new classes of astronauts who did not need to be jet qualified.

Mission specialist astronauts were broadly trained to carry out research aboard the shuttle, release satellites into orbit, perform spacewalks and organize the day-to-day operation of the space shuttle. Payload specialists were more narrowly trained to carry out specific experiments with a scientific payload aboard the shuttle.

The first group of 35 new astronauts – the 'Thirty-Five New Guys' (TFNG)– named by NASA in January 1978 for the shuttle program were a whole new kettle of fish (Figure 73). All the previous astronauts were white males. However, six of the TFNG were women, three were African-American males (Guion Bluford, Fred Gregory and Ron McNair), and one was Asian-American (Ellison Onizuka). Judy Resnik was the first Jewish-American astronaut.

There were 15 pilot astronauts in the group who would fly the shuttle and 20 mission specialist astronauts, most of whom had PhD degrees, who would be passengers doing research aboard the shuttle. These included three physicians, four physicists and one engineer, among other occupations. Nine of the mission specialists also had a military background.

I was 27 years old at the time and this was the first group of astronauts who were approximately my own age. I remember thinking that, under very different circumstances, I could conceivably have been one of this group.

By necessity, the military atmosphere of the Astronaut Office shifted as it was no longer the reserve of white male test pilots. This inclusiveness was gradually expanded to NASA as a whole. In 2016, for example, African-American former astronaut Charles Bolden was NASA Administrator, female scientist Dava Newman was Deputy NASA Administrator and Latina former astronaut Ellen Ochoa was Director of the Johnson Space Center.

What did not change was the military tradition of astronauts keeping medical and other issues private.

Figure 73: The 35 Group 8 astronauts named in January 1978 included women, African-Americans, and scientists. They were known as the 'Thirty Five New Guys' or TFNG.

© NASA

For pilots, there was nothing good that flight surgeons could do for them, but their power to ground pilots made them feared. In the Apollo era, for example, Alan Shepard kept his Meniere's disease, which caused vertigo, under wraps before secretly having surgery for it.

The death notice in July 2012 of astronaut Sally Ride, the first American woman in space, also revealed a secret – that she had a female life partner, Tam O'Shaughnessy. This was an oblique way of acknowledging Ride as the first known gay astronaut. Previously, this had been a closely guarded secret, one that even most of her own employees at her company, Sally Ride Science, did not know.

Today, NASA continues to choose astronauts in selections every two-four years. Flight opportunities for these astronauts to fly on ISS will be relatively limited until NASA rebuilds its ability to put men and women into orbit itself rather than pay the Russians increasing fees to do so. As I viewed the Apollo 11 launch in 1969, I never would have thought that 50 years later American astronauts would need to rely on the boosters of our former Cold War enemy to get to orbit.

However, eventually some of them will fly US commercial spacecraft, such as Boeing's CST-100 Starliner and Space X's Crew Dragon (see next chapter). Others will fly NASA's Orion spacecraft for space missions in lunar orbit, including riding on top of the SLS booster and ferrying modular components to build the Lunar Orbital Platform-Gateway.

Depending on how long it takes, some of the youngest new astronauts may eventually command trips to orbit and later land on Mars. The teenagers of today will comprise the men and women of their crews.

PART THREE

OUR FUTURE IN SPACE

Figure 74: The two side stages of SpaceX's Falcon Heavy rocket land almost simultaneously in February, 2018. Reusability of rockets to reduce costs has been a goal of SpaceX.

CHAPTER 20

OUR FUTURE IN EARTH ORBIT

Figure 75: The original planned crews of the first Boeing CST-100 Starliner and SpaceX Crew Dragon flights are (left to right) Sunita Williams, Josh Cassada, Eric Boe, Nicole Mann, Christopher Ferguson, Douglas Hurley, Robert Behnken, Michael Hopkins and Victor Glover.

© NASA

Young people in our time will be the space travellers of tomorrow. They will become professional astronauts, commercial astronauts hired by companies or even space tourists. But how will they get into space?

Government budget deficits continue to be a limiting factor in space advances, so the role of private companies, and the additional capital they provide, promises to be important in development of future launchers, spacecraft and space stations. Private companies also are more agile. They're able to more easily make bold decisions than government bureaucracies like NASA. And, they are also usually more efficient.

In this chapter I will first describe the new rockets being developed by private companies to send cargo into Earth orbit, and especially to the International Space Station. Then I will summarize the new manned spacecraft that have been designed by commercial companies to enable the US to resume crewed space flights on its own launchers (the space shuttle was retired in 2011). Finally, I will discuss space tourism and the contenders to send ordinary citizens to space on suborbital flights.

Overcoming Earth's gravity is the biggest hurdle, energy wise, to get into orbit around Earth. This 'gravity well' is the hard part – once in Earth orbit, the energy required to go elsewhere is just a fraction of that needed to go from rest on the ground to the required velocity of over 17,000 miles-per-hour needed to escape the binds of gravity.

Currently, there are several governments and legacy launch companies that have the capability to launch into Earth's orbit. However, the costs are quite high.

Seven countries are able to send payloads such as unmanned satellites into orbit, including the US, Russia, the European Union, China, Japan, India and Israel. These countries use multi-stage rockets largely based on old missile technology.

Today, the US relies on more advanced versions of the Atlas, Delta and Titan ICBMs originally developed in the 1960s for the US military. These advanced versions include the Atlas V, Delta IV Heavy and Titan 4 rockets. The Russians utilize an upgraded series of the Soyuz and Proton launch vehicles. The Europeans have developed the Ariane family of boosters, most recently the Ariane 5, which is launched from Kourou, French Guiana, near the Equator.

China has produced the Long March series of rockets, currently employing the Long March-7, for unmanned and manned launches. China has a new launch complex on Hainan Island (Wenchang Spacecraft Launch Site), as well as an older one in Sichuan Province (Xichang Satellite Launch Center).

Japan has progressed with its H family of rockets to put satellites and space station supplies into orbit. The H-2 rocket is launched from Tanegashima Island.

India developed its Polar Satellite Launch Vehicle (PSLV) in the early 1990s to place satellites into polar Earth orbit. PSLV is launched from India's space complex on Sriharikota Island in Andrah Pradesh State. Polar orbits are ideal for environmental remote sensing and 'spy' satellites.

Israel launches its Shavit rockets from the Palmachim Air Force Base south of Tel Aviv. They have been utilized to launch surveillance satellites for national defence.

In the US, the main consumers for Earth orbital launch services are either the American government or private industry. The military developed ICBMs in the 1950s and 1960s to carry nuclear bombs as a deterrent to potential adversaries of the United States.

These ICBMs were built by commercial contractors for the military. These same companies later went on to develop rockets based on ICBM technology for the nascent commercial space sector, including launching communications satellites, navigation satellites, weather satellites and Earth resources remote sensing satellites.

Commercial space companies more recently have begun producing their own *de novo* launchers not based on heritage ICBM technology. These companies include SpaceX, Blue Origin, Virgin Galactic and Orbital Sciences.

The most prominent of these is SpaceX, founded in 2002 by entrepreneur Elon Musk. The short-term goal of SpaceX is to reduce the cost of space exploration by making reusable rockets and spacecraft.

Musk and his colleagues developed Falcon 1, the first liquid-fuelled commercial rocket to put payloads into Earth orbit in 2008. A more advanced version, Falcon 9, orbited an unmanned Dragon spacecraft in 2010, and sent another Dragon with cargo to dock with the ISS in 2012. There are plans for Falcon 9 and Crew Dragon to ferry astronauts to ISS in late 2019.

While there was no recovery at first of the Falcon rockets, one of SpaceX's accomplishments has been to produce reusable rockets. The current wasteful paradigm is to throw away rocket stages, letting them drop into the ocean after they boost payloads to sufficient velocities. Musk's plan was to return the first stage of the Falcon 9 to Earth and have it softly land on a barge.

This goal was met in part on December 2015 when a Falcon 9 first stage successfully returned to Earth and set down on land. In April 2016, SpaceX definitively achieved this milestone when the first stage of a Falcon 9 rocket landed upright on an ocean barge off the coast of Florida. SpaceX further proved reusability in March 2017, when it launched a refurbished Falcon 9 first stage that had previously been flown.

Beyond Falcon 9, the next rocket developed by Space X was Falcon Heavy. The Falcon Heavy is more advanced and consists of a core stage derived from Falcon 9 and two attached Falcon 9 side stages. The stack stands 229 feet tall, weighs 3.1 million pounds and is powered by a total of 27 Merlin liquid-fuelled main engines. Falcon Heavy can deliver over 140,000 pounds to LEO, more than twice the payload of its major competitor, Delta 4 Heavy.

Space X's original plan was to make the Falcon Heavy suitable for a crewed flight mission, referred to in astronautic terms as 'man-rated'. However, Space X decided against it, leaving Falcon Heavy uncrewed to launch commercial, NASA and military payloads.

The first flight of Falcon Heavy on 6 February 2018 was largely successful. All stages worked well and the two side stages soft-landed simultaneously on adjacent twin pads. However, the core stage crashed in the Atlantic before it could land on a barge due to mechanical problems (see Figure 74 page 218).

Falcon Heavy's payload included a red, 2,760-pound Tesla Roadster automobile. A mannequin called 'Starman', wearing a Tesla-developed spacesuit and helmet, was seated in the driver's seat. Spectacular photographs of Starman in the Tesla, with the Earth in the background, went viral.

Of course, Tesla is one of Elon Musk's other companies, and the product placement instantly became legendary. After a six-hour coast in Earth orbit, the engines were fired again in an Earth-departure manoeuvre. The additional velocity sent the Tesla into an orbit beyond that of Mars, with the furthest point 159 million miles from the Sun.

A different vertical take-off/vertical landing launch system has been pioneered by Blue Origin, a company funded by Amazon founder Jeff Bezos. The focus of this privately owned company is to pioneer space tourism. Its initial goal is to develop a rocket and spacecraft, dubbed New Shepard after the late astronaut, to ferry up to six people on suborbital tourist missions. The system would also be used for unmanned suborbital scientific payloads. The mission profile is to fly to over 100 km and then return to a vertical soft-landing. The booster is powered by liquid oxygen and liquid hydrogen.

The program has been shrouded in secrecy, but there were at least five test flights of New Shepard 2 (NS2) in 2015 and 2016. Partially lifting the veil of secrecy, in July 2017 Bezos displayed a flown New Shepard rocket at the Experimental Aircraft Association (EAA) airshow in Wisconsin. Visitors, including the Author, were able to sit in the passenger cabin to experience a simulated suborbital flight (**Figure 76**).

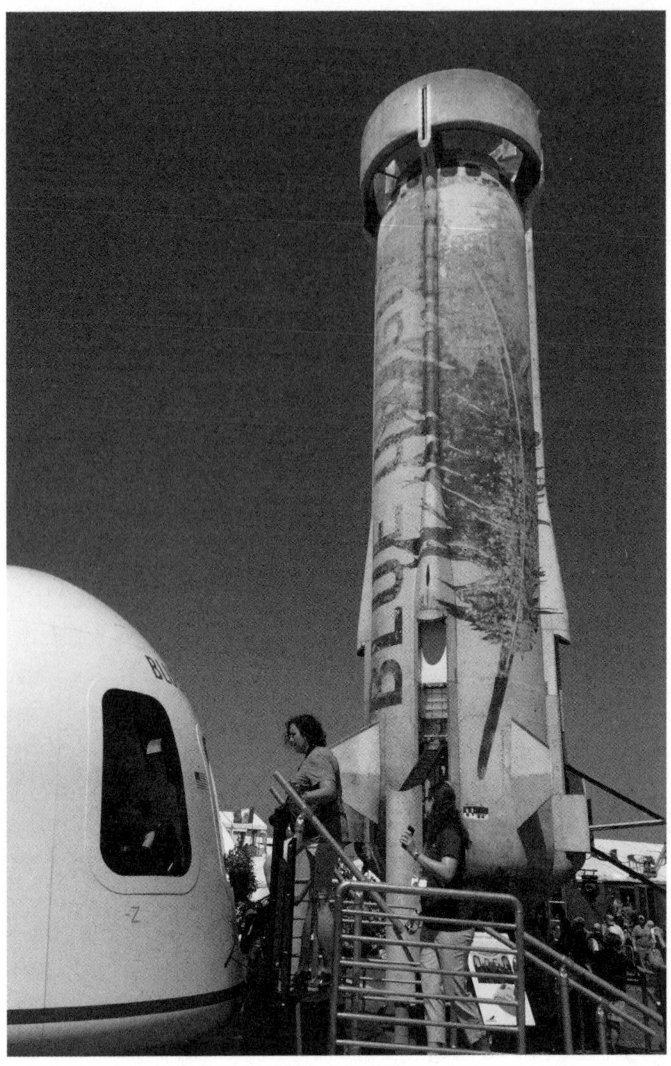

Figure 76: A flown Blue Origin New Shepard rocket was on display at the EAA airshow in Oshkosh, Wisconsin in July 2017.

© David Chudwin

On 12 December 2017, the first test of New Shepard 2 in over a year was successfully completed from a launch site in Texas. The rocket carried a dummy astronaut (with a tongue-in-cheek name, 'Mannequin Skywalker') in the capsule to over 60 miles in altitude and then soft-landed back at the launch facility.

Observers predicted flights carrying test pilots would occur in early 2019 and paying space tourist customers later in 2019, but secretive Blue Origin did not make its timetable public.

Blue Origin has also been working on an advanced rocket engine, known as the BE-4, which uses liquid hydrogen and liquid methane as fuels. The development of the BE-4 engine began in secret in 2011 and production of the first test engine was completed in 2017. Use of methane is significant because it could be potentially manufactured *in situ* on Mars as a rocket fuel. This high-tech engine also has been selected to power the successor to the Atlas V rocket, called Vulcan.

Blue Origin's own future orbital rocket has been named New Glenn, in honour of the first American in orbit. The first stage of New Glenn will have seven BE-4 engines while the second stage will have just one. The first stage will be reusable and land vertically, similar to Falcon 9.

Blue Origin built a 750,000-square-foot manufacturing facility for New Glenn adjacent to the Kennedy Space Center in Florida. Launch control for the rockets will also be located at the site, which is about ten miles from Launch Complex 36 at Kennedy Space Center, where the rocket will be launched.

Another company, Virgin Galactic, headed by Sir Richard Branson, has entered the commercial space race with a goal of developing a different type of rocket for suborbital space tourism.

A company called Scaled Composites, founded by noted aircraft designer Burt Rutan, produced SpaceShipOne, the first privately funded human spacecraft for suborbital flights. Under contract with a Virgin Galactic subsidiary, SpaceShipOne was launched mid-air from a carrier plane, named White Knight, and two test pilots flew it back to successful runway landings during a series of flights in 2004. On 4 October 2004, Scaled Composites won the $10 million Ansari X-prize for launching a reusable human spaceship into space twice within two weeks (these were suborbital missions).

The sole investor in SpaceShipOne was Paul Allen, a billionaire who was one of the founders of Microsoft along with the legendary Bill Gates.

Virgin Galactic is now working on SpaceShipTwo, a more advanced human suborbital spacecraft, as well as its carrier airplane WhiteKnightTwo. SpaceShipTwo is designed to carry six passengers and two crew members to an altitude of 68 miles and return using a re-entry system with a feathered design.

Powered test flights from Mojave, California, began in April 2013. Virgin Space Ship (VSS) Enterprise, the first SpaceShipTwo, crashed during a test flight on 31 October 2014, breaking up in the air after the feathering system was deployed prematurely. One pilot was killed and the other injured in the accident. The mishap delayed commercial use of the system for space tourism.

Test flights resumed with the second SpaceShipTwo, named VSS Unity, in 2016. After a series of captive flights attached to WhiteKnightTwo, VSS Unity separated and performed its first glide flight on 3 December 2016.

Another new launch system is Orbital Sciences' two-stage Antares rocket booster, developed to launch unmanned resupply missions to ISS. In 2008, Orbital Sciences received a $1.8 billion contract from NASA to provide development of the rocket and eight space station supply missions using what was named a Cygnus capsule on top of the Antares rocket.

The first three Antares launches from the Mid-Atlantic Regional Spaceport, in Wallops, Virginia, were successful in 2013 and 2014, but an Antares booster exploded just after take-off on 28 October 2014.

During an investigation into the accident, two additional resupply missions were flown using Atlas V rockets from Cape Canaveral. However, in October 2016, Antares successfully returned to flight with a resupply mission to the ISS from Virginia. There were additional successful cargo missions in April 2017, November 2017 and May 2018. At least two more are scheduled into 2019.

Besides these new rocket launchers, at least three private companies are also working on new crewed spacecraft to fly on existing boosters. These include Sierra Nevada, Space X and Boeing.

Sierra Nevada is a privately owned electronics corporation led by Faith and Eren Ozmen. The company's major goal is to develop and operate a new type of spacecraft that takes off on top of a rocket but lands like a glider.

Sierra Nevada's Dream Chaser is an example of such a commercially developed spacecraft. Utilizing a lifting body design, Dream Chaser will be launched into space atop conventional rockets. It will go into Earth orbit and rendezvous with the ISS, hauling cargo or, using a pressurized version, delivering astronauts to the space station. After delivery of cargo or crew to ISS, Dream Chaser will fly back and – as the space shuttle did – land like an airplane on a runway.

On 11 November 2017, the Dream Chaser vehicle successfully completed a second Approach and Landing Test. It was dropped from a mother aircraft and landed on a runway at Edwards Air Force Base in California. Sierra Nevada hopes to build two cargo Dream Chasers for flights to ISS in the last quarter of 2020 and in 2021.

Another commercial spacecraft undergoing development is Boeing's CST-100 Starliner, designed to transfer cargo and crew to ISS (**Figure 77**). CST stands for 'Crew Space Transportation'. Starliner will be launched by Atlas V rockets and will be able to carry a crew of up to seven people. NASA awarded Boeing a $4.2 billion contract in September 2014 to develop CST-100. The first flight of Starliner has been pushed back from 2017 to mid-2019 at the earliest.

Boeing is the only manufacturer of these new boosters and spacecraft that is a legacy defence and space contractor. The legacy companies offer decades of experience and reliability, but their work is costly. This is in contrast to the new space companies that have largely been funded by internet billionaires with sufficient capital necessary for new startups.

Space X's Elon Musk, New Origin's Jeff Bezos, Virgin Galactic's Sir Richard Branson and Scaled Composite's Paul Allen represent a new breed of space entrepreneurs who not only have vision to invest in space exploration, but also the hundreds of millions of dollars necessary to do so. They have provided the seed money necessary forde- sign, engineering and testing, but government support,

Figure 77: Pressure hull for the first Boeing CST-100 Starliner under construction.

mainly from NASA, has been required to pay for construction and other costs to develop a mature launch system.

SpaceX's entry into the manned spacecraft market is the Dragon spacecraft, which has both cargo-only and crewed versions. NASA has funded a series of contracts with SpaceX for Falcon 1 and Falcon 9 rockets and for Dragon cargo spacecraft. In December 2008 SpaceX was awarded a $1.6 billion contract for Dragon to carry supplies to the ISS. On 25 May 2012, Dragon became the first commercial unmanned supply vehicle to dock with ISS. By 2016, SpaceX had won additional contracts for up to 20 additional unmanned resupply missions.

Besides unmanned cargo and launch services, NASA also has had a competitive Commercial Crew Development Program (CCDev) to ferry astronauts to the ISS as successors to the space shuttle. This program has paid for a series of contracts for the planning, engineering, production and testing of proposed crewed spacecraft to carry astronauts to low Earth orbit. CCDev has had several rounds of funding to allow competing companies to produce different manned spacecraft designs.

Since the space shuttle was grounded in 2011 before any replacement was ready, the United States has needed to rely on Russian Soyuz spacecraft and rockets to ferry American astronauts to the ISS. At a cost of up to $70 million a seat, this has been an expensive arrangement; it also has been worrisome in some circles that the US was dependent on its former Cold War enemy for manned launch services and lacked a capability of its own. The failure of a Soyuz rocket in October 2018 while carrying an astronaut and cosmonaut to orbit (they survived the abort) underscored this concern about relying on the Russians.

The original schedule for CCDev was to have a US piloted spacecraft ready by 2017, but this has slipped to mid-2019 at the earliest, even assuming all tests are successful.

The first round of contracts in 2010 was split among five aerospace companies. The second round was awarded in April 2011 to four companies. In the third competitive round, announced in August 2012, Boeing was awarded $460 million for CST-100 Starliner, SpaceX received $440 million for Falcon 9 and Crew Dragon, and Sierra Nevada won $212 million for Dream Chaser.

The two final winners in 2014 of this multi-year competition were Boeing with its Atlas V/CST-100 Starliner system, and SpaceX with its Falcon 9/Crew Dragon system. In September 2014, NASA awarded contracts totaling $4.2 billion to Boeing and $2.6 billion to SpaceX to manufacture and test their manned spacecraft and launch systems.

Thus, in the near-term future, the US will have several types of new rockets and spacecraft for different missions in Earth orbit.

Robotic missions to ferry supplies to the ISS will be provided by:

1. SpaceX with its Falcon 9 rocket/Dragon spacecraft
2. Orbital Science's Antares rocket/Cygnus spacecraft
3. Sierra Nevada's Atlas V rocket/Dream Chaser space plane
4. Boeing's Atlas V/CST-100 Starliner spacecraft

Three of these same systems will be human-rated to allow transportation of astronauts to Earth orbit. These new crewed spacecraft are Crew Dragon (SpaceX), Dream Chaser (Sierra Nevada) and CST-100 Starliner (Boeing). These three space vehicles will fill the gap in US human launch capability.

NASA announced new astronaut assignments for the first flights of CST-100 Starliner and Crew Dragon on 3 August 2018, with a ceremony at the Johnson Space Center attended by NASA Administrator Jim Bridenstine (see Figure 75 page 220).

Eric Boe, Chris Ferguson and rookie Nicole Mann were assigned to fly the first crewed test flight of CST-100 Starliner aboard an Atlas V rocket, probably in late 2019. (Boe was replaced by Mike Fincke in January 2019 due to health reasons.) Sunita Williams and rookie Josh Cassada comprise the crew of the first CST-100 Starliner mission to ISS. It will stay attached to ISS for up to six months to serve as a rescue craft while its crew remains aboard the space station.

Robert Behnken and Doug Hurley were assigned the first test of Crew Dragon, which will be sent into orbit by a SpaceX Falcon 9 rocket. The launch date is likely to slip into late 2019 or early 2020. Michael Hopkins and rookie Victor Glover were scheduled to fly the first Crew Dragon mission to ISS.

Competition has been the cornerstone of the Commercial Crew program. This competition was designed to hold costs down, encourage government-private sector cooperation, and diversify US launch capabilities. NASA had made the mistake of putting all its eggs in one basket for launches with the space shuttle and was not going to go that route again.

Besides launching commercial and government payloads, space tourism has also been a major goal of the new companies. Initially these will be suborbital missions, which are safer, shorter and do not involve the higher velocities of orbital flights. The two main companies competing for the space tourism market are Virgin Galactic with its SpaceShipTwo and Blue Origin with New Shepard.

Richard Branson's Virgin Galactic was founded in 2004 with hopes of sending tourists to the edge of space within five years. These and subsequent goals proved to be unrealistic because of unknowns in developing the technology.

As noted above, the loss of SpaceShipTwo VSS Enterprise and the death of its co-pilot Michael Alsbury in October 2014 was a major blow to Virgin Galactic. A National Transportation Safety Board investigation about the accident, released in July 2015, blamed human error by Alsbury as the immediate cause, but also criticized lack of training, insufficient attention to human factors and inadequate engineering by its manufacturer, Scaled Composites. Virgin Galactic since then has made engineering, training and other changes in its system and is still pursuing tourist space flights.

Over 600 people have paid deposits of $200,000 or more each to reserve spots on the early suborbital flights of SpaceShipTwo. These pioneering space tourists will travel to an altitude of 110 km and experience weightlessness for six minutes.

On 11 January 2018 Virgin Galactic announced that VSS Unity, its new spacecraft, had successfully completed seven glide flights, the latest that day with test pilots Mark 'Forger' Stucky and Michael 'Sooch' Masucci. The glide flights tested transonic flight performance, stability and control.

The next stage of development involved powered flight tests of VSS Unity. There was a successful powered flight on 5 April 2018 that reached an altitude of 84,271 feet, and another on 29 May 2018 (Figure 78). And, on 26 July 2018, VSS Unity performed its third powered flight test with flying colours, to a record altitude of 170,800 feet.

Figure 78: Virgin Galactic's VSS Unity returns after a powered test flight in May, 2018.

© Virgin Galactic

Further crewed test flights are planned before the first tourist flight, expected in late 2019.

Virgin Galactic and Branson's main competition for the space tourism market has been Jeff Bezos' Blue Origin company. Bezos funded most of the development personally and reportedly has spent close to a billion dollars a year of his own fortune on the effort.

Bezos did not publicize Blue Origin at all until 2015. In that year and 2016, there were five successful unmanned tests of Blue Origin's New Shepard rocket and another in December 2017.

There were two additional unmanned tests in 2018, with a mission featuring the upgraded Crew Capsule 2.0 on 30 April and a high-altitude abort test on 18 July. The capsule rose to almost 390,000 feet. Overly optimistic Blue Origin officials predicted at that time that there could be a crewed test flight of New Shepard before the end of 2018.

Whether SpaceShipTwo or New Shepard will carry the first paying suborbital tourists to space, only time will tell. Development of these vehicles has taken longer than expected and forecasts of early flights were clearly unrealistic.

At the beginning of the Space Age, in the United States, only male military test pilots could hope to reach space. The space shuttle paved the way for people, both women and men, of a variety of different training and backgrounds to experience space. The new rockets and spacecraft described here will open the opportunity for space travel even more widely as space tourism eventually develops to its full potential. At long last, ordinary citizens will be able to fulfill their dreams to venture into space, even if only for brief suborbital flights to start. But where will space passengers go after they reach orbit?

CHAPTER 21

SPACE STATIONS

Figure 79: The International Space Station in Earth orbit.

© NASA

As far back as the 1940s, the possibilities of space stations in Earth orbit were considered. A space station is an orbiting habitat that allows humans to live and work in space.

A large, spinning, circular space station (as illustrated in the 1950s *Collier's* magazine series on the future of spaceflight I'd read as a child) was envisaged by Wernher von Braun and colleagues. The Disney television shows about space that I watched also depicted such a space station. Visionaries at NASA, such as Dr George Mueller, contemplated a space station in Earth's orbit as well as one in lunar orbit, with a shuttle that could ferry astronauts and supplies between the two.

Skylab was the first US space station and was operational in 1973-74. Skylab contained about 350 cubic metres (12,400 cubic feet) of habitable space and was designed for three crew members.

There was no capability for boosting it into a higher orbit, which doomed Skylab because gravity gradually lowered its orbit. It fell to Earth and broke up in a fireball over Australia in July 1979. There had been studies about using the newly developed space shuttle to extend its life by moving it to an orbit higher above the atmosphere, but delays in shuttle production and testing made that a moot point.

The Russians had the first continuously inhabited space station with the modular Mir Earth-orbiting space station. Russian and international crew members, including those from the US, flew and lived on Mir from 1986 to 2001.

The Mir core module was launched in February 1986 by a Proton rocket. Additional modules were added later, including a docking module (delivered by the US space shuttle) in 1995.

US astronauts performed joint missions with Mir from 1995 to 1998. Astronaut Norman Thagard was the first US crew member to serve on Mir. He flew to Mir aboard a Russian Soyuz rocket on 14 March 1995. A little more than three months later (27 June 1995), the space shuttle Atlantis rendezvoused and docked with Mir for the first time during a Space Transportation System (STS-71) mission. (STS with a number was used to designate space shuttle flights.) Thagard returned to Earth aboard Atlantis.

After that, the space shuttle transported additional NASA astronauts to Mir. Shannon Lucid was the next American and first American female crew member on Mir. Her 188-day stay aboard Mir set a new US space endurance record at the time, and Lucid was widely praised for her performance. The space shuttle Atlantis delivered her to Mir on 22 March 1996 and she returned safely to Earth, also aboard Atlantis, on 26 September 1996.

There were widespread concerns about the safety of the aging Mir station. Major incidents included a 1997 fire aboard Mir, a collision the same year with a Progress supply vehicle, as well as breakdowns of various systems aboard the Russian space station. US involvement with Mir ended in June 1998 when astronaut Andrew Thomas safely departed aboard STS-91, much to the relief of US astronauts and space program officials.

Meanwhile, the US began planning and construction of an International Space Station. As the Apollo program wound down, budget constraints largely due to the Vietnam War limited NASA to just one future project. NASA decided to proceed with the space shuttle program, which had nowhere to go other than low Earth orbit. As noted above, the first space shuttle flight did not occur until 12 April 1981 due to delays in the development of the partially reusable spacecraft.

With completion of shuttle development, NASA proposed that the next big US goal in space should be a large, permanently manned space station in Earth's orbit. The initial plan was called Space Station Freedom. It was announced by President Ronald Reagan in his State of the Union address in January 1984.

The design of the Space Station Freedom kept changing based on engineering and budget constraints. Between 1984 and 1987 there were three major design changes. Contracts were finally signed in September 1988 for actual construction of Space Station Freedom hardware.

There was still another design change in March 1991, with space station development over-budget and its hardware overweight. The program also faced regular yearly cuts by Congress in the White House's proposed NASA budget. Hundreds of millions of dollars were wasted between 1984 and 1993 on ever-changing Space Station Freedom development and hardware production. Space Station Freedom had lost much of its congressional support, and after the inauguration of the Clinton administration, the project was soon scrapped in 1993.

A smaller International Space Station (ISS) ultimately involving the Americans, Russians, Canadians, Japanese and the European Space Agency was proposed by NASA that same year. ISS was to be smaller in volume, though it could carry a crew of up to seven.

On-board command of ISS would rotate among all the partners. Ground control of ISS would be shared between the US and the Russians. Most importantly, costs would also be shared, with each of the partners paying for parts of ISS. The US, Russia, Japan and ESA would provide modules, while Canada was responsible for modifications of the Canadarm (robotic arm) first developed for the shuttle.

Construction of ISS began in November 1998, with the launch of a Russian power module named Zarya aboard a Proton rocket.

The first crew rotation of ISS involved astronaut William Shepherd and cosmonauts Sergei Krikalev and Yuri Gidzenko, who were launched to the space station on 31 October 2000 aboard the Russian Soyuz TM-31 spacecraft. Each crew rotation was dubbed an 'expedition', so Expedition 1 to ISS was comprised of Shepherd, Krikalev and Gidzenko.

Shuttle flights STS-91 and STS-97 then delivered additional structural parts to the ISS, including solar arrays for electric power, communications antennae and attitude support. Subsequent US modules launched by the space shuttle included the Destiny scientific laboratory, Quest airlock and additional truss structures. The Canadarm 2 grappling device was also installed.

The Columbia accident in January 2003, in which seven astronauts died when the shuttle broke up during reentry, stopped ISS construction for two years while the shuttle fleet was grounded. Construction resumed in September 2006 with arrival of STS-115 and the attachment of more solar power arrays to augment the electrical supply.

Progressive shuttle flights delivered additional structural elements, the Harmony and Tranquility nodes (which provided more work space and attachments for additional modules), ESA's Columbus scientific laboratory, and the Japanese Kibo scientific laboratory. The Russians also provided two additional scientific modules. Before the shuttle program was closed down, astronauts installed the final three US modules – the Cupola observation module, which allowed stunning views of the Earth from inside ISS, the Leonardo storage module, and a scientific payload, the Alpha Magnetic Spectrometer – aboard STS-134 in May 2011 (see Figure 79 page 238).

An additional Russian module is planned. Nauka is a large laboratory with propulsion and attitude controls and additional docking berths. Nauka, also called FGB-2, would form the basis of a Russian space station derived from ISS if the nations involved ever decided to deorbit the space station.

Currently the ISS partners (US, Russia, ESA, Canada and Japan) are committed to supporting the space station until 2024. Its fate after that is uncertain. The current ISS could be extended further, until 2028, depending on the health of its engineering systems. The alternative is that parts of ISS, or even all of it, could be deorbited into the ocean.

The US has made no definite LEO space station plans beyond 2024. It is unlikely that the US alone will have funding for its own new space station in LEO, so that international cooperation will be essential.

However, in its Fiscal Year 2019 budget, the Trump Administration proposed commercializing ISS and stopping NASA funding for it in 2025. This proposal was met with strong opposition by many in Congress, by space contractors, by the scientific community and by space enthusiasts. Doubts were expressed that commercial funding would be sufficient to cover the $3 billion annual cost of operating the space station. Critics of commercialization pointed out that over $100 billion had been spent to build ISS and that it would be wasteful to abandon it when it had additional years of useful lifespan.

The Russians, meanwhile, have proposed a plan to maintain their portion of ISS after 2024 using the planned FGB-2 module as its basis, either independently or in conjunction with the other ISS partners.

ISS has served an important purpose by giving astronauts and cosmonauts long-duration spaceflight experience. Since trips to Mars may last three years or more, it has been vital to assess the effects of long-term spaceflight in microgravity on humans.

The longest duration single space flight by US astronauts is the 340 days Scott Kelly, spent aboard ISS between March 2015 and March 2016. The US record for total time in space – 665 days – is held by astronaut Peggy Whitson, set in April 2017 while she served as ISS commander. The Russian record for a single space flight is Valeri Polyakov's 437-day stay aboard Mir in 1994-95. Cosmonauts Gennady Padalka, Sergei Krikalev and Yuri Malenchenko have each spent over 800 days in space, mainly on ISS.

These long-duration space flights are essential as experiments for prolonged human presence in microgravity, either in orbit around the Earth or Moon, or on the way to Mars. Many health issues involving radiation exposure, vision abnormalities, loss of bone and muscle mass, immune system issues and vestibular adaptation (related to the inner ear and balance) have been identified.

More generally, space stations such as Mir and ISS have proven themselves to be good locations for research in a microgravity environment. Experiments in physics, astronomy, biology, medicine, agronomy, material sciences and other fields have produced new understanding about life both in microgravity and at normal gravity.

Space stations have also been helpful as test beds for advanced materials and manufacturing, including 3-D printing. With the attachment and expansion of the Bigelow inflatable module, ISS has shown how future habitat technologies can be tested in space. The Bigelow module is an experiment sponsored by Bigelow Aerospace. Having made a fortune founding the hotel chain Budget Suites of America, Robert Bigelow has plans for hotels in Earth orbit using more advanced inflatable modules, and ISS provides a venue to test the concept.

Space station technology has come a long way from the notional versions proposed by von Braun in the 1950s to the nearly complete ISS of today.

The decades ahead should see expansion of space station activities from only around the Earth to structures in orbit around the Moon. As far back as 1969, Dr George Mueller conceptualized a future transport system to the lunar surface, as noted above. One component of this plan was to establish a space station in lunar orbit, from which astronauts would descend to land on the Moon's surface.

In March 2017, NASA laid out detailed plans for a future human-tended space station in lunar orbit called the Lunar Orbital Platform-Gateway (LOP-G). LOP-G would be the starting point for expeditions back to the Moon's surface in the late 2020s and then to Mars in the 2030s. In a series of talks to the NASA Advisory Committee and elsewhere, the agency's Associate Administrator for Human Exploration and Operations

William Gerstenmaier presented a long-term roadmap for manned space exploration beyond Earth's orbit, for the 2020s and beyond.

LOP-G is one of the centerpieces of this exploration enterprise. As currently conceived, LOP-G, also just called Gateway, would be a modular space station in orbit around the Moon that could house four astronauts for up to 45 days at a time. The plan envisages three SLS launches occurring one per year to build the Gateway space station. First human habitation is planned for 2023-24 (see **Figure 80** page 248).

The first module, to be launched into lunar orbit by a commercial rocket, would be an uncrewed propulsion and power bus that would use high-power electric propulsion to maintain LOP-G's orbit around the Moon. The 2019 NASA budget suggested that this could occur as early as 2022. The next flight would use an SLS rocket with four crew members aboard an Orion spacecraft to carry a habitation module to dock with the propulsion and power bus in lunar orbit. NASA's target date for launch of the habitation module is 2023-24. The complex would be transferred to a halo orbit around the Moon. The habitation module will be based on modules built for the space shuttle cargo bay and would allow the first crewed use of LOP-G.

The second SLS flight to LOP-G would bring a logistics module to dock with the previous two components. The third and final SLS construction flight, planned for 2026, would attach an airlock to the LOP-G for use with future flights to Mars or the lunar surface. The completed LOP-G would then serve as a gateway to return to the Moon in the late 2020s and to Mars in the 2030s.

While the US has been the main proponent for the LOP-G, the project has become more international as plans have progressed. In September 2017, the US and Russia signed an agreement at the International Astronautical Congress (IAC) to cooperate with planning, constructing and operating the LOP-G. Similar agreements with Japan, Canada and ESA are also in the works. Thus, LOP-G will operate as an international partnership similar to ISS.

In a statement at the IAC, held in Australia, the Russian space agency Roscosmos said, "The partners intend to develop international technical standards which will be used later, in particular to create a space station in lunar orbit." The statement noted, "Roscosmos and NASA have already agreed on standards for a docking unit of the future station."

In January 2018, the International Space Exploration Coordination group, a joint project of 14 different space agencies including those of the US, Russia, China and the European Union, released a third, updated edition of its Global Exploration Roadmap. This roadmap for future space exploration emphasizes LOP-G as "a small human-tended facility around the Moon which will play an important role in sustainable human space exploration. Initially, it supports human and robotic lunar exploration in a manner which creates opportunities for multiple sectors to advance."

ISS and Gateway will serve as bases for NASA's next steps into space – a return to the Moon and trips to Mars in the decades ahead.

CHAPTER 22

BACK TO THE MOON

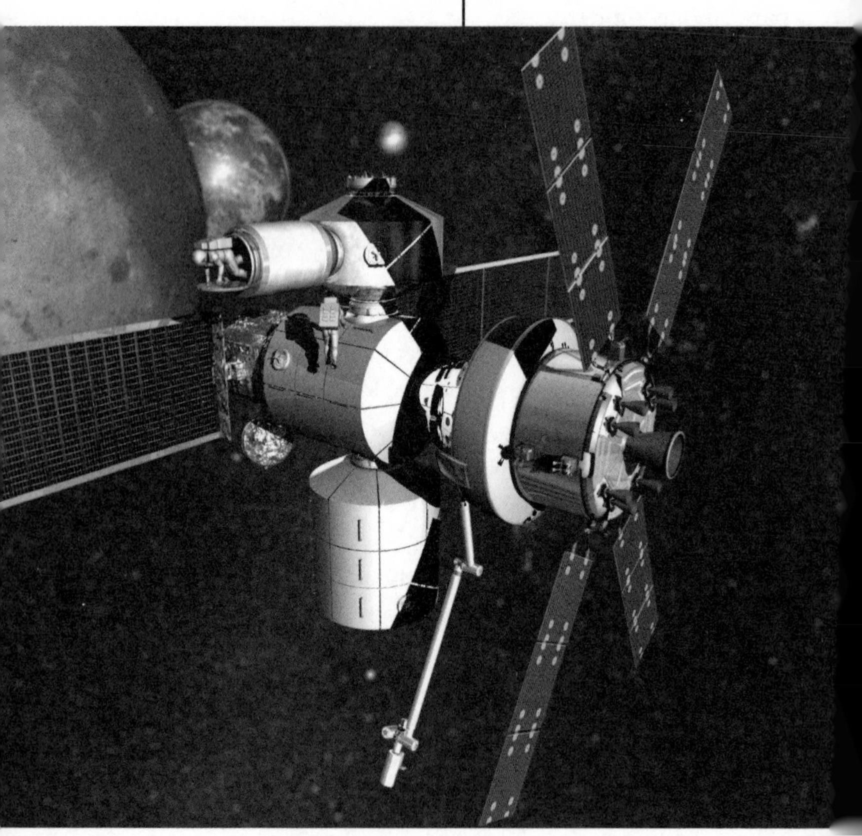

Figure 80: Early conceptual design of the Lunar Orbital Platform-Gateway space station in orbit around the Moon.

A return to the Moon in the 2020s for further human exploration and eventual colonization is now one of NASA's highest priorities.

The Moon has always been an object of fascination for humans, going back to prehistoric times. The earliest calendars were based on the 28-day lunar cycle. The Hebrew calendar, which continues to be in use, is based on the phases of the Moon. The Moon has also long been associated with both love and madness, hence the pejorative term 'lunatic'.

The Moon has also been featured in literature. Jules Verne published *From the Earth to the Moon* in 1865 about a fictional voyage to the Moon, which was prescient in some ways to the Apollo 11 mission. In the novel, a crew of three is launched from Florida to the Moon aboard a space capsule named 'Columbiad'. After landing on the Moon, the crew returns to Earth and lands in the Pacific Ocean. Many consider Jules Verne the father of science fiction because of this and other works.

In 1901, *The First Men in the Moon* by H.G. Wells was published. The novel concerns the adventures of two explorers who go to the Moon, experiencing weightlessness along the way. Once there, they encounter insect-like creatures they call Selenites. One of the men returns to Earth, but the other is captured by the alien creatures and is not heard from again.

The Moon has also been the setting for books by science fiction writers such as Robert Heinlein, whom I've cited repeatedly as a lifelong inspiration. Heinlein's 1965 novel *The Moon is a Harsh Mistress* tells the story of a penal colony on the Moon in 2075 that revolts against Earth and declares its independence. The book won the 1965 Hugo

Award for best science fiction novel. Heinlein also helped write the screenplay for a 1950 movie, *Destination Moon*, for which he also served as technical adviser. Directed by George Pal, the film was the first to realistically show the challenges and dangers of landing on the Moon.

Thus, even before Sputnik in 1957, the Moon was a significant feature in popular culture. While there were many political and practical reasons why President Kennedy decided to choose the Moon as a destination, its prominence in popular culture made that goal even more appealing to the average person.

When the late astronaut Eugene Cernan stepped off the lunar surface at the end of the Apollo 17 mission in December 1972, he said:

"This is Gene, and I'm on the surface; and, as I take man's last step from the surface, back home for some time to come – but we believe not too long into the future – I'd like to just (say) what I believe history will record: that America's challenge of today has forged man's destiny of tomorrow. And, as we leave the Moon at Taurus–Littrow, we leave as we came and, God willing, as we shall return, with peace and hope for all mankind. Godspeed the crew of Apollo 17."

At that time, no one believed that 45 years later Cernan, much to his disappointment, would still hold the distinction, until his death in January 2017, of being the last man on the Moon.

NASA's focus in the 1980s and 1990s was on flying the space shuttle. As space shuttle development costs decreased, the resulting budget 'wedge' funded Space Station Freedom and then ISS development. One of the rationales to end the space shuttle program in 2011 was to take the operational cost savings from stopping the program and use those funds to develop future programs to explore beyond Earth orbit.

An ambitious program called Constellation was proposed in 2005 by President George W. Bush to return the US to the Moon, but this never got off the ground due to inadequate funding. NASA then in 2010 stopped any plans for renewed human exploration of the Moon.

While NASA had halted any efforts for a return to the Moon, the rationale for such a program was enunciated when Constellation was first proposed. NASA in 2006 listed six reasons for a return to the Moon:

1. **Colonization** – extend human presence to the Moon to enable eventual settlement
2. **Scientific knowledge** – studying the history of the Earth, Moon and Solar System and the human place in it
3. **Exploration preparation** – study technologies, systems, flight operation and exploration techniques to prepare for manned missions to Mars
4. **Global partnerships** – provide a shared, peaceful activity which encourages nations to work together toward a common goal
5. **Economic development** – conduct lunar surface activities, which could expand Earth's economic sphere
6. **Public engagement** – encouraging students to study STEM (science, technology, engineering and mathematics) and workers to prepare for high tech jobs

Although NASA put lunar surface exploration plans on hold in 2010, the Europeans continued to consider an international effort to return to the Moon to establish a colony there. For example, an ESA working group back in 2005 proposed the following: "In 2025, Europe will begin to operate a permanently manned outpost on the Moon as part of a multi-decade, international exploration effort to serve humanity, thus increasing our knowledge and helping us to address the global challenges of the future."

In December 2016, ESA held a conference with 200 attendees from 28 countries to discuss plans for human flights to the Moon in the 2020s and a lunar colony in the 2030s. The theme of the conference was 'Moon 2020-2030 – A New Era of Coordinated Human and Robotic Exploration.'

Some of the topics discussed at the conference were integrating human and robot exploration of the Moon, the many scientific questions still unanswered about the Moon, and the US emphasis on cis-lunar space (the area between Earth and the Moon's orbit) as an important test bed for technologies required for Mars exploration.

As noted above, in March 2017 NASA announced plans for LOP-G, which would establish a small human-tended base in lunar orbit for use as a way station in a return to the Moon's surface (see **Figure 80** page 248).

While NASA has focused on lunar orbit, ESA's long-range planning has primarily addressed human lunar bases. The lunar bases would be set up under the Moon's surface to protect against the harmful radiation and micrometeorites that crews would otherwise be exposed to due to lack of an atmosphere. More recent speculation concerns the practicality of a lunar base at the North Pole of the Moon.

This was prompted by the 2009 discovery by the Chandrayaan-1 spacecraft – India's first lunar probe – of water hidden in the form of ice in craters near the poles of the Moon. The presence of water in the lunar soil was confirmed the same year by NASA's LCROSS spacecraft. The composition of the regolith – the Moon's loose surface layer of dust, soil and broken rock – was measured by remote sensing after crashing the spacecraft's Centaur upper stage into the surface.

The presence of water ice on or just below the surface of both lunar poles was directly confirmed in August 2018 with publication of data from a NASA instrument aboard Chandrayaan-1. Water is essential for human habitation of the Moon. It can be used for drinking, production of oxygen for breathing, and for manufacturing rocket fuels such as liquid hydrogen and oxygen.

Chandrayaan-2 is scheduled to be launched in 2019 to send a lander to a site 600 km from the South Pole of the Moon. This would be the first attempt to land a spacecraft in the vicinity of the Moon's poles; previous crewed and robotic missions have all landed in the Equatorial part of the Moon. One of the prime scientific objectives of Chandrayaan-2 is to look for the presence of water near the South Pole.

Besides water, two other lunar resources could make lunar settlements economically feasible. There is an excess of the isotope Helium-3 on the Moon compared to here on Earth; this substance could fuel safe nuclear fusion reactions that would provide almost unlimited energy. Apollo 17 astronaut Jack Schmitt has been a strong proponent of this futuristic technology.

The other lunar resource is the lunar soil itself. Mining the Moon has been a motif of science fiction, but use of lunar material and water could in the distant future provide structures and fuel for spacecraft headed to Mars and beyond.

The proponents of a return to the Moon argue that because it is only three days away from Earth, it is an ideal spot to develop and mature the technology to go to Mars and further out into the solar system. Developing human-tended bases in lunar orbit, such as Gateway, will likely be precursors to actual settlements on the Moon.

This could be the start of the 'spacefaring civilization' envisaged by space advocacy groups such as the L5 Society and its successor, the National Space Society. However, such an infrastructure would not be cheap to establish or maintain. International cooperation, as well as public-private partnerships, will be required to share the costs.

The Trump Administration decided in 2017 that a return to the Moon made more sense as a short-term goal for the US than a manned mission to Mars. First, the technology was not yet available to get to Mars. Second, it was logical to use cis-lunar space to develop that technology and to test future Mars spacecraft in lunar orbit. Finally, a return to the Moon was feasible within the timespan of two presidential terms so that Trump could potentially claim credit.

Vice President Mike Pence announced the pivot in US space policy at the first meeting of the re-established National Space Council on 5 October 2017:

"We will return American astronauts to the Moon, not only to leave behind footprints and flags, but to build the foundation we need to send Americans to Mars and beyond.

"The Moon will be a stepping-stone, a training ground, a venue to strengthen our commercial and international partnerships as we refocus America's space program toward human exploration."

On 12 December 2017, with Moonwalkers Buzz Aldrin and Jack Schmitt at his side, President Trump signed a formal directive to NASA to develop plans and programs for a return to the Moon. Space officials went to work in preparation for the Fiscal Year 2019 budget to determine the best path forward to accomplish this goal.

The proposed 2019 NASA budget, released in February 2018, provided that the first element of the LOP-Gateway be launched in 2022 and have it crew-tended in 2023-24. There were no additional funds for a manned lunar lander and officials suggested it would be the end of the 2020s before a return to the Moon could occur. However, funds for robotic missions to further explore the Moon's surface were included.

Jim Bridenstine, the Trump Administration's nominee for NASA Administrator, was at the forefront of arguments for a return to the Moon. After a long confirmation delay due to controversy over his past remarks about climate change, Bridenstine was sworn in as NASA's 13th administrator on 19 April 2018. In the months that followed, he visited NASA centres to introduce himself and explain Trump administration proposals to tilt from Mars to a return to the Moon, and to try to privatize ISS by 2024. In a talk to the NASA Advisory Council on 30 August 2018, Bridenstine emphasized the role of international and commercial partners in returning to the Moon. He stated that the goal is sustainable lunar exploration and not just 'flags and footprints'.

As we've said, Gene Cernan never thought he would be the last man on the Moon for so long – certainly not the length of his lifetime. How much longer will it be before another human sets foot on the lunar surface?

CHAPTER 23
MISSIONS TO MARS

Figure 81: Landing humans on Mars is the long-term goal of NASA. This picture of Mars was taken by the Hubble Space Telescope in 1999 and is a mosaic of four images.

For decades, landing humans on Mars has been the eventual long-term goal of NASA. A 1969 study on the future of NASA headed by Vice President Spiro Agnew suggested that Americans could reach Mars by the early 1980s – clearly an overly optimistic estimate. Since then, there have been regular predictions almost every decade that going to Mars was 20 years away from that particular time. Only recently has a specific roadmap and timetable to Mars been identified.

Mars has been part of human culture for centuries. The ancient stargazers noticed that certain 'stars' were not fixed in the sky, but moved in specific patterns. We know now that these 'wanderers', or planets, were Mercury, Venus, Mars, Jupiter and Saturn. Later, Uranus and Neptune were added to this list.

Mars, especially when closer to the Earth, has a definite red hue, which the ancients associated with blood. Thus, the Romans named the planet Mars, after the Roman war god. The Greeks called the planet Ares, the name of the Greek god of war. The ancient Hebrew word for Mars was Ma'adim or 'one who blushes (red)' (**Figure 81**).

The development of powerful telescopes gave astronomers the ability to see Mars as more than just a bright reddish dot. In 1877 Mars was close to Earth and the Italian astronomer Schiaparelli made a series of observations about surface markings, including linear features he described as channels. However, the English translation of 'canali' was incorrectly rendered as canals.

Thus, the idea of man-made canals was born and given impetus by the writings of American astronomer Percival Lowell, who was convinced there was intelligent life on Mars. This notion became a staple of science fiction.

Works such as *War of the Worlds* by H.G. Wells in 1898, the Barsoom books by Edgar Rice Burroughs, Ray Bradbury's award-winning *The Martian Chronicles*, and novels by Robert Heinlein, such as *Stranger in a Strange Land*, portrayed Martians as coming from a dying civilization.

The first fly-by of Mars in July 1965, by the Mariner 4 spacecraft, put a damper on speculation about dying civilizations or even any life on Mars at all. The spacecraft sent back 22 pictures showing a cratered, almost Moon-like surface, as well as data showing a very thin atmosphere (less than 7 millibars) and very cold ambient temperatures (minus 100 degrees Celsius during the day). These were not very habitable conditions, to say the least... at least not for life as we know it.

As the US space program matured, there was interest in the scientific community to look more closely for signs of life on Mars. This would require a lander that would safely touch down on the Martian surface with the ability to do biochemical investigations of the surface material.

Project Viking was a program to look for evidence of life on Mars with twin robotic explorers. Viking 1 was launched on 20 August 1975 aboard a powerful Titan III-Centaur rocket. It consisted of an orbiter and a landing vehicle and reached Mars orbit 19 June 1976. The lander made the first soft touchdown on Mars on 20 July.

Its twin spacecraft, Viking 2, was launched on 9 September 1975, orbited Mars on 7 August 1976, and the lander touched down on 3 September. The orbiters took pictures and measurements while the landers used a mini-chemistry lab to look for signs of life. Viking found evidence of a period in Martian history where there was flowing water and even floods, quite different than the bone-dry Mars of today.

The results of the biology experiments were at first thought to be negative for any signs of life. However, later interpretations of the results were more ambiguous due to the discovery in the Martian soil of oxidizing agents such as perchlorates that could have confounded the results. The question of any biological activity on Mars remains an open one over 40 years later.

Project Viking was highly sophisticated and highly successful, with both landers and orbiters lasting beyond their expected lifetimes. The Viking 1 lander remained in operation for a total of six years and three months. However, Viking was an expensive endeavour, costing the equivalent of about $11.5 billion in 2018 dollars.

It would be 20 years until the US again attempted to place a lander on the Martian surface, this time with a small 23-pound rover named Sojourner. The Pathfinder mission was designed to be relatively low-cost. The spacecraft was launched by a Delta II rocket on 4 December 1996, and landed on Mars on 4 July 1997 using a system of parachutes, solid rockets and big airbags.

Sojourner successfully rolled off the main spacecraft, named the Carl Sagan Memorial Station – after the popular astronomer, cosmologist and writer, who had just died – and performed experiments for over two-and-a-half months. The final transmission from the lander was 27 September 1997. Extensive data from both the lander and rover were consistent with the theory that water was once abundant on Mars.

Later, two rovers were launched to Mars in 2003 as part of the more sophisticated Mars Exploration Rover

(MER) program. The first one, named Spirit (MER-A), was launched by a Delta 2 rocket on 10 June 2003. The rover landed on Mars on 4 January 2004 and operated far beyond its design specifications until it got stuck in Martian soil on 1 May 2009. Communications were lost with Spirit on 22 March 2010.

Its twin rover, called Opportunity (MER-B), lifted off on 7 July 2003 and landed on a very flat plain on Mars named Meridiani Planum, on 25 January 2004. The rover had a goal of operating for 90 days but the remarkable vehicle was still active an astounding 14 years later, in 2018, before losing radio contact. Scientific payloads aboard each rover included four cameras, three spectrometers to measure chemical composition of rocks and soil, a microscopic imager and a rock abrasion tool (RAT) to allow access to the interior of rocks underneath layers of dust.

Curiosity, the most recent rover, was sent to Mars on an Atlas V rocket launched on 26 November 2011; it landed on Mars 6 August 2012 in Gale Crater. It was dispatched there as part of the Mars Science Laboratory (MSL) mission. The goals of MSL were to investigate the climate, radiation environment, geology and presence of water on Mars. Curiosity continues to explore as of 2019, sending back daily photos, climate and atmospheric data, and the results of chemical analyses of rocks and soil (**Figure 82**).

While recent Mars explorers have been rovers, NASA's InSight spacecraft is a stationary lander designed to study the deep interior of Mars, including its core, crust and mantle. It was launched 5 May 2018 by an Atlas V rocket and successfully soft-landed on Mars on 26 November. InSight will spend at least two years

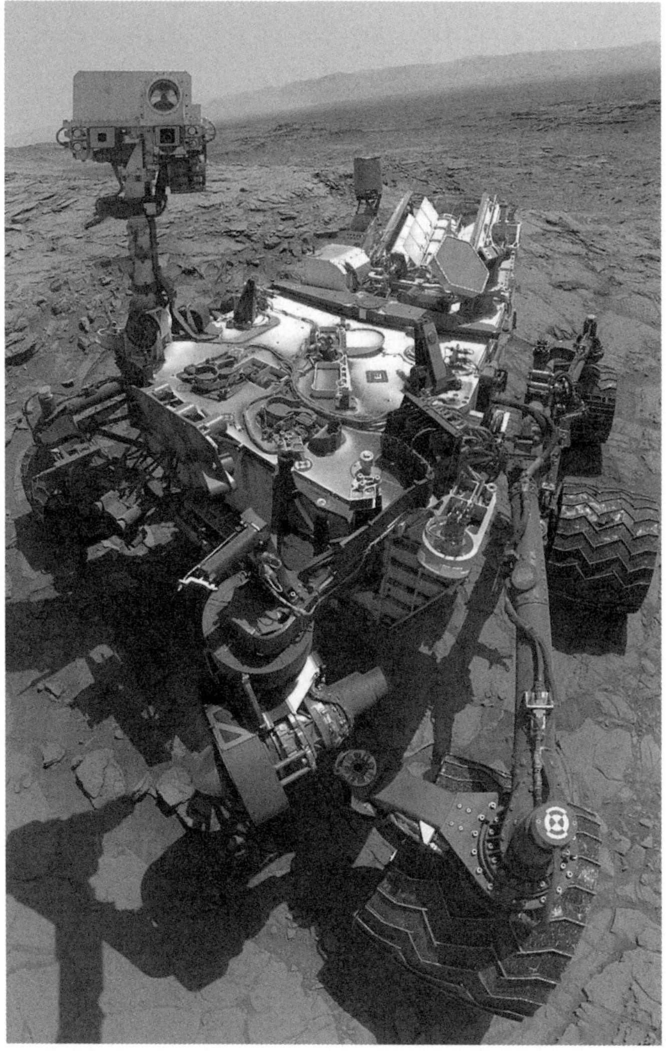

Figure 82: Curiosity rover on Mars as shown in a self-portrait in 2016.

studying Mars with a seismometer, heat probe, and a radio science instrument.

Besides landers, orbiting robotic spacecraft such as Mars Odyssey have done much to reveal the geology of Mars and the history of water there. Mars Odyssey was launched on 7 April 2001 and orbited the planet on 24 October 2001. A gamma ray spectrometer, thermal emission scanner, and radiation experiment were the main payloads. A more advanced spacecraft, Mars Reconnaissance Orbiter (MRO), lifted off 12 August 2005 aboard an Atlas and went into orbit on 10 March 2006. It is still operating 13 years later, allowing long-term follow-up on geological features with serial observations over several Martian years.

On 18 November 2013, the Mars Atmosphere and Volatile Evolution mission (MAVEN) was sent to the planet, and it successfully entered Mars' orbit on 21 September 2014. The mission's goal is to explore the planet's upper atmosphere and its interactions with the Sun and solar wind. The other major objective is to measure methane in Mars' atmosphere.

Several future scientific payloads are on the drawing boards for upcoming years. The most sophisticated is a new NASA Mars rover scheduled for a 2020 launch. A suite of instruments will seek signs of past microbial life, test whether oxygen can be extracted from Mars' atmosphere (which is comprised of largely carbon dioxide), and store rock and soil samples for a future sample return mission to Earth.

In addition, NASA is participating in the ExoMars mission, also scheduled for 2020. This robotic mission involves a lander and rover in collaboration between the European Space Agency and the Russian space agency. NASA is providing a mass spectrometer experiment that will look for signs of organic molecules, the building blocks of life, in Martian soil.

Under consideration is a proposal for a lander with the capability to explore beneath the Martian surface for water and for signs of life, protected from the harmful radiation at the surface. Still another proposal is to send a large helicopter to Mars, which would explore the lower atmosphere of the planet and take high-resolution images of large swaths of territory.

A much more complicated and costly project will be a robotic sample return mission in which Martian rocks and soil will be returned to Earth for chemical and biological studies. This has the highest scientific priority. The earliest this could occur would be 2026. A Mars Ascent Vehicle would take stored samples from the 2020 rover to Mars orbit where it would automatically dock with a spacecraft to return the samples to Earth.

The ultimate goal is to land humans on Mars, and there have been a variety of proposals to do so in the 2030s. One of the first proposals was 'Mars Direct', as suggested by futurists Robert Zubrin and David Baker in 1990. They proposed that *in situ* resource utilization would be faster, cheaper and more efficient than bringing enough fuel to Mars to return to Earth. Specifically, they planned to use carbon dioxide in the Martian atmosphere along with hydrogen fuel brought from Earth to produce oxygen and methane gas. These two substances can be used as a rocket fuel.

The 'Mars Direct' scheme would send an unmanned Earth Return Vehicle (ERV) to land on Mars, serving as a factory to produce oxygen and methane for the return trip. About 26 months later, after production of sufficient fuel, an Earth Habitat Vehicle with a minimum of four astronauts and a pressurized rover would be sent to Mars orbit and then land on the surface near the ERV. The crew would spend 18 months exploring the Martian surface before leaving for Earth aboard the ERV. The Earth Habitat unit would be left on Mars for the next crew.

Since being proposed in 1990, Mars Direct served as one of the bases for NASA concepts for a human mission to Mars, called the Mars Design Reference Missions (DRM). The plans have evolved through the years with DRM 5.0 in 2009 and an addendum in 2014.

A new NASA authorization bill signed by President Trump in March 2017 officially made landing humans on Mars NASA's eventual primary goal, but after a return to the Moon. The authorization bill made reaching Mars by 2033 a national goal. However, there were no additional appropriations to this end. This 2033 target was for a crewed Mars orbital mission and not necessarily a landing.

In its first budget, for the 2018 fiscal year, the Trump administration proposed keeping NASA funding relatively constant at $19 billion, with only about $200 million in cuts to climate research. This stable space budget was in contrast to many other civilian federal agencies that were slashed by large percentages. The final 2018 appropriation for NASA, however, was $20.74 billion, with Congress not agreeing to any cuts and adding funding for various projects, including money to add a small helicopter to the Mars 2020 mission.

Funding continues to be the rate-limiting step in Mars exploration, although some technological advancements would make the task easier.

In March 2017, NASA's Associate Administrator for Human Exploration and Operations, William Gerstenmaier, finally laid out a detailed roadmap to get to Mars. As noted above, the focus of the plan in the early 2020s is development of the LOP-G, originally called the Deep Space Gateway, a human-tended space station in lunar orbit. This modular space station would be crewed first in 2023-24 and completed in 2026.

The next step would be development of a Deep Space Transport (DST) spacecraft to carry astronauts from the Gateway to Mars and possibly other, further destinations. The DST would be reusable, utilizing electric and chemical propulsion. The DST would ferry crews to their destination, such as Martian orbit, and then return them back to the LOP-G, where the spacecraft would be serviced and sent out again.

The first flight of the DST is tentatively scheduled for 2027 and would require two SLS launches – one cargo flight and one flight for four crew members aboard an Orion spacecraft. The DST would be checked out in lunar orbit by the crew, using the LOP-G as a base.

In 2028-29, two SLS launches would provide another crew and logistics module to test the DST on an ambitious year-long flight, as a test bed for a mission to Mars. The shakedown cruise would operate in cis-lunar space and return to the LOP-G on completion.

Cis-lunar space is ideal for such a long duration test flight because communication with Mission Control is almost instantaneous and it is possible to return to Earth within three days in case of emergency. In contrast, it takes up to 30 minutes to communicate with Mars, depending on its relative distance from Earth, and it could take up to 8.5 months to travel between the two planets.

While the detailed schedule for the early 2030s has not been established, the first human mission to Mars is envisaged to occur about 2033. However, this will likely be a Mars orbit flight and not involve landing. It is planned that the astronauts on this mission will use remote control to operate robotic spacecraft on the surface to explore and obtain rock and other samples. It is possible that this mission might involve a rendezvous with the Martian moon Phobos (the innermost and larger moon of Mars, the other being Deimos).

To land humans on Mars will require Mars descent and ascent spacecraft as well as some sort of habitat for humans on the surface. This is not like likely to occur, given NASA's level funding, until the end of the 2030s because the technology required is evolving.

Besides a NASA roadmap to Mars, commercial players have also been active in the planning process. Foremost among these companies has been Lockheed Martin, the American global aerospace giant, which already has the prime contract for the Orion spacecraft.

A key concept in Lockheed Martin's detailed plan is to explore Mars using the Mars Base Camp (MBC) – a human-tended space station in Martian orbit (Figure 83). The MBC would be assembled in lunar orbit, at the LOP-G, and then sent uncrewed to orbit Mars. Exploration of the Martian surface using robotic landers sent down from the MBC is planned as a precursor to human exploration.

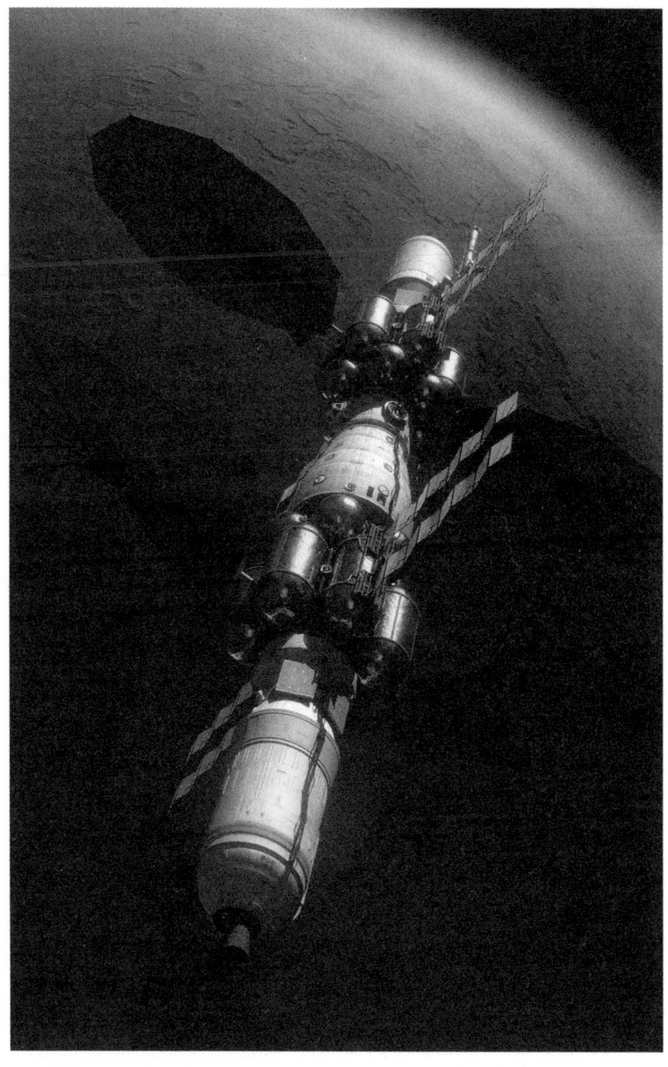

Figure 83: Mars Base Camp concept in orbit around Mars.

Later, a crew would be sent separately to Mars orbit in an Orion capsule attached to a Habitat module. Lockheed Martin has studied use of a space shuttle multi-purpose logistics module as the basis for such a Habitat module. The module would serve first as part of the structure of the LOP-G and then eventually the MBC. The existing Donatello shuttle module has been converted by Lockheed Martin to a LOP-G habitat prototype.

A Mars Ascent Descent Vehicle (MADV) would allow transfer of astronauts from the MBC to the Martian surface and back. The Lockheed Martin design would use six RL-10 engines powered by liquid hydrogen and liquid oxygen. The fuel would be produced in Mars orbit by hydrolysis of water sent from Earth via the LOP-G. The MADV would land vertically on Mars using retro-rockets, carry enough provisions for a 10-day stay, and then take off vertically to return to the MBC in orbit.

This architecture requires several SLS launches, including three to construct the LOP-G, three to build the MBC in Earth orbit, two to send the unmanned MADV to Mars orbit, and two to send astronauts to the LOP-G as a way station to Mars. Considering that SLS launches may cost as much as $1 billion each, feasibility of the plan would require either increases in NASA's budget, additional dollars from commercial sources, and/or international cooperation and funding.

However, in early 2017 SpaceX's founder Elon Musk presented a revolutionary plan to land on Mars earlier than 2033, and later to colonize Mars. Musk proposed using a giant rocket called Big Falcon Rocket (BFR) and an Interspace Transport System (ITS) to get 100 passengers at a time to the Red Planet. Musk also raised the possibility of terraforming Mars – literally transforming the planet's ecology to more closely resemble Earth's – at some point in the future. Critics called these plans unrealistic, but Musk has confounded his critics in the past.

First tests of BFR prototypes are scheduled to start in 2019 with short up-and-down flights to an altitude of several kilometers. Musk has talked about sending humans to Mars orbit as early as 2024.

However, if SpaceX's plans are unrealistic and NASA's slow but steady approach prevails, it might be 2039 or later until men and women land on Mars – 70 years after I watched Apollo 11 head for the Moon. If I live that long, I will be 89 years old, which is not an impossibility because both my parents have lived to their 90s.

Even if I don't make it to that milestone, I was privileged as a teenager to witness the Apollo 11 crew's last steps on Earth before leaving for the Moon, and, from afar, Armstrong's and Aldrin's first steps on the Moon. I hope that the teenagers of that time in the future will have the same, or even greater, enthusiasm for space exploration than was prevalent in my own generation. Colonizing the Moon and landing on Mars are worthy goals for the next generation.

EPILOGUE:

SO WHAT?

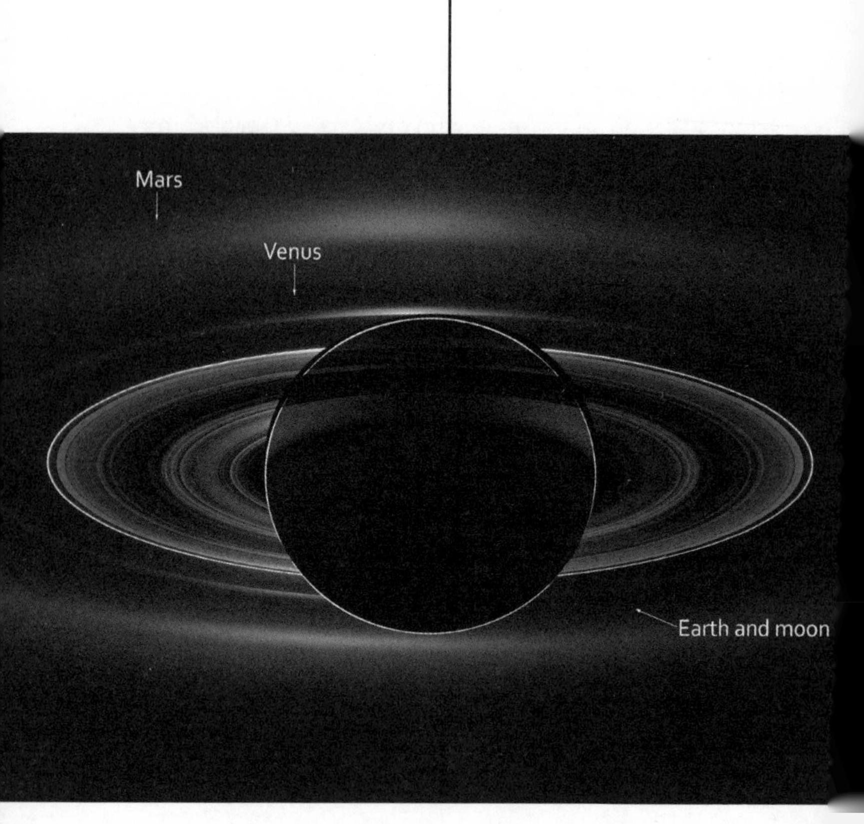

Figure 84: Image from the Cassini spacecraft orbiting Saturn showing Earth, Venus and Mars. Our home planet Earth is just a dot in the cosmos.

© NASA

It has been almost 50 years since that warm, sunny day on 16 July 1969 when I saw Armstrong, Aldrin and Collins walk down the ramp in their white spacesuits, headed for the Moon. While almost five decades gives us some historical perspective on the event, the true significance may not be clear for perhaps a century after Apollo 11 – the year 2069. Today's teenagers will be retirees then and a whole new generation of potential space explorers will arise.

Where will we be in space in 2069? One possibility is that given the huge costs of space exploration and the huge budget deficits of our time, human space endeavours will largely be limited to unmanned satellites and human-occupied, Earth-orbiting space stations. The expensive SLS rocket, with current NASA budgets (about $19 billion yearly in constant dollars), will be available only once a year, not enough to support a Moon base or to land astronauts on Mars (as opposed to orbiting the planet).

Under this pessimistic scenario, human exploration beyond LEO will be limited to lunar orbit flights without landings or a surface base. A round-trip to rendezvous with one of the Martian moons might occur in the 2030s, but there would not be enough funds for a human Mars lander and Earth Return Vehicle.

Space travel in Earth orbit would remain a curiosity, available only to rich space tourists. NASA would cede the means of Earth orbit access to commercial companies such as SpaceX or Blue Origin, but would retain a tight hold on activities beyond Earth's orbit.

If this bleak but realistic scenario plays out, then space exploration will become an endeavour just for scientists, the wealthy and 'space geeks'. It will not play a major role in the national consciousness, but rather remain a sideshow sandwiched in between the latest fictional movies and popular music culture. It will not inspire young people, for whom space travel is a relatively routine event and landings on the Moon are all but ancient history. Under this scenario, space also will not play a key role in the development of the economy of the future.

Taken in this context, the first Moon landing was of limited historical importance. As such, Armstrong and Aldrin's first steps were no different than the sea voyagers who explored the distant shores of the Atlantic and Pacific Oceans, landing on new islands and continents. These new lands on Earth would prove to be more important to mankind than landing on the dark, rocky soil of a Moon without an atmosphere some quarter-million miles away. According to this view, the launch of Apollo 11 that I witnessed in July 1969 was an interesting event, but not critical, or even that important, to the history and future of humanity.

The opposite viewpoint was best expressed by Wernher von Braun at the press conference I attended just before the Apollo 11 launch. As recounted in an earlier chapter, when the rocket scientist was asked about the significance of the upcoming event, he compared it to "aquatic life crawling on land for the first time."

This optimistic viewpoint sees the Apollo program as the first step in the human species expanding its existence to a whole New Frontier in space.

The first amphibian land dwellers millions of years ago exchanged the ocean environment for a far more complex and dangerous environment on land, allowing the expansion of species without being dependent on the oceans. Similarly, the first space travelers of our time have exchanged our Earth-centred environment for the rest of our solar system, including other planets, their moons, dwarf planets, asteroids and comets, and the billions of cubic kilometres of space in between. These new worlds and huge distances offer multiple opportunities.

In the short run, mining asteroids or the Moon could provide new sources of rare metals and gases for eventual production of almost unlimited cheap energy. The 'holy grail' of space development and settlement has been to involve commercial companies, with their access to the large amount of capital required to develop a space infrastructure for mining and other commercial activities.

It is significant that huge profits from the relatively newborn internet have been the source of much of this recent commercial space business development. Elon Musk, Jeff Bezos, Paul Allen and other digital billionaires have provided good business sense and hundreds of millions of dollars in seed money to the commercial space sector. Other entrepreneurs, such as George Bigelow and Sir Richard Branson, have taken profits from other industries, such as lodging in Bigelow's case and music and airlines with Branson, to fund start-up space ventures.

With NASA budgets unlikely to increase very much beyond inflation, commercial space companies will likely be the prime movers for making space a place for tourism, and for economic development such as mining the Moon or asteroids.

In the longer run, our Sun is a non-descript G-type star in an arm of the Milky Way galaxy. It is a middle-aged star that has been present for 4-5 billion years. It is estimated that the Sun can support life in its solar system for at least another three billion years before it consumes most of the hydrogen that serves as fuel for thermonuclear reactions. At this point, the Sun will start expanding and absorb and destroy the planets, including Earth, in its path.

One of my favourite non-fiction space books from the 1960s was authored by the late Italian journalist Oriana Fallaci. The title is *If the Sun Dies*. Published in English in 1967, the book proposes the space program as a lifeboat for humanity. Fallaci and other thinkers noted that if humankind is limited to Planet Earth, we are hostage to man-made events such as a nuclear war or environmental catastrophes, or to natural disasters ranging from an asteroid strike to eventually the death of the Sun.

In more recent years, the late physicist Stephen Hawking also championed this argument. To ensure humanity's survival, Hawking believed we would need to colonize other solar systems. "Spreading out may be the only thing that saves us from ourselves. I am convinced that humans need to leave Earth," Hawking said in 2017.

Human colonization of the solar system, initially the Moon and then perhaps Mars, provides a refuge for the human species if one of these catastrophes were to wipe out life on Earth. While human colonization would not survive the end of the solar system when the Sun expands in some 3-4 billion years, that event is so far in the future that travel to distant stars by then is not a far-fetched idea.

Seen in this light, space exploration and colonization are part of an evolutionary process necessary to save the human species. While time scales of billions of years are difficult to contemplate, recent research has revealed fossils of primitive life on Earth over three billion years old.

This is coincidentally the estimated time until the Sun expands, dooming the planets. Thus, life on Earth is approximately at half-time. On much larger time scales of billions of years, the issue is not '*If the Sun Dies*' as posited by Oriana Fallaci, because the Sun *will* eventually expand and later die – an inevitable sequence of events.

If we remain on Earth and do not expand into the solar system and later the stars, humankind will inevitably also die. In the next couple of centuries, this could occur due to a large asteroid strike, a widespread nuclear war, a deadly microbiological plague, or an environmental disaster such as severe climate change. Global warming could lead to a rapid expansion of the greenhouse effect, turning Earth into an uninhabitable Venus-like planet.

We do not know how humans will evolve over these hundreds of millions of years. Just in the last thousand years alone there have been changes in the heights of humans, in the sizes of their brains, and in their lifespans. It is estimated that the average life expectancy at birth in Medieval England was only about 30 years, while today it is over 70. Although these numbers are confounded by the deaths of countless women in childbirth during the Middle Ages, there still has been a dramatic increase in life expectancy in the last thousand years.

The ancients believed in an Earth-centred cosmos in which all the heavenly bodies rotated around the Earth. In 1543, the Polish mathematician and astronomer Nicolaus Copernicus published a book suggesting that Earth and the known planets revolved around the Sun. The demotion of the Earth from the centre of the universe to just another planet was bitterly contested and took decades to be accepted. However, it was not until the Apollo program that mankind could truly see how small the Earth is in relation to the rest of the Solar System, to the Milky Way galaxy we inhabit, and to the cosmos itself.

In judging the significance of Apollo 11, the concept of perspective is critical. One of the unexpected results of space exploration has been a better appreciation of the place of the Earth in the Universe.

As suggested earlier, the 'Earthrise' picture taken by Bill Anders from Apollo 8 in orbit around the Moon in December 1968 is likely one of the most influential photographs of all time (see Figure 19 page 74). The beauty of the blue Earth, with its oceans, continents and clouds, stands in stark contrast to the 'foreboding' lunar surface. There are no visible political boundaries. More importantly, the small size of the Earth in comparison to the rest of the cosmos is easily apparent.

Apollo 8 and 13 astronaut Jim Lovell talked about how by holding his thumb out from the vicinity of the Moon, he could totally block his view of the Earth. All of humanity's triumphs and tragedies were blanked out by a thumb in the distance.

The great astronomer Carl Sagan called Earth a 'pale blue dot',' putting it into perspective as just a single small planet in a vast cosmos. The first such image demonstrating his point came in 1990 from the Voyager 1 spacecraft, some 3.7 billion miles away from its home planet. The tiny blue dot that is our home planet was barely visible. Other views of Earth taken by robot spacecraft on Mars and later the Cassini spacecraft orbiting Saturn have given further visual proof of how small our planet is as part of the solar system, let alone the entire cosmos.

Cassini took pictures of the distant Earth on at least three separate occasions, the last of which in 2013 was dubbed *The Day the Earth Smiled* by imaging team leader Dr Carolyn Porco, who had also worked on the Voyager imaging team (see Figure 84 page 270).

This sense of perspective about how small and fragile our planet is in the cosmic scheme of things is arguably one of the reasons why Apollo 11 and the subsequent other Moon voyages are so important. As astronomer Neil DeGrasse Tyson has noted about the Apollo program, "We went to the Moon and discovered Earth." If humans only confine themselves to the Earth, then we are ignoring almost all of the universe. "Earth is the cradle of humanity, but one cannot live in the cradle forever," wrote the great Russian rocket pioneer Konstantin Tsiolkovsky.

Thus, von Braun's statement that Apollo 11 was as important as ancient aquatic life walking on land was perhaps not the hyperbole it seemed at first glance. Humanity has come to a fork in the road and either our civilization will remain Earth-centred, or men and women in the distant future will look upon Apollo 11 as the start of human expansion beyond Earth and into the solar system – perhaps eventually even to the stars.

It was a life-changing experience for a young teenager, just turned 19, to be an eyewitness to the historic events of Apollo 11.

I was privileged to meet brave astronauts like Alan Bean, Gene Cernan, Charlie Duke and Jim Irwin, who all would later walk on the Moon. I was fortunate to see first-hand the remarkable facilities NASA had constructed and perfected at Cape Kennedy in Florida. I was honoured to listen in person to space visionaries like Wernher von Braun, Robert Gilruth and George Mueller.

I had the unforgettable experience of being at the Apollo 11 walk-out as the first humans on the Moon took their last steps on Earth. I was lucky to experience the power, heat, deafening sound and physical pounding of a Saturn V launch, a spectacle that one felt as well as saw. I was fortunate to meet in person Neil Armstrong, Buzz Aldrin and Mike Collins at events in the decades following Apollo 11.

As we approach the 50th anniversary of these 1969 events in 2019, it is important to remember the time of Apollo – how a young president set a difficult goal for America in 1961 and how over 400,000 scientists, engineers and ordinary people responded with hard work, innovation, dedication and a can-do attitude over the next eight years to reach that goal.

With remarkable engineering and planning, as well as a dose of good luck, the first mission to land on the Moon took off from Earth precisely on time. The first attempt to land on the Moon and safely return was then a great success, defying the odds.

Whether it was getting a NASA press pass, obtaining Neil Armstrong's signature on a lunar orbit map, or getting a book published, I never gave up.

And for as long as I live, I can tell my children and grandchildren that I was there, in person, at the beginning of a new era. I was an eyewitness to history.

GLOSSARY

Altitude: Height, especially radial distance as measured above average sea level.

Astronaut: A human space traveller.

Atlas rocket: A family of liquid-propelled American missiles and space launch vehicles designed in the late 1950s and produced by the Convair Division of General Dynamics Corporation. The missiles saw only brief ICBM service until 1963. Atlas boosters launched the first four American astronauts to orbit (1962-3). Atlas V, a more advanced version, is still in service.

Command Module: The conical, pressurized crew quarters for three Apollo astronauts.

Cosmonaut: A space traveller from the former Soviet Union or present-day Russia.

CSM: Apollo Command and Service Modules.

Docking: The operation of mechanically connecting together orbital payloads.

EVA: Extra-vehicular activity, or spacewalk.

Go/No Go: A decision on whether to proceed with ('Go') or to stop ('No Go') a space event.

Gravity: The invisible force between objects that causes them to attract each other.

Johnson Space Center: The NASA centre near Houston, Texas, responsible for manned spaceflight and the home of the U.S. Astronaut Corps.

Kennedy Space Center: The launch site for US rockets on the Florida East Coast.

Launch: To send off a rocket vehicle under its own rocket power, as in the case of guided aircraft rockets or space vehicles.

Launch Pad: The load-bearing base or platform from which a rocket vehicle is launched.

Lift-off: The action of a rocket vehicle as it ascends vertically from its launch pad.

Lunar Module: The spacecraft designed to carry two humans to the Moon's surface and return them to the Command Module in lunar orbit.

Marshall Spaceflight Center: The NASA centre in Alabama responsible for designing and manufacturing NASA rockets, including the Saturn V.

NASA: The National Aeronautics and Space Administration, the US civilian space agency.

Nominal: Normal, without problems.

Orbit: The path followed by an object in space as it goes around another object.

Payload: Passengers, crew, instruments or equipment carried by a spacecraft.

Project Apollo: The US program to land humans on the Moon and return them to Earth using a three-man command module, a service module and a lunar landing module (flights 1968-72).

Project Gemini: A two-man US spacecraft that tested in Earth orbit techniques, such as rendezvous and docking, necessary to land on the Moon (flights 1965-66).

Project Mercury: The first American program to launch a man into space (flights 1961-63).

Re-entry: The return of a spacecraft into the Earth's atmosphere.

Redstone rocket: The rocket that launched Alan Shepard and Gus Grissom on suborbital flights, derived from the US Army Redstone ballistic missile and the first stage of the related Jupiter-C launch vehicle. To human rate it, the structure and systems were modified to improve safety and reliability.

Rendezvous: Two or more objects meeting with zero relative velocity in close proximity at a pre-planned time and place.

Rocket engine: A reaction engine that contains its own fuel and oxidizer, which allows it to burn, creating thrust.

Rocket stage: A self-propelled separable element of a rocket vehicle.

Satellite: An object that moves around a larger object.

Saturn 1B rocket: A two-stage rocket used to launch Apollo spacecraft into Earth orbit.

Saturn V rocket: A large three-stage rocket used to send American astronauts to the Moon (1968-72) and to launch the Skylab space station (1973).

Service Module: An unmanned cylindrical part of the Apollo spacecraft with rocket engines, fuel, oxygen, water and other consumables.

Soyuz: A Russian crewed spacecraft able to carry up to three passengers to Earth orbit, consisting of orbital, descent and service modules.

Spacecraft: Devices, either crewed or unmanned, which are designed to be placed into Earth orbit or into a trajectory to another celestial body.

Space station: An orbiting human habitat for working and living in space.

Space suit: A suit for wear in space, or at very low ambient pressures within the atmosphere, to permit the wearer to leave the protection of a pressurized cabin.

T minus: Time until scheduled launch.

T plus: Time after launch.

Vehicle: A structure, machine or device, such as an aircraft or rocket, designed to carry a burden through air or space.

Vostok: The Soviet spacecraft that carried the first humans into Earth orbit, with a spherical pressurized capsule housing one person and an uncrewed service module.

Weightlessness: Not feeling the effects of gravity due to microgravity environment, such as in Earth orbit.

Adapted from these sources:

https://er.jsc.nasa.gov/seh/menu.html

http://idahoptv.org/sciencetrek/topics/astronomy/glossary.cfm

https://starchild.gsfc.nasa.gov/docs/StarChild/glossary_level1/glossary_text.html

https://solarsystem.nasa.gov/basics/glossary/

ACKNOWLEDGMENTS

I owe a debt of gratitude to many people for the evolution of this book. I would first like to thank four people who have been instrumental in developing a sense of community among space enthusiasts. By their efforts, they have encouraged me to continue to pursue my lifelong interest in space exploration.

Robert Pearlman founded the *collectSPACE* website on 20 July 1999, long before social media became popular. He has been a pioneer in creating interest in space collectibles and, as an active journalist, has used the internet to investigate and inform interested readers about space history and memorabilia.

Emily Carney started the *Space Hipsters* group on Facebook in 2011, and it has grown exponentially to over 16,000 members by 2019. They are a diverse group of intelligent people who share an intense interest in all things related to space exploration, but who also have fun and a sense of humour doing it. I am proud that I was invited to be one of the earliest members of this group.

Finally, the late Kim Poor and his wife Sally founded Spacefest in 2007. Kim was a renowned space artist who had to give up painting due to a rare form of the neurologic disease called ataxia, to which he succumbed in August 2017. Kim and Sally invented the concept of Spacefest – an annual meeting of astronauts, scientists, writers, artists, autograph collectors and space enthusiasts. The gathering, usually in Tucson, has achieved almost mythical status for its lectures, art exhibits, meals with astronauts and informal gatherings of 'space nerds' from around the world. I have been thrilled to attend eight of the nine Spacefests between 2007 and 2018 and look forward to Spacefest X in August 2019.

As far as my own writing is concerned, I would like to thank my mother Caryl Chudwin and my late aunt Riss Victor for serving as examples of individuals with many other responsibilities who made the time to write professionally. I am also grateful to one of my high school English teachers, Mr J.C. Dredla, for improving my writing with his painstaking criticism of our essays in junior year high school English.

I owe a major debt of gratitude to *The Michigan Daily*, where I spent four years as a reporter and eventually became the Managing Editor during my senior year. There is no journalism school at the University of Michigan, but hundreds of professional journalists mastered their trade at *The Daily* over the last 125 years. I learned more about writing, politics, government and interpersonal relations at *The Daily* than in any of my classes.

My Apollo 11 adventure would not have been possible without my childhood friend Marvin Rubenstein, PhD. Marv was the one who suggested going to Florida to see a Saturn V launch in person. We have been friends for six decades – a friendship I value highly.

As I began this book, a number of space authors and experts were kind enough to read parts of the manuscript and make helpful suggestions. Thanks to Colin Burgess, William Callaway, Francis French, Tim Gagnon, Jay Gallentine, Richard Jurek and Jonathan Ward for their comments and advice. I appreciate Apollo astronauts Charlie Duke, Fred Haise, Jack Lousma, and Al Worden taking the time to write endorsements, as well as space historians Francis French, Jay Gallentine and Professor James R. Hansen.

I am especially grateful to Jeff Qualls, a friend and professional editor, who volunteered to copy edit the entire preliminary manuscript, and to my fiercest critic, my daughter Stacy, who closely reviewed the manuscript and always tells me the truth about my writing.

This manuscript would not have made it to print without the sage advice of my outstanding literary agent, Peter Beren. Peter took the brave step of agreeing to represent a first-time book author, for which I will always be grateful. His wisdom, experience and advice have been invaluable. For example, Peter suggested the title of the book. He also directed me to LID Publishing.

I am grateful to the team at LID Publishing, who transformed my original manuscript into the book you see today. I especially would like to thank Sara Taheri, LID's Editorial Director, for her detailed and insightful editing of my manuscript, and Marion Bernstein, LID's former Communications Manager, for planning the promotion of this book. Brian Doyle did an excellent job copy editing the final manuscript. I am grateful to LID's Designers Matthew Renaudin and Caroline Li for the cover design and interior design of the book. The team at LID is professional, organized, responsive and experienced.

Finally, I would like to thank my family, especially my wife Claudia, for putting up with hours of me writing in my basement study. This basement room has space art and memorabilia filling the walls, and a walk-in closet with shelves stacked with books and other materials. It has been my 'spaceman's cave' for the two-and-a-half years it has taken to write these words, in between my medical practice and other responsibilities.

Claudia passed away suddenly on 24 August 2018, just a few hours after I had signed a contract with LID Publishing for this book. She had boundless patience for my writing, even though it kept me away, and was happy for me to sign the contract. Rest in peace.

When I was at Cape Canaveral in July 1969, it was a life-changing experience. I knew I had been an eyewitness to history and vowed that I would tell my story, especially to younger people of the next generation. This book is part of that quest. I believe the future of mankind lies in space and it was my privilege to be there in person at the start of a new era.

ABOUT THE AUTHOR

David Chudwin MD was the only college journalist accredited by NASA to cover the 1969 Apollo 11 launch and first landing on the Moon. At age 19, he was one of only a handful of teenagers with official press passes at the Kennedy Space Center for the launch.

Chudwin has been a writer since high school, when he was a reporter and an editor of his high school newspaper, *The Torch*. He then attended the University of Michigan where he was a reporter and an editor of *The Michigan Daily*, becoming the Managing Editor for the Class of 1972. During this time, he covered the Apollo 11 launch for the College Press Service Wire Network and *The Daily*. He was also selected to attend a summer journalism program at Ohio State University that involved an internship on the copy desk of *The Cleveland Press*.

He decided to go into medicine instead of journalism, but as a result of his Apollo 11 experiences he developed a life-long interest in space exploration. Chudwin has written about Apollo 11 in a variety of media, including magazines (*Spaceflight*), hobby publications (*Astrophile*) and online (*collectSPACE* and a Facebook series of 70 daily posts in 2014). He has spoken about Apollo 11 at schools and at space meetings, including Spacefest in 2016. Chudwin is well known in the space community, and Apollo astronauts such as Charlie Duke, Fred Haise, Jack Lousma and Al Worden wrote endorsements for this book.

He has been an active blogger online, participating in blogs about space history, space memorabilia, unmanned planetary exploration and the Apollo program. Chudwin is one of the original members of the *Space Hipsters* group on Facebook, comprising over 16,000 of the most dedicated and influential space enthusiasts around the world.

Chudwin received his medical degree from the University of Michigan and had further medical training at the University of Wisconsin, Madison, and the University of California, San Francisco. He is a practicing allergist/immunologist in the Chicago suburbs. He is the author of over 30 medical research publications and has been a peer reviewer for research articles about space medicine.

He was married and has two grown children, Adam and Stacy, both of whom are interested in the space program but not to the same extent as their dad. He lives in the northern suburbs of Chicago.

davidchudwin.com
david.chudwin@gmail.com